THE GLASS
MENAGERIE

by TENNESSEE WILLIAMS

Nobody, not even the rain, has such small hands.
E. E. CUMMINGS

THE NEW CLASSICS

A NEW DIRECTIONS BOOK

FIRST PUBLISHED BY RANDOM HOUSE IN 1945

FIRST NEW CLASSICS EDITION 1949

FIRST PUBLISHED AS ND PAPERBOOK 218 IN 1966;
RESET EDITION, IN 1970.

Manufactured in the United States of America
Published in Canada by Penguin Books Canada Limited
New Directions books are printed on acid-free paper

New Directions Books are published for James Laughlin
by New Directions Publishing Corporation,
80 Eighth Avenue, New York 10011

THIRTY-SIXTH PRINTING

The Glass Menagerie was first produced by Eddie Dowling and Louis J. Singer at the Civic Theatre, Chicago, Ill., on December 26, 1944, and at the Playhouse Theatre, New York City, on March 31, 1945. The setting was designed and lighted by Jo Mielziner; original music was composed by Paul Bowles; the play was staged by Eddie Dowling and Margo Jones. The cast was as follows:

THE MOTHER	Laurette Taylor
HER SON	Eddie Dowling
HER DAUGHTER	Julie Haydon
THE GENTLEMAN CALLER	Anthony Ross

SCENE: *An Alley in St. Louis*

    Part I. Preparation for a Gentleman Caller.
    Part II. The Gentleman calls.

Time: Now and the Past.

AMANDA WINGFIELD (*the mother*)

A little woman of great but confused vitality clinging frantically to another time and place. Her characterization must be carefully created, not copied from type. She is not paranoiac, but her life is paranoia. There is much to admire in Amanda, and as much to love and pity as there is to laugh at. Certainly she has endurance and a kind of heroism, and though her foolishness makes her unwittingly cruel at times, there is tenderness in her slight person.

LAURA WINGFIELD (*her daughter*)

Amanda, having failed to establish contact with reality, continues to live vitally in her illusions, but Laura's situation is even graver. A childhood illness has left her crippled, one leg slightly shorter than the other, and held in a brace. This defect need not be more than suggested on the stage. Stemming from this, Laura's separation increases till she is like a piece of her own glass collection, too exquisitely fragile to move from the shelf.

TOM WINGFIELD (*her son*)

And the narrator of the play. A poet with a job in a warehouse. His nature is not remorseless, but to escape from a trap he has to act without pity.

JIM O'CONNOR (*the gentleman caller*)

A nice, ordinary, young man.

5

PRODUCTION NOTES

Being a "memory play," *The Glass Menagerie* can be presented with unusual freedom of convention. Because of its considerably delicate or tenuous material, atmospheric touches and subtleties of direction play a particularly important part. Expressionism and all other unconventional techniques in drama have only one valid aim, and that is a closer approach to truth. When a play employs unconventional techniques, it is not, or certainly shouldn't be, trying to escape its responsibility of dealing with reality, or interpreting experience, but is actually or should be attempting to find a closer approach, a more penetrating and vivid expression of things as they are. The straight realistic play with its genuine Frigidaire and authentic ice-cubes, its characters who speak exactly as its audience speaks, corresponds to the academic landscape and has the same virtue of a photographic likeness. Everyone should know nowadays the unimportance of the photographic in art: that truth, life, or reality is an organic thing which the poetic imagination can represent or suggest, in essence, only through transformation, through changing into other forms than those which were merely present in appearance.

These remarks are not meant as a preface only to this particular play. They have to do with a conception of a new, plastic theatre which must take the place of the exhausted theatre of realistic conventions if the theatre is to resume vitality as a part of our culture.

7

THE SCREEN DEVICE: There is *only one important difference between the original and the acting version of the play* and that is the *omission* in the latter of the device that I tentatively included in my *original* script. This device was the use of a screen on which were projected magic-lantern slides bearing images or titles. I do not regret the omission of this device from the original Broadway production. The extraordinary power of Miss Taylor's performance made it suitable to have the utmost simplicity in the physical production. But I think it may be interesting to some readers to see how this device was conceived. So I am putting it into the published manuscript. These images and legends, projected from behind, were cast on a section of wall between the front-room and dining-room areas, which should be indistinguishable from the rest when not in use.

The purpose of this will probably be apparent. It is to give accent to certain values in each scene. Each scene contains a particular point (or several) which is structurally the most important. In an episodic play, such as this, the basic structure or narrative line may be obscured from the audience; the effect may seem fragmentary rather than architectural. This may not be the fault of the play so much as a lack of attention in the audience. The legend or image upon the screen will strengthen the effect of what is merely allusion in the writing and allow the primary point to be made more simply and lightly than if the entire responsibility were on the spoken lines. Aside from this structural value, I think the screen will have a definite emotional appeal, less definable but just as important. An imaginative producer or director may invent many other uses for this device than those indicated in the present script. In fact the possibilities of the device seem much larger to me than the instance of this play can possibly utilize.

THE MUSIC: Another extra-literary accent in this play is provided by the use of music. A single recurring tune, "The Glass Menagerie," is used to give emotional emphasis to suitable passages. This tune is like circus music, not when you are on the grounds or in the immediate vicinity of the parade, but when you are at some distance and very likely thinking of something else. It seems under those circumstances to continue almost interminably and it weaves in and out of your preoccupied consciousness; then it is the lightest, most delicate music in the world and perhaps the saddest. It expresses the surface vivacity of life with the underlying strain of immutable and inexpressible sorrow. When you look at a piece of delicately spun glass you think of two things: how beautiful it is and how easily it can be broken. Both of those ideas should be woven into the recurring tune, which dips in and out of the play as if it were carried on a wind that changes. It serves as a thread of connection and allusion between the narrator with his separate point in time and space and the subject of his story. Between each episode it returns as reference to the emotion, nostalgia, which is the first condition of the play. It is primarily Laura's music and therefore comes out most clearly when the play focuses upon her and the lovely fragility of glass which is her image.

THE LIGHTING: The lighting in the play is not realistic. In keeping with the atmosphere of memory, the stage is dim. Shafts of light are focused on selected areas or actors, sometimes in contradistinction to what is the apparent center. For instance, in the quarrel scene between Tom and Amanda, in which Laura has no active part, the clearest pool of light is on her figure. This is also true of the supper scene, when her silent figure on the sofa should remain the visual center. The light upon Laura should be distinct from the others, having a peculiar pristine clarity such as light used in early religious

9

portraits of female saints or madonnas. A certain correspond-ence to light in religious paintings, such as El Greco's, where the figures are radiant in atmosphere that is relatively dusky, could be effectively used throughout the play. (It will also permit a more effective use of the screen.) A free, imaginative use of light can be of enormous value in giving a mobile, plastic quality to plays of a more or less static nature.

Tennessee Williams

THE CATASTROPHE OF SUCCESS

[This essay was first published in "The New York Times," later reprinted in "Story," and is now included, as an introduction, in The New Classics edition of this play.]

This winter marked the third anniversary of the Chicago opening of "The Glass Menagerie," an event that terminated one part of my life and began another about as different in all external circumstances as could well be imagined. I was snatched out of virtual oblivion and thrust into sudden prominence, and from the precarious tenancy of furnished rooms about the country I was removed to a suite in a first-class Manhattan hotel. My experience was not unique. Success has often come that abruptly into the lives of Americans. The Cinderella story is our favorite national myth, the cornerstone of the film industry if not of the Democracy itself. I have seen it enacted on the screen so often that I was now inclined to yawn at it, not with disbelief but with an attitude of Who Cares! Anyone with such beautiful teeth and hair as the screen protagonist of such a story was bound to have a good time one way or another, and you could bet your bottom dollar and all the tea in China that that one would not be caught dead or alive at any meeting involving a social conscience.

No, my experience was not exceptional, but neither was it quite ordinary, and if you are willing to accept the somewhat eclectic proposition that I had not been writing with such an experience in mind—and many people are not willing to believe that a playwright is interested in anything but popular success—there may be some point in comparing the two estates.

The sort of life that I had had previous to this popular

11

success was one that required endurance, a life of clawing and scratching along a sheer surface and holding on tight with raw fingers to every inch of rock higher than the one caught hold of before, but it was a good life because it was the sort of life for which the human organism is created.

I was not aware of how much vital energy had gone into this struggle until the struggle was removed. I was out on a level plateau with my arms still thrashing and my lungs still grabbing at air that no longer resisted. This was security at last.

I sat down and looked about me and was suddenly very depressed. I thought to myself, this is just a period of adjustment. Tomorrow morning I will wake up in this first-class hotel suite above the discreet hum of an East Side boulevard and I will appreciate its elegance and luxuriate in its comforts and know that I have arrived at our American plan of Olympus. Tomorrow morning when I look at the green satin sofa I will fall in love with it. It is only temporarily that the green satin looks like slime on stagnant water.

But in the morning the inoffensive little sofa looked more revolting than the night before and I was already getting too fat for the $125 suit which a fashionable acquaintance had selected for me. In the suite things began to break accidentally. An arm came off the sofa. Cigarette burns appeared on the polished surface of the furniture. Windows were left open and a rain storm flooded the suite. But the maid always put it straight and the patience of the management was inexhaustible. Late parties could not offend them seriously. Nothing short of a demolition bomb seemed to bother my neighbors.

I lived on room service. But in this, too, there was a disenchantment. Some time between the moment when I ordered dinner over the phone and when it was rolled into my living room like a corpse on a rubber-wheeled table, I lost all interest in it. Once I ordered a sirloin steak and a chocolate sundae, but everything was so cunningly disguised on the table that

I mistook the chocolate sauce for gravy and poured it over the sirloin steak.

Of course all this was the more trivial aspect of a spiritual dislocation that began to manifest itself in far more disturbing ways. I soon found myself becoming indifferent to people. A well of cynicism rose in me. Conversations all sounded as if they had been recorded years ago and were being played back on a turntable. Sincerity and kindliness seemed to have gone out of my friends' voices. I suspected them of hypocrisy. I stopped calling them, stopped seeing them. I was impatient of what I took to be inane flattery.

I got so sick of hearing people say, "I loved your play!" that I could not say thank you any more. I choked on the words and turned rudely away from the usually sincere person. I no longer felt any pride in the play itself but began to dislike it, probably because I felt too lifeless inside ever to create another. I was walking around dead in my shoes and I knew it but there were no friends I knew or trusted sufficiently, at that time, to take them aside and tell them what was the matter.

This curious condition persisted about three months, till late spring, when I decided to have another eye operation mainly because of the excuse it gave me to withdraw from the world behind a gauze mask. It was my fourth eye operation, and perhaps I should explain that I had been afflicted for about five years with a cataract on my left eye which required a series of needling operations and finally an operation on the muscle of the eye. (The eye is still in my head. So much for that.)

Well, the gauze mask served a purpose. While I was resting in the hospital the friends whom I had neglected or affronted in one way or another began to call on me and now that I was in pain and darkness, their voices seemed to have changed, or rather that unpleasant mutation which I had suspected earlier in the season had now disappeared and they sounded now as they had used to sound in the lamented days of my obscurity. Once more they were sincere and kindly voices with the ring of truth in them and that quality of understanding for which I had originally sought them out.

As far as my physical vision was concerned, this last operation was only relatively successful (although it left me with an apparently clear black pupil in the right position, or nearly so) but in another, figurative way, it had served a much deeper purpose.

When the gauze mask was removed I found myself in a readjusted world. I checked out of the handsome suite at the first-class hotel, packed my papers and a few incidental belongings and left for Mexico, an elemental country where you can quickly forget the false dignities and conceits imposed by success, a country where vagrants innocent as children curl up to sleep on the pavements and human voices, especially when their language is not familiar to the ear, are soft as birds'. My public self, that artifice of mirrors, did not exist here and so my natural being was resumed.

Then, as a final act of restoration, I settled for a while at Chapala to work on a play called "The Poker Night," which later became "A Streetcar Named Desire." It is only in his work that an artist can find reality and satisfaction, for the actual world is less intense than the world of his invention and consequently his life, without recourse to violent disorder, does not seem very substantial. The right condition for him is that in which his work is not only convenient but unavoidable.

For me a convenient place to work is a remote place among strangers where there is good swimming. But life should require a certain minimal effort. You should not have too many people waiting on you, you should have to do most things for yourself. Hotel service is embarrassing. Maids, waiters, bellhops, porters and so forth are the most embarrassing people in the world for they continually remind you of inequities which we accept as the proper thing. The sight of an ancient woman, gasping and wheezing as she drags a heavy pail of water down a hotel corridor to mop up the mess of some drunken overprivileged guest, is one that sickens and weighs upon the heart and withers it with shame for this world in which it is not only tolerated but regarded as proof positive that the wheels of Democracy are functioning as they should without interference from above or below. Nobody should have to clean up anybody else's mess in this world. It is terribly bad for both parties, but probably worse for the one receiving the service.

I have been corrupted as much as anyone else by the vast number of menial services which our society has grown to expect and depend on. We should do for ourselves or let the machines do for us, the glorious technology that is supposed to be the new light of the world. We are like a man who has bought a great amount of equipment for a camping trip, who has the canoe and the tent and the fishing lines and the axe and the guns, the mackinaw and the blankets, but who now, when all the preparations and the provisions are piled expertly together, is suddenly too timid to set out on the journey but remains where he was yesterday and the day before and the day before that, looking suspiciously through white lace curtains at the clear sky he distrusts. Our great technology is a God-given chance for adventure and for progress which we are afraid to attempt. Our ideas and our ideals remain exactly what they were and where they were three centuries ago. No. I beg your pardon. It is no longer safe for a man even to declare them!

This is a long excursion from a small theme into a large one which I did not intend to make, so let me go back to what I was saying before.

This is an oversimplification. One does not escape that

15

easily from the seduction of an effete way of life. You cannot arbitrarily say to yourself, I will now continue my life as it was before this thing, Success, happened to me. But once you fully apprehend the vacuity of a life without struggle you are equipped with the basic means of salvation. Once you know this is true, that the heart of man, his body and his brain, are forged in a white-hot furnace for the purpose of conflict (the struggle of creation) and that with the conflict removed, the man is a sword cutting daisies, that not privation but luxury is the wolf at the door and that the fangs of this wolf are all the little vanities and conceits and laxities that Success is heir to—why, then with this knowledge you are at least in a position of knowing where danger lies.

You know, then, that the public Somebody you are when you "have a name" is a fiction created with mirrors and that the only somebody worth being is the solitary and unseen you that existed from your first breath and which is the sum of your actions and so is constantly in a state of becoming under your own violation—and knowing these things, you can even survive the catastrophe of Success!

It is never altogether too late, unless you embrace the Bitch Goddess, as William James called her, with both arms and find in her smothering caresses exactly what the homesick little boy in you always wanted, absolute protection and utter effortlessness. Security is a kind of death, I think, and it can come to you in a storm of royalty checks beside a kidney-shaped pool in Beverly Hills or anywhere at all that is removed from the conditions that made you an artist, if that's what you are or were or intended to be. Ask anyone who has experienced the kind of success I am talking about— What good is it? Perhaps to get an honest answer you will have to give him a shot of truth serum but the word he will finally groan is unprintable in genteel publications.

Then what is good? The obsessive interest in human affairs,

16

plus a certain amount of compassion and moral conviction, that first made the experience of living something that must be translated into pigment or music or bodily movement or poetry or prose or anything that's dynamic and expressive— that's what's good for you if you're at all serious in your aims. William Saroyan wrote a great play on this theme, that purity of heart is the one success worth having. "In the time of your life—live!" That time is short and it doesn't return again. It is slipping away while I write this and while you read it, and the monosyllable of the clock is Loss, loss, loss, unless you devote your heart to its opposition.

THE GLASS MENAGERIE

The Wingfield apartment is in the rear of the building, one of those vast hive-like conglomerations of cellular living-units that flower as warty growths in overcrowded urban centers of lower middle-class population and are symptomatic of the impulse of this largest and fundamentally enslaved section of American society to avoid fluidity and differentiation and to exist and function as one interfused mass of automatism.

The apartment faces an alley and is entered by a fire escape, a structure whose name is a touch of accidental poetic truth, for all of these huge buildings are always burning with the slow and implacable fires of human desperation. The fire escape is part of what we see—that is, the landing of it and steps descending from it.

The scene is memory and is therefore nonrealistic. Memory takes a lot of poetic license. It omits some details; others are exaggerated, according to the emotional value of the articles it touches, for memory is seated predominantly in the heart. The interior is therefore rather dim and poetic.

At the rise of the curtain, the audience is faced with the dark, grim rear wall of the Wingfield tenement. This building is flanked on both sides by dark, narrow alleys which run into murky canyons of tangled clotheslines, garbage cans, and the sinister latticework of neighboring fire escapes. It is up and down these side alleys that exterior entrances and exits are made during the play. At the end of Tom's opening commentary, the dark tenement wall slowly becomes transparent and reveals the interior of the ground-floor Wingfield apartment.

Nearest the audience is the living room, which also serves as a sleeping room for Laura, the sofa unfolding to make her

21

bed. *Just beyond, separated from the living room by a wide
arch or second proscenium with transparent faded portieres
(or second curtain), is the dining room. In an old-fashioned
whatnot in the living room are seen scores of transparent
glass animals. A blown-up photograph of the father hangs on
the wall of the living room, to the left of the archway. It is
the face of a very handsome young man in a doughboy's
First World War cap. He is gallantly smiling, ineluctably
smiling, as if to say "I will be smiling forever."*

*Also hanging on the wall, near the photograph, are a type-
writer keyboard chart and a Gregg shorthand diagram. An
upright typewriter on a small table stands beneath the charts.*

*The audience hears and sees the opening scene in the dining
room through both the transparent fourth wall of the building
and the transparent gauze portieres of the dining-room arch.
It is during this revealing scene that the fourth wall slowly
ascends, out of sight. This transparent exterior wall is not
brought down again until the very end of the play, during
Tom's final speech.*

*The narrator is an undisguised convention of the play. He
takes whatever license with dramatic convention is convenient
to his purposes.*

*Tom enters, dressed as a merchant sailor, and strolls across
to the fire escape. There he stops and lights a cigarette. He
addresses the audience.*

TOM: Yes, I have tricks in my pocket, I have things up my
sleeve. But I am the opposite of a stage magician. He gives
you illusion that has the appearance of truth. I give you truth
in the pleasant disguise of illusion.

To begin with, I turn back time. I reverse it to that quaint period, the thirties, when the huge middle class of America was matriculating in a school for the blind. Their eyes had failed them, or they had failed their eyes, and so they were having their fingers pressed forcibly down on the fiery Braille alphabet of a dissolving economy.

In Spain there was revolution. Here there was only shouting and confusion. In Spain there was Guernica. Here there were disturbances of labor, sometimes pretty violent, in otherwise peaceful cities such as Chicago, Cleveland, Saint Louis . . . This is the social background of the play.

[*Music begins to play.*]

The play is memory. Being a memory play, it is dimly lighted, it is sentimental, it is not realistic. In memory everything seems to happen to music. That explains the fiddle in the wings.

I am the narrator of the play, and also a character in it. The other characters are my mother, Amanda, my sister, Laura, and a gentleman caller who appears in the final scenes. He is the most realistic character in the play, being an emissary from a world of reality that we were somehow set apart from. But since I have a poet's weakness for symbols, I am using this character also as a symbol; he is the long-delayed but always expected something that we live for.

There is a fifth character in the play who doesn't appear except in this larger-than-life-size photograph over the mantel. This is our father who left us a long time ago. He was a telephone man who fell in love with long distances; he gave up his job with the telephone company and skipped the light fantastic out of town . . .

The last we heard of him was a picture postcard from Mazatlan, on the Pacific coast of Mexico, containing a message of two words: "Hello—Goodbye!" and no address.

I think the rest of the play will explain itself. . . .

23

[*Amanda's voice becomes audible through the portieres.*]

[*Legend on screen:* "Ou sont les neiges."]

[*Tom divides the portieres and enters the dining room. Amanda and Laura are seated at a drop-leaf table. Eating is indicated by gestures without food or utensils. Amanda faces the audience. Tom and Laura are seated in profile. The interior has lit up softly and through the scrim we see Amanda and Laura seated at the table.*]

AMANDA [*calling*]: Tom?

TOM: Yes, Mother.

AMANDA: We can't say grace until you come to the table!

TOM: Coming, Mother. [*He bows slightly and withdraws, reappearing a few moments later in his place at the table.*]

AMANDA [*to her son*]: Honey, don't *push* with your *fingers*. If you have to push with something, the thing to push with is a crust of bread. And chew—chew! Animals have secretions in their stomachs which enable them to digest food without mastication, but human beings are supposed to chew their food before they swallow it down. Eat food leisurely, son, and really enjoy it. A well-cooked meal has lots of delicate flavors that have to be held in the mouth for appreciation. So chew your food and give your salivary glands a chance to function!

[*Tom deliberately lays his imaginary fork down and pushes his chair back from the table.*]

TOM: I haven't enjoyed one bite of this dinner because of your constant directions on how to eat it. It's you that make me rush through meals with your hawklike attention to every bite I take. Sickening—spoils my appetite—all this discussion of—animals' secretion—salivary glands—mastication!

AMANDA [*lightly*] : Temperament like a Metropolitan star!

[*Tom rises and walks toward the living room.*]

You're not excused from the table.

TOM: I'm getting a cigarette.

AMANDA: You smoke too much.

[*Laura rises.*]

LAURA: I'll bring in the blanc mange.

[*Tom remains standing with his cigarette by the portieres.*]

AMANDA [*rising*] : No, sister, no, sister—you be the lady this time and I'll be the darky.

LAURA: I'm already up.

AMANDA: Resume your seat, little sister—I want you to stay fresh and pretty—for gentlemen callers!

LAURA [*sitting down*] : I'm not expecting any gentlemen callers.

AMANDA [*crossing out to the kitchenette, airily*] : Sometimes they come when they are least expected! Why, I remember one Sunday afternoon in Blue Mountain—

[*She enters the kitchenette.*]

TOM: I know what's coming!

LAURA: Yes. But let her tell it.

TOM: Again?

LAURA: She loves to tell it.

[*Amanda returns with a bowl of dessert*].

25

AMANDA: One Sunday afternoon in Blue Mountain—your mother received—*seventeen!*—gentlemen callers! Why, sometimes there weren't chairs enough to accommodate them all. We had to send the nigger over to bring in folding chairs from the parish house.

TOM [*remaining at the portieres*]: How did you entertain those gentlemen callers?

AMANDA: I understood the art of conversation!

TOM: I bet you could talk.

AMANDA: Girls in those days *knew* how to talk, I can tell you.

TOM: Yes?

[*Image on screen*: Amanda as a girl on a porch, greeting callers.]

AMANDA: They knew how to entertain their gentlemen callers. It wasn't enough for a girl to be possessed of a pretty face and a graceful figure—although I wasn't slighted in either respect. She also needed to have a nimble wit and a tongue to meet all occasions.

TOM: What did you talk about?

AMANDA: Things of importance going on in the world! Never anything coarse or common or vulgar.

[*She addresses Tom as though he were seated in the vacant chair at the table though he remains by the portieres. He plays this scene as though reading from a script.*]

My callers were gentlemen—all! Among my callers were some of the most prominent young planters of the Mississippi Delta—planters and sons of planters!

26

[*Tom motions for music and a spot of light on Amanda. Her eyes lift, her face glows, her voice becomes rich and elegiac.*]

[*Screen legend*: "Ou sont les neiges d'antan?"]

There was young Champ Laughlin who later became vice-president of the Delta Planters Bank. Hadley Stevenson who was drowned in Moon Lake and left his widow one hundred and fifty thousand in Government bonds. There were the Cutrere brothers, Wesley and Bates. Bates was one of my bright particular beaux! He got in a quarrel with that wild Wainwright boy. They shot it out on the floor of Moon Lake Casino. Bates was shot through the stomach. Died in the ambulance on his way to Memphis. His widow was also well provided-for, came into eight or ten thousand acres, that's all. She married him on the rebound—never loved her—carried my picture on him the night he died! And there was that boy that every girl in the Delta had set her cap for! That beautiful, brilliant young Fitzhugh boy from Greene County!

TOM: What did he leave his widow?

AMANDA: He never married! Gracious, you talk as though all of my old admirers had turned up their toes to the daisies!

TOM: Isn't this the first you've mentioned that still survives?

AMANDA: That Fitzhugh boy went North and made a fortune—came to be known as the Wolf of Wall Street! He had the Midas touch, whatever he touched turned to gold! And I could have been Mrs. Duncan J. Fitzhugh, mind you! But—I picked your *father!*

LAURA [*rising*]: Mother, let me clear the table.

AMANDA: No, dear, you go in front and study your typewriter chart. Or practice your shorthand a little. Stay fresh

27

and pretty!—It's almost time for our gentlemen callers to start arriving. [*She flounces girlishly toward the kitchenette*] How many do you suppose we're going to entertain this afternoon?

[*Tom throws down the paper and jumps up with a groan.*]

LAURA [*alone in the dining room*]: I don't believe we're going to receive any, Mother.

AMANDA [*reappearing, airily*]: What? No one—not one? You must be joking!

[*Laura nervously echoes her laugh. She slips in a fugitive manner through the half-open portieres and draws them gently behind her. A shaft of very clear light is thrown on her face against the faded tapestry of the curtains. Faintly the music of "The Glass Menagerie" is heard as she continues, lightly:*]

Not one gentleman caller? It can't be true! There must be a flood, there must have been a tornado!

LAURA: It isn't a flood, it's not a tornado, Mother. I'm just not popular like you were in Blue Mountain. . . .

[*Tom utters another groan. Laura glances at him with a faint, apologetic smile. Her voice catches a little:*]

Mother's afraid I'm going to be an old maid.

[*The scene dims out with the "Glass Menagerie" music.*]

SCENE TWO

On the dark stage the screen is lighted with the image of blue roses. Gradually Laura's figure becomes apparent and the screen goes out. The music subsides.

Laura is seated in the delicate ivory chair at the small claw-foot table. She wears a dress of soft violet material for a kimono—her hair is tied back from her forehead with a ribbon. She is washing and polishing her collection of glass. Amanda appears on the fire escape steps. At the sound of her ascent, Laura catches her breath, thrusts the bowl of ornaments away, and seats herself stiffly before the diagram of the typewriter keyboard as though it held her spellbound. Something has happened to Amanda. It is written in her face as she climbs to the landing: a look that is grim and hopeless and a little absurd. She has on one of those cheap or imitation velvety-looking cloth coats with imitation fur collar. Her hat is five or six years old, one of those dreadful cloche hats that were worn in the late Twenties, and she is clutching an enormous black patent-leather pocketbook with nickel clasps and initials. This is her full-dress outfit, the one she usually wears to the D.A.R. Before entering she looks through the door. She purses her lips, opens her eyes very wide, rolls them upward and shakes her head. Then she slowly lets herself in the door. Seeing her mother's expression Laura touches her lips with a nervous gesture.

LAURA: Hello, Mother, I was— [She makes a nervous gesture toward the chart on the wall. Amanda leans against the shut door and stares at Laura with a martyred look.]

AMANDA: Deception? Deception? [She slowly removes her hat and gloves, continuing the sweet suffering stare. She lets the hat and gloves fall on the floor—a bit of acting.]

29

LAURA [*shakily*]: How was the D.A.R. meeting?

[*Amanda slowly opens her purse and removes a dainty white handkerchief which she shakes out delicately and delicately touches to her lips and nostrils.*]

Didn't you go to the D.A.R. meeting, Mother?

AMANDA [*faintly, almost inaudibly*]: —No.—No. [*then more forcibly:*] I did not have the strength—to go to the D.A.R. In fact, I did not have the courage! I wanted to find a hole in the ground and hide myself in it forever! [*She crosses slowly to the wall and removes the diagram of the typewriter keyboard. She holds it in front of her for a second, staring at it sweetly and sorrowfully—then bites her lips and tears it in two pieces.*]

LAURA [*faintly*]: Why did you do that, Mother?

[*Amanda repeats the same procedure with the chart of the Gregg Alphabet.*]

Why are you—

AMANDA: Why? Why? How old are you, Laura?

LAURA: Mother, you know my age.

AMANDA: I thought that you were an adult; it seems that I was mistaken. [*She crosses slowly to the sofa and sinks down and stares at Laura.*]

LAURA: Please don't stare at me, Mother.

[*Amanda closes her eyes and lowers her head. There is a ten-second pause.*]

AMANDA: What are we going to do, what is going to become of us, what is the future?

[*There is another pause.*]

LAURA: Has something happened, Mother?

[*Amanda draws a long breath, takes out the handkerchief again, goes through the dabbing process.*]

Mother, has—something happened?

AMANDA: I'll be all right in a minute, I'm just bewildered —[*She hesitates.*]—by life. . . .

LAURA: Mother, I wish that you would tell me what's happened!

AMANDA: As you know, I was supposed to be inducted into my office at the D.A.R. this afternoon.

[*Screen image*: A swarm of typewriters.]

But I stopped off at Rubicam's Business College to speak to your teachers about your having a cold and ask them what progress they thought you were making down there.

LAURA: Oh. . . .

AMANDA: I went to the typing instructor and introduced myself as your mother. She didn't know who you were. "Wingfield," she said, "We don't have any such student enrolled at the school!"
I assured her she did, that you had been going to classes since early in January.
"I wonder," she said, "If you could be talking about that terribly shy little girl who dropped out of school after only a few days' attendance?"
"No," I said, "Laura, my daughter, has been going to school every day for the past six weeks!"
"Excuse me," she said. She took the attendance book out and there was your name, unmistakably printed, and all the dates you were absent until they decided that you had dropped out of school.

I still said, "No, there must have been some mistake! There must have been some mix-up in the records!"

And she said, "No—I remember her perfectly now. Her hands shook so that she couldn't hit the right keys! The first time we gave a speed test, she broke down completely—was sick at the stomach and almost had to be carried into the wash room! After that morning she never showed up any more. We phoned the house but never got any answer"—While I was working at Famous–Barr, I suppose, demonstrating those—

[*She indicates a brassiere with her hands.*]

Oh! I felt so weak I could barely keep on my feet! I had to sit down while they got me a glass of water! Fifty dollars' tuition, all of our plans—my hopes and ambitions for you— just gone up the spout, just gone up the spout like that.

[*Laura draws a long breath and gets awkwardly to her feet. She crosses to the Victrola and winds it up.*]

What are you doing?

LAURA: Oh! [*She releases the handle and returns to her seat.*]

AMANDA: Laura, where have you been going when you've gone out pretending that you were going to business college?

LAURA: I've just been going out walking.

AMANDA: That's not true.

LAURA: It is. I just went walking.

AMANDA: Walking? Walking? In winter? Deliberately courting pneumonia in that light coat? Where did you walk to, Laura?

LAURA: All sorts of places—mostly in the park.

AMANDA: Even after you'd started catching that cold?

LAURA: It was the lesser of two evils, Mother.

[*Screen image*: Winter scene in a park.]

I couldn't go back there. I—threw up—on the floor!

AMANDA: From half past seven till after five every day you mean to tell me you walked around in the park, because you wanted to make me think that you were still going to Rubicam's Business College?

LAURA: It wasn't as bad as it sounds. I went inside places to get warmed up.

AMANDA: Inside where?

LAURA: I went in the art museum and the bird houses at the Zoo. I visited the penguins every day! Sometimes I did without lunch and went to the movies. Lately I've been spending most of my afternoons in the Jewel Box, that big glass house where they raise the tropical flowers.

AMANDA: You did all this to deceive me, just for deception?

[*Laura looks down.*] Why?

LAURA: Mother, when you're disappointed, you get that awful suffering look on your face, like the picture of Jesus' mother in the museum!

AMANDA: Hush!

LAURA: I couldn't face it.

[*There is a pause. A whisper of strings is heard. Legend on screen*: "The Crust of Humility."]

AMANDA [*hopelessly fingering the huge pocketbook*]: So what are we going to do the rest of our lives? Stay home and

33

watch the parades go by? Amuse ourselves with the glass menagerie, darling? Eternally play those worn-out phonograph records your father left as a painful reminder of him? We won't have a business career—we've given that up because it gave us nervous indigestion! [*She laughs wearily.*] What is there left but dependency all our lives? I know so well what becomes of unmarried women who aren't prepared to occupy a position. I've seen such pitiful cases in the South— barely tolerated spinsters living upon the grudging patronage of sister's husband or brother's wife!—stuck away in some little mousetrap of a room—encouraged by one in-law to visit another—little birdlike women without any nest—eating the crust of humility all their life!

Is that the future that we've mapped out for ourselves? I swear it's the only alternative I can think of! [*She pauses.*] It isn't a very pleasant alternative, is it? [*She pauses again.*] Of course—some girls *do marry.*

[*Laura twists her hands nervously.*]

Haven't you ever liked some boy?

LAURA: Yes. I liked one once. [*She rises.*] I came across his picture a while ago.

AMANDA [*with some interest*]: He gave you his picture?

LAURA: No, it's in the yearbook.

AMANDA [*disappointed*]: Oh—a high school boy.

[*Screen image*: Jim as the high school hero bearing a silver cup.]

LAURA: Yes. His name was Jim. [*She lifts the heavy annual from the claw-foot table.*] Here he is in *The Pirates of Penzance.*

AMANDA [*absently*]: The what?

34

LAURA: The operetta the senior class put on. He had a wonderful voice and we sat across the aisle from each other Mondays, Wednesdays and Fridays in the Aud. Here he is with the silver cup for debating! See his grin?

AMANDA [*absently*]: He must have had a jolly disposition.

LAURA: He used to call me—Blue Roses.

[*Screen image*: Blue roses.]

AMANDA: Why did he call you such a name as that?

LAURA: When I had that attack of pleurosis—he asked me what was the matter when I came back. I said pleurosis—he thought that I said Blue Roses! So that's what he always called me after that. Whenever he saw me, he'd holler, "Hello, Blue Roses!" I didn't care for the girl that he went out with. Emily Meisenbach. Emily was the best-dressed girl at Soldan. She never struck me, though, as being sincere . . . It says in the Personal Section—they're engaged. That's—six years ago! They must be married by now.

AMANDA: Girls that aren't cut out for business careers usually wind up married to some nice man. [*She gets up with a spark of revival.*] Sister, that's what you'll do!

[*Laura utters a startled, doubtful laugh. She reaches quickly for a piece of glass.*]

LAURA: But, Mother—

AMANDA: Yes? [*She goes over to the photograph.*]

LAURA [*in a tone of frightened apology*]: I'm—crippled!

AMANDA: Nonsense! Laura, I've told you never, never to use that word. Why, you're not crippled, you just have a little defect—hardly noticeable, even! When people have some

35

slight disadvantage like that, they cultivate other things to make up for it—develop charm—and vivacity—and—*charm!* That's all you have to do! [*She turns again to the photograph.*] One thing your father had *plenty of*—was *charm!*

[*The scene fades out with music.*]

SCENE THREE

Legend on screen: "After the fiasco—"

Tom speaks from the fire escape landing.

TOM: After the fiasco at Rubicam's Business College, the idea of getting a gentleman caller for Laura began to play a more and more important part in Mother's calculations. It became an obsession. Like some archetype of the universal unconscious, the image of the gentleman caller haunted our small apartment. . . .

[*Screen image*: A young man at the door of a house with flowers.]

An evening at home rarely passed without some allusion to this image, this specter, this hope. . . . Even when he wasn't mentioned, his presence hung in Mother's preoccupied look and in my sister's frightened, apologetic manner—hung like a sentence passed upon the Wingfields!

Mother was a woman of action as well as words. She began to take logical steps in the planned direction. Late that winter and in the early spring—realizing that extra money would be needed to properly feather the nest and plume the bird—she conducted a vigorous campaign on the telephone, roping in subscribers to one of those magazines for matrons called *The Homemaker's Companion,* the type of journal that features the serialized sublimations of ladies of letters who think in terms of delicate cuplike breasts, slim, tapering waists, rich, creamy thighs, eyes like wood smoke in autumn, fingers that soothe and caress like strains of music, bodies as powerful as Etruscan sculpture.

[*Screen image*: The cover of a glamor magazine.]

37

[*Amanda enters with the telephone on a long extension cord. She is spotlighted in the dim stage.*]

AMANDA: Ida Scott? This is Amanda Wingfield! We *missed* you at the D.A.R. last Monday! I said to myself: She's probably suffering with that sinus condition! How is that sinus condition?

Horrors! Heaven have mercy!—You're a Christian martyr, yes, that's what your are, a Christian martyr!

Well, I just now happened to notice that your subscription to the *Companion*'s about to expire! Yes, it expires with the next issue, honey!—just when that wonderful new serial by Bessie Mae Hopper is getting off to such an exciting start. Oh, honey, it's something that you can't miss! You remember how *Gone with the Wind* took everybody by storm? You simply couldn't go out if you hadn't read it. All everybody *talked* was Scarlett O'Hara. Well, this is a book that critics already compare to *Gone with the Wind*. It's the *Gone with the Wind* of the post-World-War generation!—What?—Burning?—Oh, honey, don't let them burn, go take a look in the oven and I'll hold the wire! Heavens—I think she's hung up!

[*The scene dims out.*]

[*Legend on screen*: "You think I'm in love with Continental Shoemakers?"]

[*Before the lights come up again, the violent voices of Tom and Amanda are heard. They are quarreling behind the portieres. In front of them stands Laura with clenched hands and panicky expression. A clear pool of light is on her figure throughout this scene.*]

TOM: What in Christ's name am I—

AMANDA [*shrilly*]: Don't you use that—

TOM: —supposed to do!

AMANDA: —expression! Not in my—

TOM: Ohhh!

AMANDA: —presence! Have you gone out of your senses?

TOM: I have, that's true, *driven* out!

AMANDA: What is the matter with you, you—big—big—
IDIOT!

TOM: Look!—I've got *no thing,* no single thing—

AMANDA: Lower your voice!

TOM: —in my life here that I can call my OWN! Everything
is—

AMANDA: Stop that shouting!

TOM: Yesterday you confiscated my books! You had the
nerve to—

AMANDA: I took that horrible novel back to the library—
yes! That hideous book by that insane Mr. Lawrence.

[*Tom laughs wildly.*]

I cannot control the output of diseased minds or people who
cater to them—

[*Tom laughs still more wildly.*]

BUT I WON'T ALLOW SUCH FILTH BROUGHT INTO MY HOUSE!
No, no, no, no, no!

TOM: House, house! Who pays rent on it, who makes a
slave of himself to—

AMANDA [*fairly screeching*]: Don't you DARE to—

39

TOM: No, no, *I* mustn't say things! *I've* got to just—

AMANDA: Let me tell you—

TOM: I don't want to hear any more!

[*He tears the portieres open. The dining-room area is lit with a turgid smoky red glow. Now we see Amanda; her hair is in metal curlers and she is wearing a very old bath-robe, much too large for her slight figure, a relic of the faithless Mr. Wingfield. The upright typewriter now stands on the drop-leaf table, along with a wild disarray of manu-scripts. The quarrel was probably precipitated by Amanda's interruption of Tom's creative labor. A chair lies over-thrown on the floor. Their gesticulating shadows are cast on the ceiling by the fiery glow.*]

AMANDA: You *will* hear more, you—

TOM: No, I won't hear more, I'm going out!

AMANDA: You come right back in—

TOM: Out, out, out! Because I'm—

AMANDA: Come back here, Tom Wingfield! I'm not through talking to you!

TOM: Oh, go—

LAURA [*desperately*]: —Tom!

AMANDA: You're going to listen, and no more insolence from you! I'm at the end of my patience!

[*He comes back toward her.*]

TOM: What do you think I'm at? Aren't I supposed to have any patience to reach the end of, Mother? I know, I know. It seems unimportant to you, what I'm *doing*—what I *want* to

40

do—having a little *difference* between them! You don't think that—

AMANDA: I think you've been doing things that you're ashamed of. That's why you act like this. I don't believe that you go every night to the movies. Nobody goes to the movies night after night. Nobody in their right minds goes to the movies as often as you pretend to. People don't go to the movies at nearly midnight, and movies don't let out at two A.M. Come in stumbling. Muttering to yourself like a maniac! You get three hours' sleep and then go to work. Oh, I can picture the way you're doing down there. Moping, doping, because you're in no condition.

TOM [*wildly*]: No, I'm in no condition!

AMANDA: What right have you got to jeopardize your job? Jeopardize the security of us all? How do you think we'd manage if you were—

TOM: Listen! You think I'm crazy about the *warehouse?* [*He bends fiercely toward her slight figure.*] You think I'm in love with the Continental Shoemakers? You think I want to spend fifty-five *years* down there in that—*celotex interior!* with—*fluorescent—tubes!* Look! I'd rather somebody picked up a crowbar and battered out my brains—than go back mornings! I *go!* Every time you come in yelling that God-damn *"Rise and Shine!" "Rise and Shine!"* I say to myself, "How *lucky dead* people are!" But I get up. I *go!* For sixty-five dollars a month I give up all that I dream of doing and being *ever!* And you say self—*self's* all I ever think of. Why, listen, if self is what I thought of, Mother, I'd be where he is—GONE! [*He points to his father's picture.*] As far as the system of transportation reaches! [*He starts past her. She grabs his arm.*] Don't grab at me, Mother!

AMANDA: Where are you going?

41

TOM: I'm going to the *movies!*

AMANDA: I don't believe that lie!

[*Tom crouches toward her, overtowering her tiny figure. She backs away, gasping.*]

TOM: I'm going to opium dens! Yes, opium dens, dens of vice and criminals' hangouts, Mother. I've joined the Hogan Gang, I'm a hired assassin, I carry a tommy gun in a violin case! I run a string of cat houses in the Valley! They call me Killer, Killer Wingfield, I'm leading a double-life, a simple, honest warehouse worker by day, by night a dynamic *czar* of the *underworld, Mother.* I go to gambling casinos, I spin away fortunes on the roulette table! I wear a patch over one eye and a false mustache, sometimes I put on green whiskers. On those occasions they call me—*El Diablo!* Oh, I could tell you many things to make you sleepless! My enemies plan to dynamite this place. They're going to blow us all sky-high some night! I'll be glad, very happy, and so will you! You'll go up, up on a broomstick, over Blue Mountain with seventeen gentlemen callers! You ugly—babbling old—*witch.* . . . [*He goes through a series of violent, clumsy movements, seizing his overcoat, lunging to the door, pulling it fiercely open. The women watch him, aghast. His arm catches in the sleeve of the coat as he struggles to pull it on. For a moment he is pinioned by the bulky garment. With an outraged groan he tears the coat off again, splitting the shoulder of it, and hurls it across the room. It strikes against the shelf of Laura's glass collection, and there is a tinkle of shattering glass. Laura cries out as if wounded.*]

[*Music.*]

[*Screen legend*: "The Glass Menagerie."]

LAURA [*shrilly*]: *My glass!*—menagerie. . . . [*She covers her face and turns away.*]

[*But Amanda is still stunned and stupefied by the "ugly witch" so that she barely notices this occurrence. Now she recovers her speech.*]

AMANDA [*in an awful voice*]: I won't speak to you—until you apologize!

[*She crosses through the portieres and draws them together behind her. Tom is left with Laura. Laura clings weakly to the mantel with her face averted. Tom stares at her stupidly for a moment. Then he crosses to the shelf. He drops awkwardly on his knees to collect the fallen glass, glancing at Laura as if he would speak but couldn't.*]

[*"The Glass Menagerie" music steals in as the scene dims out.*]

The interior of the apartment is dark. There is a faint light in the alley. A deep-voiced bell in a church is tolling the hour of five.

Tom appears at the top of the alley. After each solemn boom of the bell in the tower, he shakes a little noisemaker or rattle as if to express the tiny spasm of man in contrast to the sustained power and dignity of the Almighty. This and the unsteadiness of his advance make it evident that he has been drinking. As he climbs the few steps to the fire escape landing light steals up inside. Laura appears in the front room in a nightdress. She notices that Tom's bed is empty. Tom fishes in his pockets for his door key, removing a motley assortment of articles in the search, including a shower of movie ticket stubs and an empty bottle. At last he finds the key, but just as he is about to insert it, it slips from his fingers. He strikes a match and crouches below the door.

TOM [*bitterly*]: One crack—and it falls through!

[*Laura opens the door.*]

LAURA: Tom! Tom, what are you doing?

TOM: Looking for a door key.

LAURA: Where have you been all this time?

TOM: I have been to the movies.

LAURA: All this time at the movies?

TOM: There was a very long program. There was a Garbo picture and a Mickey Mouse and a travelogue and a newsreel and a preview of coming attractions. And there was an organ solo and a collection for the Milk Fund—simultaneously—

which ended up in a terrible fight between a fat lady and an usher!

LAURA [*innocently*]: Did you have to stay through everything?

TOM: Of course! And, oh, I forgot! There was a big stage show! The headliner on this stage show was Malvolio the Magician. He performed wonderful tricks, many of them, such as pouring water back and forth between pitchers. First it turned to wine and then it turned to beer and then it turned to whisky. I know it was whisky it finally turned into because he needed somebody to come up out of the audience to help him, and I came up—both shows! It was Kentucky Straight Bourbon. A very generous fellow, he gave souvenirs. [*He pulls from his back pocket a shimmering rainbow-colored scarf.*] He gave me this. This is his magic scarf. You can have it, Laura. You wave it over a canary cage and you get a bowl of goldfish. You wave it over the goldfish bowl and they fly away canaries. . . . But the wonderfullest trick of all was the coffin trick. We nailed him into a coffin and he got out of the coffin without removing one nail. [*He has come inside.*] There is a trick that would come in handy for me—get me out of this two-by-four situation! [*He flops onto the bed and starts removing his shoes.*]

LAURA: Tom—shhh!

TOM: What're you shushing me for?

LAURA: You'll wake up Mother.

TOM: Goody, goody! Pay 'er back for all those "Rise an' Shines." [*He lies down, groaning.*] You know it don't take much intelligence to get yourself into a nailed-up coffin, Laura. But who in hell ever got himself out of one without removing one nail?

45

[*As if in answer, the father's grinning photograph lights up. The scene dims out.*]

[*Immediately following, the church bell is heard striking six. At the sixth stroke the alarm clock goes off in Amanda's room, and after a few moments we hear her calling: "Rise and Shine! Rise and Shine! Laura, go tell your brother to rise and shine!"*]

TOM [*sitting up slowly*]: I'll rise—but I won't shine.

[*The light increases.*]

AMANDA: Laura, tell your brother his coffee is ready.

[*Laura slips into the front room.*]

LAURA: Tom!—It's nearly seven. Don't make Mother nervous.

[*He stares at her stupidly.*]

[*beseechingly*:] Tom, speak to Mother this morning. Make up with her, apologize, speak to her!

TOM: She won't to me. It's her that started not speaking.

LAURA: If you just say you're sorry she'll start speaking.

TOM: Her not speaking—is that such a tragedy?

LAURA: Please—please!

AMANDA [*calling from the kitchenette*]: Laura, are you going to do what I asked you to do, or do I have to get dressed and go out myself?

LAURA: Going, going—soon as I get on my coat!

[*She pulls on a shapeless felt hat with a nervous, jerky movement, pleadingly glancing at Tom. She rushes awk-*

wardly for her coat. The coat is one of Amanda's, inaccurately made-over, the sleeves too short for Laura.]

Butter and what else?

AMANDA [*entering from the kitchenette*]: Just butter. Tell them to charge it.

LAURA: Mother, they make such faces when I do that.

AMANDA: Sticks and stones can break our bones, but the expression on Mr. Garfinkel's face won't harm us! Tell your brother his coffee is getting cold.

LAURA [*at the door*]: Do what I asked you, will you, will you, Tom?

[*He looks sullenly away.*]

AMANDA: Laura, go now or just don't go at all!

LAURA [*rushing out*]: Going—going!

[*A second later she cries out. Tom springs up and crosses to the door. Tom opens the door.*]

TOM: Laura?

LAURA: I'm all right. I slipped, but I'm all right.

AMANDA [*peering anxiously after her*]: If anyone breaks a leg on those fire-escape steps, the landlord ought to be sued for every cent he possesses! [*She shuts the door. Now she remembers she isn't speaking to Tom and returns to the other room.*]

[*As Tom comes listlessly for his coffee, she turns her back to him and stands rigidly facing the window on the gloomy gray vault of the areaway. Its light on her face with its aged but childish features is cruelly sharp, satirical as a Daumier print.*]

47

[*The music of "Ave Maria," is heard softly.*]

[*Tom glances sheepishly but sullenly at her averted figure and slumps at the table. The coffee is scalding hot; he sips it and gasps and spits it back in the cup. At his gasp, Amanda catches her breath and half turns. Then she catches herself and turns back to the window. Tom blows on his coffee, glancing sidewise at his mother. She clears her throat. Tom clears his. He starts to rise, sinks back down again, scratches his head, clears his throat again. Amanda coughs. Tom raises his cup in both hands to blow on it, his eyes staring over the rim of it at his mother for several moments. Then he slowly sets the cup down and awkwardly and hesitantly rises from the chair.*]

TOM [*hoarsely*]: Mother. I—I apologize, Mother.

[*Amanda draws a quick, shuddering breath. Her face works grotesquely. She breaks into childlike tears.*]

I'm sorry for what I said, for everything that I said, I didn't mean it.

AMANDA [*sobbingly*]: My devotion has made me a witch and so I make myself hateful to my children!

TOM: *No,* you *don't.*

AMANDA: I worry so much, don't sleep, it makes me nervous!

TOM [*gently*]: I understand that.

AMANDA: I've had to put up a solitary battle all these years. But you're my right-hand bower! Don't fall down, don't fail!

TOM [*gently*]: I try, Mother.

AMANDA [*with great enthusiasm*]: Try and you will *succeed!* [*The notion makes her breathless.*] Why, you—you're just *full* of natural endowments! Both of my children— they're *unusual* children! Don't you think I know it? I'm so —*proud!* Happy and—feel I've—so much to be thankful for but— promise me one thing, son!

TOM: What, Mother?

AMANDA: Promise, son, you'll—never be a drunkard!

TOM [*turns to her grinning*]: I will never be a drunkard, Mother.

AMANDA: That's what frightened me so, that you'd be drinking! Eat a bowl of Purina!

TOM: Just coffee, Mother.

AMANDA: Shredded wheat biscuit?

TOM: No. No, Mother, just coffee.

AMANDA: You can't put in a day's work on an empty stomach. You've got ten minutes—don't gulp! Drinking too-hot liquids makes cancer of the stomach. . . . Put cream in.

TOM: No, thank you.

AMANDA: To cool it.

TOM: No! No, thank you, I want it black.

AMANDA: I know, but it's not good for you. We have to do all that we can to build ourselves up. In these trying times we live in, all that we have to cling to is—each other. . . . That's why it's so important to— Tom, I— I sent out your sister so I could discuss something with you. If you hadn't spoken I would have spoken to you. [*She sits down.*]

49

TOM [*gently*]: What is it, Mother, that you want to discuss?

AMANDA: *Laura!*

[*Tom puts his cup down slowly.*]

[*Legend on screen*: "Laura." *Music*: *"The Glass Menagerie."*]

TOM: —Oh.—Laura . . .

AMANDA [*touching his sleeve*]: You know how Laura is. So quiet but—still water runs deep! She notices things and I think she—broods about them.

[*Tom looks up.*]

A few days ago I came in and she was crying.

TOM: What about?

AMANDA: You.

TOM: Me?

AMANDA: She has an idea that you're not happy here.

TOM: What gave her that idea?

AMANDA: What gives her any idea? However, you do act strangely. I—I'm not criticizing, understand *that!* I know your ambitions do not lie in the warehouse, that like everybody in the whole wide world—you've had to—make sacrifices, but— Tom—Tom—life's not easy, it calls for—Spartan endurance! There's so many things in my heart that I cannot describe to you! I've never told you but I—*loved* your father. . . .

TOM [*gently*]: I know that, Mother.

AMANDA: And you—when I see you taking after his ways! Staying out late—and—well, you *had* been drinking the night you were in that—terrifying condition! Laura says that you hate the apartment and that you go out nights to get away from it! Is that true, Tom?

TOM: No. You say there's so much in your heart that you can't describe to me. That's true of me, too. There's so much in my heart that I can't describe to *you!* So let's respect each other's—

AMANDA: But, why—*why*, Tom—are you always so *restless?* Where do you *go* to, nights?

TOM: I—go to the movies.

AMANDA: Why do you go to the movies so much, Tom?

TOM: I go to the movies because—I like adventure. Adventure is something I don't have much of at work, so I go to the movies.

AMANDA: But, Tom, you go to the movies *entirely* too *much!*

TOM: I like a lot of adventure.

[*Amanda looks baffled, then hurt. As the familiar inquisition resumes, Tom becomes hard and impatient again. Amanda slips back into her querulous attitude toward him.*]

[*Image on screen*: A sailing vessel with Jolly Roger.]

AMANDA: Most young men find adventure in their careers.

TOM: Then most young men are not employed in a warehouse.

AMANDA: The world is full of young men employed in warehouses and offices and factories.

TOM: Do all of them find adventure in their careers?

51

AMANDA: They do or they do without it! Not everybody has a craze for adventure.

TOM: Man is by instinct a lover, a hunter, a fighter, and none of those instincts are given much play at the warehouse!

AMANDA: Man is by instinct! Don't quote instinct to me! Instinct is something that people have got away from! It belongs to animals! Christian adults don't want it!

TOM: What do Christian adults want, then, Mother?

AMANDA: Superior things! Things of the mind and the spirit! Only animals have to satisfy instincts! Surely your aims are somewhat higher than theirs! Than monkeys—pigs—

TOM: I reckon they're not.

AMANDA: You're joking. However, that isn't what I wanted to discuss.

TOM [*rising*]: I haven't much time.

AMANDA [*pushing his shoulders*]: Sit down.

TOM: You want me to punch in red at the warehouse, Mother?

AMANDA: You have five minutes. I want to talk about Laura.

[*Screen legend*: "Plans and Provisions."]

TOM: All right! What about Laura?

AMANDA: We have to be making some plans and provisions for her. She's older than you, two years, and nothing has happened. She just drifts along doing nothing. It frightens me terribly how she just drifts along.

TOM: I guess she's the type that people call home girls.

AMANDA: There's no such type, and if there is, it's a pity! That is unless the home is hers, with a husband!

TOM: What?

AMANDA: Oh, I can see the handwriting on the wall as plain as I see the nose in front of my face! It's terrifying! More and more you remind me of your father! He was out all hours without explanation!—Then *left! Goodbye!* And me with the bag to hold. I saw that letter you got from the Merchant Marine. I know what you're dreaming of. I'm not standing here blindfolded. [*She pauses.*] Very well, then. Then *do* it! But not till there's somebody to take your place.

TOM: What do you mean?

AMANDA: I mean that as soon as Laura has got somebody to take care of her, married, a home of her own, independent —why, then you'll be free to go wherever you please, on land, on sea, whichever way the wind blows you! But until that time you've got to look out for your sister. I don't say me because I'm old and don't matter! I say for your sister because she's young and dependent.

I put her in business college—a dismal failure! Frightened her so it made her sick at the stomach. I took her over to the Young People's League at the church. Another fiasco. She spoke to nobody, nobody spoke to her. Now all she does is fool with those pieces of glass and play those worn-out records. What kind of a life is that for a girl to lead?

TOM: What can I do about it?

AMANDA: Overcome selfishness! Self, self, self is all that you ever think of!

[*Tom springs up and crosses to get his coat. It is ugly and bulky. He pulls on a cap with earmuffs.*]

53

Where is your muffler? Put your wool muffler on!

[*He snatches it angrily from the closet, tosses it around his neck and pulls both ends tight.*]

Tom! I haven't said what I had in mind to ask you.

TOM: I'm too late to—

AMANDA [*catching his arm—very importunately; then shyly*]: Down at the warehouse, aren't there some—nice young men?

TOM: No!

AMANDA: There *must* be—*some* . . .

TOM: Mother—[*He gestures.*]

AMANDA: Find out one that's clean-living—doesn't drink and ask him out for sister!

TOM: What?

AMANDA: For *sister!* To *meet!* Get *acquainted!*

TOM [*stamping to the door*]: Oh, my *go-osh!*

AMANDA: Will you?

[*He opens the door. She says, imploringly:*]

Will you?

[*He starts down the fire escape.*]

Will you? *Will* you, dear?

TOM [*calling back*]: *Yes!*

[*Amanda closes the door hesitantly and with a troubled but faintly hopeful expression.*]

[*Screen image*: The cover of a glamor magazine.]

[*The spotlight picks up Amanda at the phone.*]

AMANDA: Ella Cartwright? This is Amanda Wingfield!
How are you, honey?
How is that kidney condition?

[*There is a five-second pause.*]

Horrors!

[*There is another pause.*]

You're a Christian martyr, yes, honey, that's what you are, a
Christian martyr! Well, I just now happened to notice in
my little red book that your subscription to the *Companion*
has just run out! I knew that you wouldn't want to miss out
on the wonderful serial starting in this new issue. It's by Bessie
Mae Hopper, the first thing she's written since *Honeymoon for
Three.* Wasn't that a strange and interesting story? Well, this
one is even lovelier, I believe. It has a sophisticated, society
background. It's all about the horsey set on Long Island!

[*The light fades out.*]

55

SCENE FIVE

Legend on the screen: "Annunciation."

Music is heard as the light slowly comes on.

It is early dusk of a spring evening. Supper has just been finished in the Wingfield apartment. Amanda and Laura, in light-colored dresses, are removing dishes from the table in the dining room, which is shadowy, their movements formalized almost as a dance or ritual, their moving forms as pale and silent as moths. Tom, in white shirt and trousers, rises from the table and crosses toward the fire escape.

AMANDA [*as he passes her*]: Son, will you do me a favor?

TOM: What?

AMANDA: Comb your hair! You look so pretty when your hair is combed!

[*Tom slouches on the sofa with the evening paper. Its enormous headline reads: "Franco Triumphs."*]

There is only one respect in which I would like you to emulate your father.

TOM: What respect is that?

AMANDA: The care he always took of his appearance. He never allowed himself to look untidy.

[*He throws down the paper and crosses to the fire escape.*]

Where are you going?

TOM: I'm going out to smoke.

AMANDA: You smoke too much. A pack a day at fifteen cents a pack. How much would that amount to in a month?

56

Thirty times fifteen is how much, Tom? Figure it out and you will be astounded at what you could save. Enough to give you a night-school course in accounting at Washington U.! Just think what a wonderful thing that would be for you, son!

[*Tom is unmoved by the thought.*]

TOM: I'd rather smoke. [*He steps out on the landing, letting the screen door slam.*]

AMANDA [*sharply*]: I know! That's the tragedy of it. . . . [*Alone, she turns to look at her husband's picture.*]

[*Dance music: "The World Is Waiting for the Sunrise!"*]

TOM [*to the audience*]: Across the alley from us was the Paradise Dance Hall. On evenings in spring the windows and doors were open and the music came outdoors. Sometimes the lights were turned out except for a large glass sphere that hung from the ceiling. It would turn slowly about and filter the dusk with delicate rainbow colors. Then the orchestra played a waltz or a tango, something that had a slow and sensuous rhythm. Couples would come outside, to the relative privacy of the alley. You could see them kissing behind ash pits and telephone poles. This was the compensation for lives that passed like mine, without any change or adventure. Adventure and change were imminent in this year. They were waiting around the corner for all these kids. Suspended in the mist over Berchtesgaden, caught in the folds of Chamberlain's umbrella. In Spain there was Guernica! But here there was only hot swing music and liquor, dance halls, bars, and movies, and sex that hung in the gloom like a chandelier and flooded the world with brief, deceptive rainbows. . . . All the world was waiting for bombardments!

[*Amanda turns from the picture and comes outside.*]

57

AMANDA [*sighing*]: A fire escape landing's a poor excuse for a porch. [*She spreads a newspaper on a step and sits down, gracefully and demurely as if she were settling into a swing on a Mississippi veranda.*] What are you looking at?

TOM: The moon.

AMANDA: Is there a moon this evening?

TOM: It's rising over Garfinkel's Delicatessen.

AMANDA: So it is! A little silver slipper of a moon. Have you made a wish on it yet?

TOM: Um-hum.

AMANDA: What did you wish for?

TOM: That's a secret.

AMANDA: A secret, huh? Well, I won't tell mine either. I will be just as mysterious as you.

TOM: I bet I can guess what yours is.

AMANDA: Is my head so transparent?

TOM: You're not a sphinx.

AMANDA: No, I don't have secrets. I'll tell you what I wished for on the moon. Success and happiness for my precious children! I wish for that whenever there's a moon, and when there isn't a moon, I wish for it, too.

TOM: I thought perhaps you wished for a gentleman caller.

AMANDA: Why do you say that?

TOM: Don't you remember asking me to fetch one?

AMANDA: I remember suggesting that it would be nice for your sister if you brought home some nice young man from the warehouse. I think that I've made that suggestion more than once.

TOM: Yes, you have made it repeatedly.

AMANDA: Well?

TOM: We are going to have one.

AMANDA: *What?*

TOM: A gentleman caller!

[*The annunciation is celebrated with music.*]

[*Amanda rises.*]

[*Image on screen*: A caller with a bouquet.]

AMANDA: You mean you have asked some nice young man to come over?

TOM: Yep. I've asked him to dinner.

AMANDA: You really did?

TOM: I did!

AMANDA: You did, and did he—*accept?*

TOM: He did!

AMANDA: Well, well—well, well! That's—lovely!

TOM: I thought that you would be pleased.

AMANDA: It's definite then?

TOM: Very definite.

AMANDA: Soon?

TOM: Very soon.

AMANDA: For heaven's sake, stop putting on and tell me some things, will you?

TOM: What things do you want me to tell you?

AMANDA: *Naturally* I would like to know when he's *coming!*

TOM: He's coming tomorrow.

AMANDA: *Tomorrow?*

TOM: Yep. Tomorrow.

AMANDA: But, Tom!

TOM: Yes, Mother?

AMANDA: Tomorrow gives me no time!

TOM: Time for what?

AMANDA: Preparations! Why didn't you phone me at once, as soon as you asked him, the minute that he accepted? Then, don't you see, I could have been getting ready!

TOM: You don't have to make any fuss.

AMANDA: Oh, Tom, Tom, Tom, of course I have to make a fuss! I want things nice, not sloppy! Not thrown together. I'll certainly have to do some fast thinking, won't I?

TOM: I don't see why you have to think at all.

AMANDA: You just don't know. We can't have a gentleman caller in a pigsty! All my wedding silver has to be polished, the monogrammed table linen ought to be laundered! The windows have to be washed and fresh curtains put up. And how about clothes? We have to *wear* something, don't we?

TOM: Mother, this boy is no one to make a fuss over!

60

AMANDA: Do you realize he's the first young man we've introduced to your sister? It's terrible, dreadful, disgraceful that poor little sister has never received a single gentleman caller! Tom, come inside! [*She opens the screen door.*]

TOM: What for?

AMANDA: I want to ask you some things.

TOM: If you're going to make such a fuss, I'll call it off, I'll tell him not to come!

AMANDA: You certainly won't do anything of the kind. Nothing offends people worse than broken engagements. It simply means I'll have to work like a Turk! We won't be brilliant, but we will pass inspection. Come on inside.

[*Tom follows her inside, groaning.*]

Sit down.

TOM: Any particular place you would like me to sit?

AMANDA: Thank heavens I've got that new sofa! I'm also making payments on a floor lamp I'll have sent out! And put the chintz covers on, they'll brighten things up! Of course I'd hoped to have these walls re-papered. . . . What is the young man's name?

TOM: His name is O'Connor.

AMANDA: That, of course, means fish—tomorrow is Friday! I'll have that salmon loaf—with Durkee's dressing! What does he do? He works at the warehouse?

TOM: Of course! How else would I—

AMANDA: Tom, he—doesn't drink?

TOM: Why do you ask me that?

61

AMANDA: Your father *did!*

TOM: Don't get started on that!

AMANDA: He *does* drink, then?

TOM: Not that I know of!

AMANDA: Make sure, be certain! The last thing I want for my daughter's a boy who drinks!

TOM: Aren't you being a little bit premature? Mr. O'Connor has not yet appeared on the scene!

AMANDA: But will tomorrow. To meet your sister, and what do I know about his character? Nothing! Old maids are better off than wives of drunkards!

TOM: Oh, my God!

AMANDA: Be still!

TOM [*leaning forward to whisper*]: Lots of fellows meet girls whom they don't marry!

AMANDA: Oh, talk sensibly, Tom—and don't be sarcastic! [*She has gotten a hairbrush.*]

TOM: What are you doing?

AMANDA: I'm brushing that cowlick down! [*She attacks his hair with the brush.*] What is this young man's position at the warehouse?

TOM [*submitting grimly to the brush and the interrogation*]: This young man's position is that of a shipping clerk, Mother.

AMANDA: Sounds to me like a fairly responsible job, the sort of a job *you* would be in if you just had more *get-up.* What is his salary? Have you any idea?

TOM: I would judge it to be approximately eighty-five dollars a month.

AMANDA: Well—not princely, but—

TOM: Twenty more than I make.

AMANDA: Yes, how well I know! But for a family man, eighty-five dollars a month is not much more than you can just get by on. . . .

TOM: Yes, but Mr. O'Connor is not a family man.

AMANDA: He might be, mightn't he? Some time in the future?

TOM: I see. Plans and provisions.

AMANDA: You are the only young man that I know of who ignores the fact that the future becomes the present, the present the past, and the past turns into everlasting regret if you don't plan for it!

TOM: I will think that over and see what I can make of it.

AMANDA: Don't be supercilious with your mother! Tell me some more about this—what do you call him?

TOM: James D. O'Connor. The D. is for Delaney.

AMANDA: Irish on *both* sides! *Gracious!* And doesn't drink?

TOM: Shall I call him up and ask him right this minute?

AMANDA: The only way to find out about those things is to make discreet inquiries at the proper moment. When I was a girl in Blue Mountain and it was suspected that a young man drank, the girl whose attentions he had been receiving, if any girl *was*, would sometimes speak to the minister of his

63

church, or rather her father would if her father was living, and sort of feel him out on the young man's character. That is the way such things are discreetly handled to keep a young woman from making a tragic mistake!

TOM: Then how did you happen to make a tragic mistake?

AMANDA: That innocent look of your father's had everyone fooled! He *smiled*—the world was *enchanted!* No girl can do worse than put herself at the mercy of a handsome appearance! I hope that Mr. O'Connor is not too good-looking.

TOM: No, he's not too good-looking. He's covered with freckles and hasn't too much of a nose.

AMANDA: He's not right-down homely, though?

TOM: Not right-down homely. Just medium homely, I'd say.

AMANDA: Character's what to look for in a man.

TOM: That's what I've always said, Mother.

AMANDA: You've never said anything of the kind and I suspect you would never give it a thought.

TOM: Don't be so suspicious of me.

AMANDA: At least I hope he's the type that's up and coming.

TOM: I think he really goes in for self-improvement.

AMANDA: What reason have you to think so?

TOM: He goes to night school.

AMANDA [*beaming*]: Splendid! What does he do, I mean study?

TOM: Radio engineering and public speaking!

64

AMANDA: Then he has visions of being advanced in the world! Any young man who studies public speaking is aiming to have an executive job some day! And radio engineering? A thing for the future! Both of these facts are very illuminating. Those are the sort of things that a mother should know concerning any young man who comes to call on her daughter. Seriously or—not.

TOM: One little warning. He doesn't know about Laura. I didn't let on that we had dark ulterior motives. I just said, why don't you come and have dinner with us? He said okay and that was the whole conversation.

AMANDA: I bet it was! You're eloquent as an oyster. However, he'll know about Laura when he gets here. When he sees how lovely and sweet and pretty she is, he'll thank his lucky stars he was asked to dinner.

TOM: Mother, you mustn't expect too much of Laura.

AMANDA: What do you mean?

TOM: Laura seems all those things to you and me because she's ours and we love her. We don't even notice she's crippled any more.

AMANDA: Don't say crippled! You know that I never allow that word to be used!

TOM: But face facts, Mother. She is and—that's not all—

AMANDA: What do you mean "not all"?

TOM: Laura is very different from other girls.

AMANDA: I think the difference is all to her advantage.

TOM: Not quite all—in the eyes of others—strangers—she's terribly shy and lives in a world of her own and those

65

things make her seem a little peculiar to people outside the house.

AMANDA: Don't say peculiar.

TOM: Face the facts. She is.

[*The dance hall music changes to a tango that has a minor and somewhat ominous tone.*]

AMANDA: In what way is she peculiar—may I ask?

TOM [*gently*]: She lives in a world of her own—a world of little glass ornaments, Mother. . . .

[*He gets up. Amanda remains holding the brush, looking at him, troubled.*]

She plays old phonograph records and—that's about all— [*He glances at himself in the mirror and crosses to the door.*]

AMANDA [*sharply*]: Where are you going?

TOM: I'm going to the movies. [*He goes out the screen door.*]

AMANDA: Not to the movies, every night to the movies! [*She follows quickly to the screen door.*] I don't believe you always go to the movies!

[*He is gone. Amanda looks worriedly after him for a moment. Then vitality and optimism return and she turns from the door, crossing to the portieres.*]

Laura! Laura!

[*Laura answers from the kitchenette.*]

LAURA: Yes, Mother.

AMANDA: Let those dishes go and come in front!

[*Laura appears with a dish towel. Amanda speaks to her gaily.*]

Laura, come here and make a wish on the moon!

[*Screen image*: The Moon.]

LAURA [*entering*]: Moon—moon?

AMANDA: A little silver slipper of a moon. Look over your left shoulder, Laura, and make a wish!

[*Laura looks faintly puzzled as if called out of sleep. Amanda seizes her shoulders and turns her at an angle by the door.*]

Now! Now, darling, *wish!*

LAURA: What shall I wish for, Mother?

AMANDA [*her voice trembling and her eyes suddenly filling with tears*]: Happiness! Good fortune!

[*The sound of the violin rises and the stage dims out.*]

SCENE SIX

The light comes up on the fire escape landing. Tom is leaning against the grill, smoking.

[*Screen image*: The high school hero.]

TOM: And so the following evening I brought Jim home to dinner. I had known Jim slightly in high school. In high school Jim was a hero. He had tremendous Irish good nature and vitality with the scrubbed and polished look of white chinaware. He seemed to move in a continual spotlight. He was a star in basketball, captain of the debating club, president of the senior class and the glee club and he sang the male lead in the annual light operas. He was always running or bounding, never just walking. He seemed always at the point of defeating the law of gravity. He was shooting with such velocity through his adolescence that you would logically expect him to arrive at nothing short of the White House by the time he was thirty. But Jim apparently ran into more interference after his graduation from Soldan. His speed had definitely slowed. Six years after he left high school he was holding a job that wasn't much better than mine.

[*Screen image*: The Clerk.]

He was the only one at the warehouse with whom I was on friendly terms. I was valuable to him as someone who could remember his former glory, who had seen him win basketball games and the silver cup in debating. He knew of my secret practice of retiring to a cabinet of the washroom to work on poems when business was slack in the warehouse. He called me Shakespeare. And while the other boys in the warehouse regarded me with suspicious hostility, Jim took a humorous attitude toward me. Gradually his attitude affected the others, their hostility wore off and they also began to smile at me as

68

people smile at an oddly fashioned dog who trots across their path at some distance.

I knew that Jim and Laura had known each other at Soldan, and I had heard Laura speak admiringly of his voice. I didn't know if Jim remembered her or not. In high school Laura had been as unobtrusive as Jim had been astonishing. If he did remember Laura, it was not as my sister, for when I asked him to dinner, he grinned and said, "You know, Shakespeare, I never thought of you as having folks!"

He was about to discover that I did. . . .

[*Legend on screen*: "The accent of a coming foot."]

[*The light dims out on Tom and comes up in the Wingfield living room—a delicate lemony light. It is about five on a Friday evening of late spring which comes "scattering poems in the sky."*]

[*Amanda has worked like a Turk in preparation for the gentleman caller. The results are astonishing. The new floor lamp with its rose silk shade is in place, a colored paper lantern conceals the broken light fixture in the ceiling, new billowing white curtains are at the windows, chintz covers are on the chairs and sofa, a pair of new sofa pillows make their initial appearance. Open boxes and tissue paper are scattered on the floor.*]

[*Laura stands in the middle of the room with lifted arms while Amanda crouches before her, adjusting the hem of a new dress, devout and ritualistic. The dress is colored and designed by memory. The arrangement of Laura's hair is changed; it is softer and more becoming. A fragile, unearthly prettiness has come out in Laura: she is like a piece of translucent glass touched by light, given a momentary radiance, not actual, not lasting.*]

AMANDA [*impatiently*]: Why are you trembling?

69

LAURA: Mother, you've made me so nervous!

AMANDA: How have I made you nervous?

LAURA: By all this fuss! You make it seem so important!

AMANDA: I don't understand you, Laura. You couldn't be satisfied with just sitting home, and yet whenever I try to arrange something for you, you seem to resist it. [*She gets up.*] Now take a look at yourself. No, wait! Wait just a moment—I have an idea!

LAURA: What is it now?

[*Amanda produces two powder puffs which she wraps in handkerchiefs and stuffs in Laura's bosom.*]

LAURA: Mother, what are you doing?

AMANDA: They call them "Gay Deceivers"!

LAURA: I won't wear them!

AMANDA: You will!

LAURA: Why should I?

AMANDA: Because, to be painfully honest, your chest is flat.

LAURA: You make it seem like we were setting a trap.

AMANDA: All pretty girls are a trap, a pretty trap, and men expect them to be.

[*Legend on screen*: "A pretty trap."]

Now look at yourself, young lady. This is the prettiest you will ever be! [*She stands back to admire Laura.*] I've got to fix myself now! You're going to be surprised by your mother's appearance!

70

[*Amanda crosses through the portieres, humming gaily. Laura moves slowly to the long mirror and stares solemnly at herself. A wind blows the white curtains inward in a slow, graceful motion and with a faint, sorrowful sighing.*]

AMANDA [*from somewhere behind the portieres*]: It isn't dark enough yet.

[*Laura turns slowly before the mirror with a troubled look.*]

[*Legend on screen*: "This is my sister: Celebrate her with strings!" *Music plays.*]

AMANDA [*laughing, still not visible*]: I'm going to show you something. I'm going to make a spectacular appearance!

LAURA: What is it, Mother?

AMANDA: Possess your soul in patience—you will see! Something I've resurrected from that old trunk! Styles haven't changed so terribly much after all. . . . [*She parts the portieres.*] Now just look at your mother! [*She wears a girlish frock of yellowed voile with a blue silk sash. She carries a bunch of jonquils—the legend of her youth is nearly revived. Now she speaks feverishly:*] This is the dress in which I led the cotillion. Won the cakewalk twice at Sunset Hill, wore one Spring to the Governor's Ball in Jackson! See how I sashayed around the ballroom, Laura? [*She raises her skirt and does a mincing step around the room.*] I wore it on Sundays for my gentlemen callers! I had it on the day I met your father. . . . I had malaria fever all that Spring. The change of climate from East Tennessee to the Delta—weakened resistance. I had a little temperature all the time—not enough to be serious—just enough to make me restless and giddy! Invitations poured in—parties all over the Delta! "Stay in bed," said Mother, "you have a fever!"—but I just wouldn't. I took quinine but kept on going, going! Evenings, dances!

71

Afternoons, long, long rides! Picnics—lovely! So lovely, that country in May—all lacy with dogwood, literally flooded with jonquils! That was the spring I had the craze for jonquils. Jonquils became an absolute obsession. Mother said, "Honey, there's no more room for jonquils." And still I kept on bringing in more jonquils. Whenever, wherever I saw them, I'd say, "Stop! Stop! I see jonquils!" I made the young men help me gather the jonquils! It was a joke, Amanda and her jonquils. Finally there were no more vases to hold them, every available space was filled with jonquils. No vases to hold them? All right, I'll hold them myself! And then I—[*She stops in front of the picture. Music plays.*] met your father! Malaria fever and jonquils and then—this—boy. . . . [*She switches on the rose-colored lamp.*] I hope they get here before it starts to rain. [*She crosses the room and places the jonquils in a bowl on the table.*] I gave your brother a little extra change so he and Mr. O'Connor could take the service car home.

LAURA [*with an altered look*]: What did you say his name was?

AMANDA: O'Connor.

LAURA: What is his first name?

AMANDA: I don't remember. Oh, yes, I do. It was—Jim!

[*Laura sways slightly and catches hold of a chair.*]

[*Legend on screen*: "Not Jim!"]

LAURA [*faintly*]: Not—Jim!

AMANDA: Yes, that was it, it was Jim! I've never known a Jim that wasn't nice!

[*The music becomes ominous.*]

LAURA: Are you sure his name is Jim O'Connor?

AMANDA: Yes. Why?

LAURA: Is he the one that Tom used to know in high school?

AMANDA: He didn't say so. I think he just got to know him at the warehouse.

LAURA: There was a Jim O'Connor we both knew in high school—[*then, with effort*] If that is the one that Tom is bringing to dinner—you'll have to excuse me, I won't come to the table.

AMANDA: What sort of nonsense is this?

LAURA: You asked me once if I'd ever liked a boy. Don't you remember I showed you this boy's picture?

AMANDA: You mean the boy you showed me in the yearbook?

LAURA: Yes, that boy.

AMANDA: Laura, Laura, were you in love with that boy?

LAURA: I don't know, Mother. All I know is I couldn't sit at the table if it was him!

AMANDA: It won't be him! It isn't the least bit likely. But whether it is or not, you will come to the table. You will not be excused.

LAURA: I'll have to be, Mother.

AMANDA: I don't intend to humor your silliness, Laura. I've had too much from you and your brother, both! So just sit down and compose yourself till they come. Tom has forgotten his key so you'll have to let them in, when they arrive.

LAURA [*panicky*]: Oh, Mother—*you* answer the door!

AMANDA [*lightly*]: I'll be in the kitchen—busy!

LAURA: Oh, Mother, please answer the door, don't make me do it!

AMANDA [*crossing into the kitchenette*]: I've got to fix the dressing for the salmon. Fuss, fuss—silliness!—over a gentleman caller!

[*The door swings shut. Laura is left alone.*]

[*Legend on screen*: "Terror!"]

[*She utters a low moan and turns off the lamp—sits stiffly on the edge of the sofa, knotting her fingers together.*]

[*Legend on screen*: "The Opening of a Door!"]

[*Tom and Jim appear on the fire escape steps and climb to the landing. Hearing their approach, Laura rises with a panicky gesture. She retreats to the portieres. The doorbell rings. Laura catches her breath and touches her throat. Low drums sound.*]

AMANDA [*calling*]: Laura, sweetheart! The door!

[*Laura stares at it without moving.*]

JIM: I think we just beat the rain.

TOM: Uh-huh. [*He rings again, nervously. Jim whistles and fishes for a cigarette.*]

AMANDA [*very, very gaily*]: Laura, that is your brother and Mr. O'Connor! Will you let them in, darling?

[*Laura crosses toward the kitchenette door.*]

LAURA [*breathlessly*]: Mother—you go to the door!

*Amanda steps out of the kitchenette and stares furiously
at Laura. She points imperiously at the door.*]

LAURA: Please, please!

AMANDA [*in a fierce whisper*]: What is the matter with
you, you silly thing?

LAURA [*desperately*]: Please, you answer it, *please!*

AMANDA: I told you I wasn't going to humor you, Laura.
Why have you chosen this moment to lose your mind?

LAURA: Please, please, please, you go!

AMANDA: You'll have to go to the door because I can't!

LAURA [*despairingly*]: I can't either!

AMANDA: *Why?*

LAURA: I'm *sick!*

AMANDA: I'm sick, too—of your nonsense! Why can't
you and your brother be normal people? Fantastic whims and
behavior!

[*Tom gives a long ring.*]

Preposterous goings on! Can you give me one reason—
[*She calls out lyrically.*] Coming! Just one second!—why you
should be afraid to open a door? Now you answer it, Laura!

LAURA: Oh, oh, oh . . . [*She returns through the portieres,
darts to the Victrola, winds it frantically and turns it on.*]

AMANDA: Laura Wingfield, you march right to that door!

LAURA: *Yes—yes, Mother!*

[*A faraway, scratchy rendition of "Dardanella" softens the
air and gives her strength to move through it. She slips to*

the door and draws it cautiously open. Tom enters with the caller, Jim O'Connor.]

TOM: Laura, this is Jim. Jim, this is my sister, Laura.

JIM [*stepping inside*]: I didn't know that Shakespeare had a sister!

LAURA [*retreating, stiff and trembling, from the door*]: How—how do you do?

JIM [*heartily, extending his hand*]: Okay!

[*Laura touches it hesitantly with hers.*]

JIM: Your hand's *cold*, Laura!

LAURA: Yes, well—I've been playing the Victrola. . . .

JIM: Must have been playing classical music on it! You ought to play a little hot swing music to warm you up!

LAURA: Excuse me—I haven't finished playing the Victrola. . . . [*She turns awkwardly and hurries into the front room. She pauses a second by the Victrola. Then she catches her breath and darts through the portieres like a frightened deer.*]

JIM [*grinning*]: What was the matter?

TOM: Oh—with Laura? Laura is—terribly shy.

JIM: Shy, huh? It's unusual to meet a shy girl nowadays. I don't believe you ever mentioned you had a sister.

TOM: Well, now you know. I have one. Here is the *Post Dispatch*. You want a piece of it?

JIM: Uh-huh.

TOM: What piece? The comics?

JIM: Sports! [*He glances at it.*] Ole Dizzy Dean is on his bad behavior.

TOM [*uninterested*]: Yeah? [*He lights a cigarette and goes over to the fire-escape door.*]

JIM: Where are *you* going?

TOM: I'm going out on the terrace.

JIM [*going after him*]: You know, Shakespeare—I'm going to sell you a bill of goods!

TOM: What goods?

JIM: A course I'm taking.

TOM: Huh?

JIM: In public speaking! You and me, we're not the warehouse type.

TOM: Thanks—that's good news. But what has public speaking got to do with it?

JIM: It fits you for—executive positions!

TOM: Awww.

JIM: I tell you it's done a helluva lot for me.

[*Image on screen*: Executive at his desk.]

TOM: In what respect?

JIM: In every! Ask yourself what is the difference between you an' me and men in the office down front? Brains?—No! —Ability?—No! Then what? Just one little thing—

TOM: What is that one little thing?

JIM: Primarily it amounts to—social poise! Being able to square up to people and hold your own on any social level!

AMANDA [*from the kitchenette*]:Tom?

TOM: Yes, Mother?

AMANDA: Is that you and Mr. O'Connor?

TOM: Yes, Mother.

AMANDA: Well, you just make yourselves comfortable in there.

TOM: Yes, Mother.

AMANDA: Ask Mr. O'Connor if he would like to wash his hands.

JIM: Aw, no—no—thank you—I took care of that at the warehouse. Tom—

TOM: Yes?

JIM: Mr. Mendoza was speaking to me about you.

TOM: Favorably?

JIM: What do you think?

TOM: Well—

JIM: You're going to be out of a job if you don't wake up.

TOM: I am waking up—

JIM: You show no signs.

TOM: The signs are interior.

[*Image on screen*: The sailing vessel with the Jolly Roger again.]

TOM: I'm planning to change. [*He leans over the fire-escape rail, speaking with quiet exhilaration. The incandescent marquees and signs of the first-run movie houses light his face from across the alley. He looks like a voyager.*] I'm right at the point of committing myself to a future that doesn't include the warehouse and Mr. Mendoza or even a night-school course in public speaking.

JIM: What are you gassing about?

TOM: I'm tired of the movies.

JIM: Movies!

TOM: Yes, movies! Look at them— [*a wave toward the marvels of Grand Avenue*] All of those glamorous people— having adventures—hogging it all, gobbling the whole thing up! You know what happens? People go to the *movies* instead of *moving!* Hollywood characters are supposed to have all the adventures for everybody in America, while everybody in America sits in a dark room and watches them have them! Yes, until there's a war. That's when adventure becomes available to the masses! *Everyone's* dish, not only Gable's! Then the people in the dark room come out of the dark room to have some adventures themselves—goody, goody! It's our turn now, to go to the South Sea Island—to make a safari— to be exotic, far-off! But I'm not patient. I don't want to wait till then. I'm tired of the *movies* and I am *about* to *move!*

JIM [*incredulously*]: Move?

TOM: Yes.

JIM: When?

TOM: Soon!

JIM: Where? Where?

[*The music seems to answer the question, while Tom thinks it over. He searches in his pockets.*]

TOM: I'm starting to boil inside. I know I seem dreamy, but inside—well, I'm boiling! Whenever I pick up a shoe, I shudder a little thinking how short life is and what I am doing! Whatever that means, I know it doesn't mean shoes —except as something to wear on a traveler's feet! [*He finds what he has been searching for in his pockets and holds out a paper to Jim.*] Look—

JIM: What?

TOM: I'm a member.

JIM [*reading*]: The Union of Merchant Seamen.

TOM: I paid my dues this month, instead of the light bill.

JIM: You will regret it when they turn the lights off.

TOM: I won't be here.

JIM: How about your mother?

TOM: I'm like my father. The bastard son of a bastard! Did you notice how he's grinning in his picture in there? And he's been absent going on sixteen years!

JIM: You're just talking, you drip. How does your mother feel about it?

TOM: Shhh! Here comes Mother! Mother is not acquainted with my plans!

AMANDA [*coming through the portieres*]: Where are you all?

TOM: On the terrace, Mother.

[*They start inside. She advances to them. Tom is distinctly shocked at her appearance. Even Jim blinks a little. He is making his first contact with girlish Southern vivacity and in spite of the night-school course in public speaking is*]

*somewhat thrown off the beam by the unexpected outlay of
social charm. Certain responses are attempted by Jim but
are swept aside by Amanda's gay laughter and chatter. Tom
is embarrassed but after the first shock Jim reacts very
warmly. He grins and chuckles, is altogether won over.*]

[*Image on screen*: Amanda as a girl.]

AMANDA [*coyly smiling, shaking her girlish ringlets*]:
Well, well, well, so this is Mr. O'Connor. Introductions entirely unnecessary. I've heard so much about you from my
boy. I finally said to him, Tom—good gracious!—why don't
you bring this paragon to supper? I'd like to meet this nice
young man at the warehouse!—instead of just hearing him
sing your praises so much! I don't know why my son is so
stand-offish—that's not Southern behavior!

Let's sit down and—I think we could stand a little more
air in here! Tom, leave the door open. I felt a nice fresh
breeze a moment ago. Where has it gone to? Mmm, so warm
already! And not quite summer, even. We're going to burn
up when summer really gets started. However, we're having—
we're having a very light supper. I think light things are
better fo' this time of year. The same as light clothes are. Light
clothes an' light food are what warm weather calls fo'. You
know our blood gets so thick during th' winter—it takes a
while fo' us to *adjust* ou'selves!—when the season changes . . .
It's come so quick this year. I wasn't prepared. All of a sudden
—heavens! Already summer! I ran to the trunk an' pulled
out this light dress—terribly old! Historical almost! But feels
so good—so good an' co-ol, y' know. . . .

TOM: Mother—

AMANDA: Yes, honey?

TOM: How about—supper?

81

AMANDA: Honey, you go ask Sister if supper is ready! You know that Sister is in full charge of supper! Tell her you hungry boys are waiting for it. [*to Jim*] Have you met Laura?

JIM: She—

AMANDA: Let you in? Oh, good, you've met already! It's rare for a girl as sweet an' pretty as Laura to be domestic! But Laura is, thank heavens, not only pretty but also very domestic. I'm not at all. I never was a bit. I never could make a thing but angel-food cake. Well, in the South we had so many servants. Gone, gone, gone. All vestige of gracious living! Gone completely! I wasn't prepared for what the future brought me. All of my gentlemen callers were sons of planters and so of course I assumed that I would be married to one and raise my family on a large piece of land with plenty of servants. But man proposes—and woman accepts the proposal! To vary that old, old saying a little bit—I married no planter! I married a man who worked for the telephone company! That gallantly smiling gentleman over there! [*She points to the picture.*] A telephone man who—fell in love with long-distance! Now he travels and I don't even know where! But what am I going on for about my—tribulations? Tell me yours—I hope you don't have any! Tom?

TOM [*returning*]: Yes, Mother?

AMANDA: Is supper nearly ready?

TOM: It looks to me like supper is on the table.

AMANDA: Let me look— [*She rises prettily and looks through the portieres.*] Oh, lovely! But where is Sister?

TOM: Laura is not feeling well and she says that she thinks she'd better not come to the table.

AMANDA: What? Nonsense! Laura? Oh, Laura!

LAURA [*from the kitchenette, faintly*]: Yes, Mother.

AMANDA: You really must come to the table. We won't be seated until you come to the table! Come in, Mr. O'Connor. You sit over there, and I'll. . . . Laura? Laura Wingfield! You're keeping us waiting, honey! We can't say grace until you come to the table!

[*The kitchenette door is pushed weakly open and Laura comes in. She is obviously quite faint, her lips trembling, her eyes wide and staring. She moves unsteadily toward the table.*]

[*Screen legend*: "Terror!"]

[*Outside a summer storm is coming on abruptly. The white curtains billow inward at the windows and there is a sorrowful murmur from the deep blue dusk.*]

[*Laura suddenly stumbles; she catches at a chair with a faint moan.*]

TOM: Laura!

AMANDA: Laura!

[*There is a clap of thunder.*]

[*Screen legend*: "Ah!"]

[*despairingly*] Why, Laura, you *are* ill, darling! Tom, help your sister into the living room, dear! Sit in the living room, Laura—rest on the sofa. Well! [*to Jim as Tom helps his sister to the sofa in the living room*] Standing over the hot stove made her ill! I told her that it was just too warm this evening, but—

[*Tom comes back to the table.*]

83

Is Laura all right now?

TOM: Yes.

AMANDA: What *is* that? Rain? A nice cool rain has come up! [*She gives Jim a frightened look.*] I think we may—have grace—now . . .

[*Tom looks at her stupidly.*] Tom, honey—you say grace!

TOM: Oh . . . "For these and all thy mercies—"

[*They bow their heads, Amanda stealing a nervous glance at Jim. In the living room Laura, stretched on the sofa, clenches her hand to her lips, to hold back a shuddering sob.*]

God's Holy Name be praised—

[*The scene dims out.*]

SCENE SEVEN

It is half an hour later. Dinner is just being finished in the dining room, Laura is still huddled upon the sofa, her feet drawn under her, her head resting on a pale blue pillow, her eyes wide and mysteriously watchful. The new floor lamp with its shade of rose-colored silk gives a soft, becoming light to her face, bringing out the fragile, unearthly prettiness which usually escapes attention. From outside there is a steady murmur of rain, but it is slackening and soon stops; the air outside becomes pale and luminous as the moon breaks through the clouds. A moment after the curtain rises, the lights in both rooms flicker and go out.

JIM: Hey, there, Mr. Light Bulb!

[*Amanda laughs nervously.*]

[*Legend on screen*: "Suspension of a public service."]

AMANDA: Where was Moses when the lights went out? Ha-ha. Do you know the answer to that one, Mr. O'Connor?

JIM: No, Ma'am, what's the answer?

AMANDA: In the dark!

[*Jim laughs appreciatively.*]

Everybody sit still. I'll light the candles. Isn't it lucky we have them on the table? Where's a match? Which of you gentlemen can provide a match?

JIM: Here.

AMANDA: Thank you, Sir.

JIM: Not at all, Ma'am!

AMANDA [*as she lights the candles*]: I guess the fuse has burnt out. Mr. O'Connor, can you tell a burnt-out fuse? I know I can't and Tom is a total loss when it comes to mechanics.

[*They rise from the table and go into the kitchenette, from where their voices are heard.*]

Oh, be careful you don't bump into something. We don't want our gentleman caller to break his neck. Now wouldn't that be a fine howdy-do?

JIM: Ha-ha! Where is the fuse-box?

AMANDA: Right here next to the stove. Can you see anything?

JIM: Just a minute.

AMANDA: Isn't electricity a mysterious thing? Wasn't it Benjamin Franklin who tied a key to a kite? We live in such a mysterious universe, don't we? Some people say that science clears up all the mysteries for us. In my opinion it only creates more! Have you found it yet?

JIM: No, Ma'am. All these fuses look okay to me.

AMANDA: Tom!

TOM: Yes, Mother?

AMANDA: That light bill I gave you several days ago. The one I told you we got the notices about?

[*Legend on screen*: "Ha!"]

TOM: Oh—yeah.

AMANDA: You didn't neglect to pay it by any chance?

TOM: Why, I—

AMANDA: Didn't! I might have known it!

JIM: Shakespeare probably wrote a poem on that light bill, Mrs. Wingfield.

AMANDA: I might have known better than to trust him with it! There's such a high price for negligence in this world!

JIM: Maybe the poem will win a ten-dollar prize.

AMANDA: We'll just have to spend the remainder of the evening in the nineteenth century, before Mr. Edison made the Mazda lamp!

JIM: Candlelight is my favorite kind of light.

AMANDA: That shows you're romantic! But that's no excuse for Tom. Well, we got through dinner. Very considerate of them to let us get through dinner before they plunged us into everlasting darkness, wasn't it, Mr. O'Connor?

JIM: Ha-ha!

AMANDA: Tom, as a penalty for your carelessness you can help me with the dishes.

JIM: Let me give you a hand.

AMANDA: Indeed you will not!

JIM: I ought to be good for something.

AMANDA: Good for something? [*Her tone is rhapsodic.*] *You?* Why, Mr. O'Connor, nobody, *nobody's* given me this much entertainment in years—as you have!

JIM: Aw, now, Mrs. Wingfield!

AMANDA: I'm not exaggerating, not one bit! But Sister is all by her lonesome. You go keep her company in the parlor! I'll give you this lovely old candelabrum that used to be on the

87

altar at the Church of the Heavenly Rest. It was melted a little out of shape when the church burnt down. Lightning struck it one spring. Gypsy Jones was holding a revival at the time and he intimated that the church was destroyed because the Episcopalians gave card parties.

JIM: Ha-ha.

AMANDA: And how about you coaxing Sister to drink a little wine? I think it would be good for her! Can you carry both at once?

JIM: Sure. I'm Superman!

AMANDA: Now, Thomas, get into this apron!

[*Jim comes into the dining room, carrying the candela-brum, its candles lighted, in one hand and a glass of wine in the other. The door of the kitchenette swings closed on Amanda's gay laughter; the flickering light approaches the portieres. Laura sits up nervously as Jim enters. She can hardly speak from the almost intolerable strain of being alone with a stranger.*]

[*Screen legend*: "I don't suppose you remember me at all!"]

[*At first, before Jim's warmth overcomes her paralyzing shyness, Laura's voice is thin and breathless, as though she had just run up a steep flight of stairs. Jim's attitude is gently humorous. While the incident is apparently unimportant, it is to Laura the climax of her secret life.*]

JIM: Hello there, Laura.

LAURA [*faintly*]: Hello.

[*She clears her throat.*]

JIM: How are you feeling now? Better?

LAURA: Yes. Yes, thank you.

JIM: This is for you. A little dandelion wine. [*He extends the glass toward her with extravagant gallantry.*]

LAURA: Thank you.

JIM: Drink it—but don't get drunk!

[*He laughs heartily. Laura takes the glass uncertainly; she laughs shyly.*]

Where shall I set the candles?

LAURA: Oh—oh, anywhere . . .

JIM: How about here on the floor? Any objections?

LAURA: No.

JIM: I'll spread a newspaper under to catch the drippings. I like to sit on the floor. Mind if I do?

LAURA: Oh, no.

JIM: Give me a pillow?

LAURA: What?

JIM: A pillow!

LAURA: Oh . . . [*She hands him one quickly.*]

JIM: How about you? Don't you like to sit on the floor?

LAURA: Oh—yes.

JIM: Why don't you, then?

LAURA: I—will.

JIM: Take a pillow!

89

[*Laura does. She sits on the floor on the other side of the candelabrum. Jim crosses his legs and smiles engagingly at her.*] I can't hardly see you sitting way over there.

LAURA: I can—see you.

JIM: I know, but that's not fair, I'm in the limelight.

[*Laura moves her pillow closer.*]

Good! Now I can see you! Comfortable?

LAURA: Yes.

JIM: So am I. Comfortable as a cow! Will you have some gum?

LAURA: No, thank you.

JIM: I think that I will indulge, with your permission. [*He musingly unwraps a stick of gum and holds it up.*] Think of the fortune made by the guy that invented the first piece of chewing gum. Amazing, huh? The Wrigley Building is one of the sights of Chicago—I saw it when I went up to the Century of Progress. Did you take in the Century of Progress?

LAURA: No, I didn't.

JIM: Well, it was quite a wonderful exposition. What impressed me most was the Hall of Science. Gives you an idea of what the future will be in America, even more wonderful than the present time is! [*There is a pause. Jim smiles at her.*] Your brother tells me you're shy. Is that right, Laura?

LAURA: I—don't know.

JIM: I judge you to be an old-fashioned type of girl. Well, I think that's a pretty good type to be. Hope you don't think I'm being too personal—do you?

LAURA [*hastily, out of embarrassment*]: I believe I *will* take a piece of gum, if you—don't mind. [*clearing her throat*] Mr. O'Connor, have you—kept up with your singing?

JIM: Singing? Me?

LAURA: Yes. I remember what a beautiful voice you had.

JIM: When did you hear me sing?

[*Laura does not answer, and in the long pause which follows a man's voice is heard singing offstage.*]

VOICE:
O blow, ye winds, heigh-ho,
A-roving I will go!
   I'm off to my love
    With a boxing glove—
Ten thousand miles away!

JIM: You say you've heard me sing?

LAURA: Oh, yes! Yes, very often . . . I—don't suppose—you remember me—at all?

JIM [*smiling doubtfully*]: You know I have an idea I've seen you before. I had that idea soon as you opened the door. It seemed almost like I was about to remember your name. But the name that I started to call you—wasn't a name! And so I stopped myself before I said it.

LAURA: Wasn't it—Blue Roses?

JIM [*springing up, grinning*]: Blue Roses! My gosh, yes— Blue Roses! That's what I had on my tongue when you opened the door! Isn't it funny what tricks your memory plays? I didn't connect you with high school somehow or other. But that's where it was; it was high school. I didn't even know you were Shakespeare's sister! Gosh, I'm sorry.

91

LAURA: I didn't expect you to. You—barely knew me!

JIM: But we did have a speaking acquaintance, huh?

LAURA: Yes, we—spoke to each other.

JIM: When did you recognize me?

LAURA: Oh, right away!

JIM: Soon as I came in the door?

LAURA: When I heard your name I thought it was probably you. I knew that Tom used to know you a little in high school. So when you came in the door—well, then I was—sure.

JIM: Why didn't you *say* something, then?

LAURA [*breathlessly*]: I didn't know what to say, I was —too surprised!

JIM: For goodness' sakes! You know, this sure is funny!

LAURA: Yes! Yes, isn't it, though . . .

JIM: Didn't we have a class in something together?

LAURA: Yes, we did.

JIM: What class was that?

LAURA: It was—singing—chorus!

JIM: Aw!

LAURA: I sat across the aisle from you in the Aud.

JIM: Aw.

LAURA: Mondays, Wednesdays, and Fridays.

JIM: Now I remember—you always came in late.

LAURA: Yes, it was so hard for me, getting upstairs. I had that brace on my leg—it clumped so loud!

JIM: I never heard any clumping.

LAURA [*wincing at the recollection*]: To me it sounded like—thunder!

JIM: Well, well, well, I never even noticed.

LAURA: And everybody was seated before I came in. I had to walk in front of all those people. My seat was in the back row. I had to go clumping all the way up the aisle with everyone watching!

JIM: You shouldn't have been self-conscious.

LAURA: I know, but I was. It was always such a relief when the singing started.

JIM: Aw, yes, I've placed you now! I used to call you Blue Roses. How was it that I got started calling you that?

LAURA: I was out of school a little while with pleurosis. When I came back you asked me what was the matter. I said I had pleurosis—you thought I said *Blue Roses.* That's what you always called me after that!

JIM: I hope you didn't mind.

LAURA: Oh, no—I liked it. You see, I wasn't acquainted with many—people. . . .

JIM: As I remember you sort of stuck by yourself.

LAURA: I—I—never have had much luck at—making friends.

JIM: I don't see why you wouldn't.

LAURA: Well, I—started out badly.

JIM: You mean being—

LAURA: Yes, it sort of—stood between me—

JIM: You shouldn't have let it!

LAURA: I know, but it did, and—

JIM: You were shy with people!

LAURA: I tried not to be but never could—

JIM: Overcome it?

LAURA: No, I—I never could!

JIM: I guess being shy is something you have to work out of kind of gradually.

LAURA [*sorrowfully*]: Yes—I guess it—

JIM: Takes time!

LAURA: Yes—

JIM: People are not so dreadful when you know them. That's what you have to remember! And everybody has problems, not just you, but practically everybody has got some problems. You think of yourself as having the only problems, as being the only one who is disappointed. But just look around you and you will see lots of people as disappointed as you are. For instance, I hoped when I was going to high school that I would be further along at this time, six years later, than I am now. You remember that wonderful write-up I had in *The Torch?*

LAURA: Yes! [*She rises and crosses to the table.*]

JIM: It said I was bound to succeed in anything I went into!

[*Laura returns with the high school yearbook.*]

Holy Jeez! *The Torch!*

[*He accepts it reverently. They smile across the book with mutual wonder. Laura crouches beside him and they begin to turn the pages. Laura's shyness is dissolving in his warmth.*]

LAURA: Here you are in *The Pirates of Penzance!*

JIM [*wistfully*]: I sang the baritone lead in that operetta.

LAURA [*raptly*]: So—*beautifully!*

JIM [*protesting*]: Aw—

LAURA: Yes, yes—beautifully—beautifully!

JIM: You heard me?

LAURA: All three times!

JIM: No!

LAURA: Yes!

JIM: All three performances?

LAURA [*looking down*]: Yes.

JIM: Why?

LAURA: I—wanted to ask you to—autograph my program. [*She takes the program from the back of the yearbook and shows it to him.*]

JIM: Why didn't you ask me to?

LAURA: You were always surrounded by your own friends so much that I never had a chance to.

JIM: You should have just—

95

LAURA: Well, I—thought you might think I was—

JIM: Thought I might think you was—what?

LAURA: Oh—

JIM [*with reflective relish*]: I was beleaguered by females in those days.

LAURA: You were terribly popular!

JIM: Yeah—

LAURA: You had such a—friendly way—

JIM: I was spoiled in high school.

LAURA: Everybody—liked you!

JIM: Including you?

LAURA: I—yes, I—did, too— [*She gently closes the book in her lap.*]

JIM: Well, well, well! Give me that program, Laura.

[*She hands it to him. He signs it with a flourish.*]

There you are—better late than never!

LAURA: Oh, I—what a—surprise!

JIM: My signature isn't worth very much right now. But some day—maybe—it will increase in value! Being disappointed is one thing and being discouraged is something else. I am disappointed but I am not discouraged. I'm twenty-three years old. How old are you?

LAURA: I'll be twenty-four in June.

JIM: That's not old age!

LAURA: No, but—

JIM: You finished high school?

LAURA [*with difficulty*]: I didn't go back.

JIM: You mean you dropped out?

LAURA: I made bad grades in my final examinations. [*She rises and replaces the book and the program on the table. Her voice is strained.*] How is—Emily Meisenbach getting along?

JIM: Oh, that kraut-head!

LAURA: Why do you call her that?

JIM: That's what she was.

LAURA: You're not still—going with her?

JIM: I never see her.

LAURA: It said in the "Personal" section that you were—engaged!

JIM: I know, but I wasn't impressed by that—propaganda!

LAURA: It wasn't—the truth?

JIM: Only in Emily's optimistic opinion!

LAURA: Oh—

[*Legend:* "What have you done since high school?"]

[*Jim lights a cigarette and leans indolently back on his elbows smiling at Laura with a warmth and charm which lights her inwardly with altar candles. She remains by the table, picks up a piece from the glass menagerie collection, and turns it in her hands to cover her tumult.*]

JIM [*after several reflective puffs on his cigarette*]: What have you done since high school?

97

[*She seems not to hear him.*]

Huh?

[*Laura looks up.*]

I said what have you done since high school, Laura?

LAURA: Nothing much.

JIM: You must have been doing something these six long years.

LAURA: Yes.

JIM: Well, then, such as what?

LAURA: I took a business course at business college—

JIM: How did that work out?

LAURA: Well, not very—well—I had to drop out, it gave me—indigestion—

[*Jim laughs gently.*]

JIM: What are you doing now?

LAURA: I don't do anything—much. Oh, please don't think I sit around doing nothing! My glass collection takes up a good deal of time. Glass is something you have to take good care of.

JIM: What did you say—about glass?

LAURA: Collection I said—I have one— [*She clears her throat and turns away again, acutely shy.*]

JIM [*abruptly*]: You know what I judge to be the trouble with you? Inferiority complex! Know what that is? That's what they call it when someone low-rates himself! I understand it because I had it, too. Although my case was not so

98

aggravated as yours seems to be. I had it until I took up public speaking, developed my voice, and learned that I had an aptitude for science. Before that time I never thought of myself as being outstanding in any way whatsoever! Now I've never made a regular study of it, but I have a friend who says I can analyze people better than doctors that make a profession of it. I don't claim that to be necessarily true, but I can sure guess a person's psychology, Laura! [*He takes out his gum.*] Excuse me, Laura. I always take it out when the flavor is gone. I'll use this scrap of paper to wrap it in. I know how it is to get it stuck on a shoe. [*He wraps the gum in paper and puts it in his pocket.*] Yep—that's what I judge to be your principal trouble. A lack of confidence in yourself as a person. You don't have the proper amount of faith in yourself. I'm basing that fact on a number of your remarks and also on certain observations I've made. For instance that clumping you thought was so awful in high school. You say that you even dreaded to walk into class. You see what you did? You dropped out of school, you gave up an education because of a clump, which as far as I know was practically non-existent! A little physical defect is what you have. Hardly noticeable even! Magnified thousands of times by imagination! You know what my strong advice to you is? Think of yourself as *superior* in some way!

LAURA: In what way would I think?

JIM: Why, man alive, Laura! Just look about you a little. What do you see? A world full of common people! All of 'em born and all of 'em going to die! Which of them has one-tenth of your good points! Or mine! Or anyone else's, as far as that goes—gosh! Everybody excels in some one thing. Some in many! [*He unconsciously glances at himself in the mirror.*] All you've got to do is discover in *what!* Take me, for instance. [*He adjusts his tie at the mirror.*] My interest happens to lie

99

in electro-dynamics. I'm taking a course in radio engineering at night school, Laura, on top of a fairly responsible job at the warehouse. I'm taking that course and studying public speaking.

LAURA: Ohhhh.

JIM: Because I believe in the future of television! [*turning his back to her.*] I wish to be ready to go up right along with it. Therefore I'm planning to get in on the ground floor. In fact I've already made the right connections and all that remains is for the industry itself to get under way! Full steam —[*His eyes are starry.*] *Knowledge*—Zzzzzp! *Money*— Zzzzzzp!—*Power!* That's the cycle democracy is built on!

[*His attitude is convincingly dynamic. Laura stares at him, even her shyness eclipsed in her absolute wonder. He suddenly grins.*]

I guess you think I think a lot of myself!

LAURA: No—o-o-o, I—

JIM: Now how about you? Isn't there something you take more interest in than anything else?

LAURA: Well, I do—as I said—have my—glass collection—

[*A peal of girlish laughter rings from the kitchenette.*]

JIM: I'm not right sure I know what you're talking about. What kind of glass is it?

LAURA: Little articles of it, they're ornaments mostly! Most of them are little animals made out of glass, the tiniest little animals in the world. Mother calls them a glass menagerie! Here's an example of one, if you'd like to see it! This one is one of the oldest. It's nearly thirteen.

[*Music*: "The Glass Menagerie."]

100

[*He stretches out his hand.*]

Oh, be careful—if you breathe, it breaks!

JIM: I'd better not take it. I'm pretty clumsy with things.

LAURA: Go on, I trust you with him! [*She places the piece in his palm.*] There now—you're holding him gently! Hold him over the light, he loves the light! You see how the light shines through him?

JIM: It sure does shine!

LAURA: I shouldn't be partial, but he is my favorite one.

JIM: What kind of a thing is this one supposed to be?

LAURA: Haven't you noticed the single horn on his forehead?

JIM: A unicorn, huh?

LAURA: Mmmm-hmmm!

JIM: Unicorns—aren't they extinct in the modern world?

LAURA: I know!

JIM: Poor little fellow, he must feel sort of lonesome.

LAURA [*smiling*]: Well, if he does, he doesn't complain about it. He stays on a shelf with some horses that don't have horns and all of them seem to get along nicely together.

JIM: How do you know?

LAURA [*lightly*]: I haven't heard any arguments among them!

JIM [*grinning*]: No arguments, huh? Well, that's a pretty good sign! Where shall I set him?

101

LAURA: Put him on the table. They all like a change of scenery once in a while!

JIM: Well, well, well, well—[*He places the glass piece on the table, then raises his arms and stretches.*] Look how big my shadow is when I stretch!

LAURA: Oh, oh, yes—it stretches across the ceiling!

JIM [*crossing to the door*]: I think it's stopped raining. [*He opens the fire-escape door and the background music changes to a dance tune.*] Where does the music come from?

LAURA: From the Paradise Dance Hall across the alley.

JIM: How about cutting the rug a little, Miss Wingfield?

LAURA: Oh, I—

JIM: Or is your program filled up? Let me have a look at it. [*He grasps an imaginary card.*] Why, every dance is taken! I'll just have to scratch some out.

[*Waltz music*: "La Golondrina."]

Ahhh, a waltz! [*He executes some sweeping turns by himself, then holds his arms toward Laura.*]

LAURA [*breathlessly*]: I—can't dance!

JIM: There you go, that inferiority stuff!

LAURA: I've never danced in my life!

JIM: Come on, try!

LAURA: Oh, but I'd step on you!

JIM: I'm not made out of glass.

LAURA: How—how—how do we start?

JIM: Just leave it to me. You hold your arms out a little.

LAURA: Like this?

JIM [*taking her in his arms*]: A little bit higher. Right. Now don't tighten up, that's the main thing about it—relax.

LAURA [*laughing breathlessly*]: It's hard not to.

JIM: Okay.

LAURA: I'm afraid you can't budge me.

JIM: What do you bet I can't? [*He swings her into motion.*]

LAURA: Goodness, yes, you can!

JIM: Let yourself go, now, Laura, just let yourself go.

LAURA: I'm—

JIM: Come on!

LAURA:—trying!

JIM: Not so stiff—easy does it!

LAURA: I know but I'm—

JIM: Loosen th' backbone! There now, that's a lot better.

LAURA: Am I?

JIM: Lots, lots better! [*He moves her about the room in a clumsy waltz.*]

LAURA: Oh, my!

JIM: Ha-ha!

LAURA: Oh, my goodness!

JIM: Ha-ha-ha!

[*They suddenly bump into the table, and the glass piece on it falls to the floor. Jim stops the dance.*]

103

What did we hit on?

LAURA: Table.

JIM: Did something fall off it? I think—

LAURA: Yes.

JIM: I hope that it wasn't the little glass horse with the horn!

LAURA: Yes. [*She stoops to pick it up.*]

JIM: Aw, aw, aw. Is it broken?

LAURA: Now it is just like all the other horses.

JIM: It's lost its—

LAURA: Horn! It doesn't matter. Maybe it's a blessing in disguise.

JIM: You'll never forgive me. I bet that that was your favorite piece of glass.

LAURA: I don't have favorites much. It's no tragedy, Freckles. Glass breaks so easily. No matter how careful you are. The traffic jars the shelves and things fall off them.

JIM: Still I'm awfully sorry that I was the cause.

LAURA [*smiling*]: I'll just imagine he had an operation. The horn was removed to make him feel less—freakish!

[*They both laugh.*]

Now he will feel more at home with the other horses, the ones that don't have horns. . . .

JIM: Ha-ha, that's very funny! [*Suddenly he is serious.*] I'm glad to see that you have a sense of humor. You know

104

—you're—well—very different! Surprisingly different from anyone else I know! [*His voice becomes soft and hesitant with a genuine feeling.*] Do you mind me telling you that?

[*Laura is abashed beyond speech.*]

I mean it in a nice way—

[*Laura nods shyly, looking away.*]

You make me feel sort of—I don't know how to put it! I'm usually pretty good at expressing things, but—this is something that I don't know how to say!

[*Laura touches her throat and clears it—turns the broken unicorn in her hands. His voice becomes softer.*]

Has anyone ever told you that you were pretty?

[*There is a pause, and the music rises slightly. Laura looks up slowly, with wonder, and shakes her head.*]

Well, you are! In a very different way from anyone else. And all the nicer because of the difference, too.

[*His voice becomes low and husky. Laura turns away, nearly faint with the novelty of her emotions.*]

I wish that you were my sister. I'd teach you to have some confidence in yourself. The different people are not like other people, but being different is nothing to be ashamed of. Because other people are not such wonderful people. They're one hundred times one thousand. You're one times one! They walk all over the earth. You just stay here. They're common as—weeds, but—you—well, you're—*Blue Roses!*

[*Image on screen*: Blue Roses.]

[*The music changes.*]

105

LAURA: But blue is wrong for—roses. . . .

JIM: It's right for you! You're—pretty!

LAURA: In what respect am I pretty?

JIM: In all respects—believe me! Your eyes—your hair—are pretty! Your hands are pretty! [*He catches hold of her hand.*] You think I'm making this up because I'm invited to dinner and have to be nice. Oh, I could do that! I could put on an act for you, Laura, and say lots of things without being very sincere. But this time I am. I'm talking to you sincerely. I happened to notice you had this inferiority complex that keeps you from feeling comfortable with people. Somebody needs to build your confidence up and make you proud instead of shy and turning away and—blushing. Somebody—ought to—*kiss* you, Laura!

[*His hand slips slowly up her arm to her shoulder as the music swells tumultuously. He suddenly turns her about and kisses her on the lips. When he releases her, Laura sinks on the sofa with a bright, dazed look. Jim backs away and fishes in his pocket for a cigarette.*]

[*Legend on screen*: "A souvenir."]

Stumblejohn!

[*He lights the cigarette, avoiding her look. There is a peal of girlish laughter from Amanda in the kitchenette. Laura slowly raises and opens her hand. It still contains the little broken glass animal. She looks at it with a tender, bewildered expression.*]

Stumblejohn! I shouldn't have done that—that was way off the beam. You don't smoke, do you?

[*She looks up, smiling, not hearing the question. He sits beside her rather gingerly. She looks at him speechlessly—*

waiting. He coughs decorously and moves a little farther aside as he considers the situation and senses her feelings, dimly, with perturbation. He speaks gently.]

Would you—care for a—mint?

[*She doesn't seem to hear him but her look grows brighter even.*]

Peppermint? Life Saver? My pocket's a regular drugstore —wherever I go . . . . [*He pops a mint in his mouth. Then he gulps and decides to make a clean breast of it. He speaks slowly and gingerly.*] Laura, you know, if I had a sister like you, I'd do the same thing as Tom. I'd bring out fellows and —introduce her to them. The right type of boys—of a type to —appreciate her. Only—well—he made a mistake about me. Maybe I've got no call to be saying this. That may not have been the idea in having me over. But what if it was? There's nothing wrong about that. The only trouble is that in my case—I'm not in a situation to—do the right thing. I can't take down your number and say I'll phone. I can't call up next week and—ask for a date. I thought I had better explain the situation in case you—misunderstood it and—I hurt your feelings. . . .

[*There is a pause. Slowly, very slowly, Laura's look changes, her eyes returning slowly from his to the glass figure in her palm. Amanda utters another gay laugh in the kitchenette.*]

LAURA [*faintly*]: You—won't—call again?

JIM: No, Laura, I can't. [*He rises from the sofa.*] As I was just explaining, I've—got strings on me. Laura, I've— been going steady! I go out all the time with a girl named Betty. She's a home-girl like you, and Catholic, and Irish, and in a great many ways we—get along fine. I met her last

107

summer on a moonlight boat trip up the river to Alton, on the *Majestic*. Well—right away from the start it was—love!

[*Legend*: Love!]

[*Laura sways slightly forward and grips the arm of the sofa. He fails to notice. now enrapt in his own comfortable being.*]

Being in love has made a new man of me!

[*Leaning stiffly forward, clutching the arm of the sofa, Laura struggles visibly with her storm. But Jim is oblivious; she is a long way off.*]

The power of love is really pretty tremendous! Love is something that—changes the whole world, Laura!

[*The storm abates a little and Laura leans back. He notices her again.*]

It happened that Betty's aunt took sick, she got a wire and had to go to Centralia. So Tom—when he asked me to dinner—I naturally just accepted the invitation, not knowing that you—that he—that I— [*He stops awkwardly.*] Huh—I'm a stumblejohn!

[*He flops back on the sofa. The holy candles on the altar of Laura's face have been snuffed out. There is a look of almost infinite desolation. Jim glances at her uneasily.*]

I wish that you would—say something.

[*She bites her lip which was trembling and then bravely smiles. She opens her hand again on the broken glass figure. Then she gently takes his hand and raises it level with her own. She carefully places the unicorn in the palm of his hand, then pushes his fingers closed upon it.*]

What are you—doing that for? You want me to have him?
Laura?

[*She nods.*]

What for?

LAURA: A—souvenir . . . .

[*She rises unsteadily and crouches beside the Victrola to wind it up.*]

[*Legend on screen*: "Things have a way of turning out so badly!" *Or image*: "Gentleman caller waving goodbye—gaily."]

[*At this moment Amanda rushes brightly back into the living room. She bears a pitcher of fruit punch in an old-fashioned cut-glass pitcher, and a plate of macaroons. The plate has a gold border and poppies painted on it.*]

AMANDA: Well, well, well! Isn't the air delightful after the shower? I've made you children a little liquid refreshment.

[*She turns gaily to Jim.*] Jim, do you know that song about lemonade?

"Lemonade, lemonade
Made in the shade and stirred with a spade—
Good enough for any old maid!"

JIM [*uneasily*]: Ha-ha! No—I never heard it.

AMANDA: Why, Laura! You look so serious!

JIM: We were having a serious conversation.

AMANDA: Good! Now you're better acquainted!

JIM [*uncertainly*]: Ha-ha! Yes.

AMANDA: You modern young people are much more serious-minded than my generation. I was so gay as a girl!

JIM: You haven't changed, Mrs. Wingfield.

AMANDA: Tonight I'm rejuvenated! The gaiety of the occasion, Mr. O'Connor! [*She tosses her head with a peal of laughter, spilling some lemonade.*] Oooo! I'm baptizing myself!

JIM: Here—let me—

AMANDA [*setting the pitcher down*]: There now. I discovered we had some maraschino cherries. I dumped them in, juice and all!

JIM: You shouldn't have gone to that trouble, Mrs. Wingfield.

AMANDA: Trouble, trouble? Why, it was loads of fun! Didn't you hear me cutting up in the kitchen? I bet your ears were burning! I told Tom how outdone with him I was for keeping you to himself so long a time! He should have brought you over much, much sooner! Well, now that you've found your way, I want you to be a very frequent caller! Not just occasional but all the time. Oh, we're going to have a lot of gay times together! I see them coming! Mmm, just breathe that air! So fresh, and the moon's so pretty! I'll skip back out—I know where my place is when young folks are having a—serious conversation!

JIM: Oh, don't go out, Mrs. Wingfield. The fact of the matter is I've got to be going.

AMANDA: Going, now? You're joking! Why, it's only the shank of the evening, Mr. O'Connor!

JIM: Well, you know how it is.

AMANDA: You mean you're a young workingman and have to keep workingmen's hours. We'll let you off early tonight. But only on the condition that next time you stay later. What's the best night for you? Isn't Saturday night the best night for you workingmen?

JIM: I have a couple of time-clocks to punch, Mrs. Wingfield. One at morning, another one at night!

AMANDA: My, but you *are* ambitious! You work at night, too?

JIM: No, Ma'am, not work but—Betty!

[*He crosses deliberately to pick up his hat. The band at the Paradise Dance Hall goes into a tender waltz.*]

AMANDA: Betty? Betty? Who's—Betty!

[*There is an ominous cracking sound in the sky.*]

JIM: Oh, just a girl. The girl I go steady with!

[*He smiles charmingly. The sky falls.*]

[*Legend*: "The Sky Falls."]

AMANDA [*a long-drawn exhalation*]: Ohhhh . . . Is it a serious romance, Mr. O'Connor?

JIM: We're going to be married the second Sunday in June.

AMANDA: Ohhhh—how nice! Tom didn't mention that you were engaged to be married.

JIM: The cat's not out of the bag at the warehouse yet. You know how they are. They call you Romeo and stuff like that. [*He stops at the oval mirror to put on his hat. He carefully shapes the brim and the crown to give a discreetly dashing effect.*] It's been a wonderful evening, Mrs. Wingfield. I guess this is what they mean by Southern hospitality.

111

AMANDA: It really wasn't anything at all.

JIM: I hope it don't seem like I'm rushing off. But I promised Betty I'd pick her up at the Wabash depot, an' by the time I get my jalopy down there her train'll be in. Some women are pretty upset if you keep 'em waiting.

AMANDA: Yes, I know—the tyranny of women! [*She extends her hand.*] Goodbye, Mr. O'Connor. I wish you luck— and happiness—and success! All three of them, and so does Laura! Don't you, Laura?

LAURA: Yes!

JIM [*taking Laura's hand*]: Goodbye, Laura. I'm certainly going to treasure that souvenir. And don't you forget the good advice I gave you. [*He raises his voice to a cheery shout.*] So long, Shakespeare! Thanks again, ladies. Good night!

[*He grins and ducks jauntily out. Still bravely grimacing, Amanda closes the door on the gentleman caller. Then she turns back to the room with a puzzled expression. She and Laura don't dare to face each other. Laura crouches beside the Victrola to wind it.*]

AMANDA [*faintly*]: Things have a way of turning out so badly. I don't believe that I would play the Victrola. Well, well—well! Our gentleman caller was engaged to be married! [*She raises her voice.*] Tom!

TOM [*from the kitchenette*]: Yes, Mother?

AMANDA: Come in here a minute. I want to tell you something awfully funny.

TOM [*entering with a macaroon and a glass of the lemonade*]: Has the gentleman caller gotten away already?

AMANDA: The gentleman caller has made an early departure. What a wonderful joke you played on us!

TOM: How do you mean?

AMANDA: You didn't mention that he was engaged to be married.

TOM: Jim? Engaged?

AMANDA: That's what he just informed us.

TOM: I'll be jiggered! I didn't know about that.

AMANDA: That seems very peculiar.

TOM: What's peculiar about it?

AMANDA: Didn't you call him your best friend down at the warehouse?

TOM: He is, but how did I know?

AMANDA: It seems extremely peculiar that you wouldn't know your best friend was going to be married!

TOM: The warehouse is where I work, not where I know things about people!

AMANDA: You don't know things anywhere! You live in a dream; you manufacture illusions!

[*He crosses to the door.*]

Where are you going?

TOM: I'm going to the movies.

AMANDA: That's right, now that you've had us make such fools of ourselves. The effort, the preparations, all the expense! The new floor lamp, the rug, the clothes for Laura! All for what? To entertain some other girl's fiancé! Go to the

113

movies, go! Don't think about us, a mother deserted, an un-married sister who's crippled and has no job! Don't let any-thing interfere with your selfish pleasure! Just go, go, go—to the movies!

TOM: All right, I will! The more you shout about my selfishness to me the quicker I'll go, and I won't go to the movies!

AMANDA: Go, then! Go to the moon—you selfish dreamer!

[*Tom smashes his glass on the floor. He plunges out on the fire escape, slamming the door. Laura screams in fright. The dance-hall music becomes louder. Tom stands on the fire escape, gripping the rail. The moon breaks through the storm clouds, illuminating his face.*]

[*Legend on screen*: "And so goodbye . . ."]

[*Tom's closing speech is timed with what is happening inside the house. We see, as though through soundproof glass, that Amanda appears to be making a comforting speech to Laura, who is huddled upon the sofa. Now that we cannot hear the mother's speech, her silliness is gone and she has dignity and tragic beauty. Laura's hair hides her face until, at the end of the speech, she lifts her head to smile at her mother. Amanda's gestures are slow and graceful, almost dancelike, as she comforts her daughter. At the end of her speech she glances a moment at the father's picture—then withdraws through the portieres. At the close of Tom's speech, Laura blows out the candles, ending the play.*]

TOM: I didn't go to the moon, I went much further—for time is the longest distance between two places. Not long after that I was fired for writing a poem on the lid of a shoe-box. I left Saint Louis. I descended the steps of this fire escape for a last time and followed, from then on, in my father's footsteps, attempting to find in motion what was lost in space. I traveled around a great deal. The cities swept about me like dead leaves, leaves that were brightly colored but torn away from the branches. I would have stopped, but I was pursued by something. It always came upon me unawares, taking me altogether by surprise. Perhaps it was a familiar bit of music. Perhaps it was only a piece of transparent glass. Perhaps I am walking along a street at night, in some strange city, before I have found companions. I pass the lighted window of a shop where perfume is sold. The window is filled with pieces of colored glass, tiny transparent bottles in delicate colors, like bits of a shattered rainbow. Then all at once my sister touches my shoulder. I turn around and look into her eyes. Oh, Laura, Laura, I tried to leave you behind me, but I am more faithful than I intended to be! I reach for a cigarette, I cross the street, I run into the movies or a bar, I buy a drink, I speak to the nearest stranger—anything that can blow your candles out!

[*Laura bends over the candles.*]

For nowadays the world is lit by lightning! Blow out your candles, Laura—and so goodbye. . . .

[*She blows the candles out.*]

New Directions Paperbooks—A Partial Listing

For a complete listing request free catalog from
New Directions, 80 Eighth Avenue, New York 10011   †Bilingual

For a complete listing request free catalog from
New Directions, 80 Eighth Avenue, New York 10011

THE

BIRTH OF

LIBERAL GUILT

IN THE

ENGLISH NOVEL

THE BIRTH OF LIBERAL

IN THE ENGLISH NOVEL

CHARLES DICKENS TO H. G. WELLS

BY DANIEL BORN

THE UNIVERSITY OF NORTH CAROLINA PRESS

CHAPEL HILL & LONDON

The paper in this book meets the guidelines for permanence and durability of the Committee on Production Guidelines for Book Longevity of the Council on Library Resources.

Library of Congress Cataloging-in-Publication Data

Born, Daniel.

The birth of liberal guilt in the English novel: Charles Dickens to H. G. Wells / by Daniel Born.

p. cm.

Includes bibliographical references and index.

ISBN 0-8078-2241-8 (cloth : alk. paper). — ISBN 0-8078-4544-2 (pbk. : alk. paper)

1. English fiction—19th century—History and criticism. 2. Guilt in literature. 3. English fiction—20th century—History and criticism. 4. Liberalism in literature. 5. Social problems in literature. 6. Literature and society—Great Britain. 7. Politics and literature—Great Britain. I. Title.

PR878.G84B67 1995 95-11705

823'.809358—dc20

CIP

Portions of this work appeared earlier, in somewhat different form, in "Echoes of Kipling in Marlow's 'Privileged Man'?," *Conradiana: A Journal of Joseph Conrad Studies* 24 (Summer 1992): 100–115, and "Private Gardens, Public Swamps: *Howards End* and the Revaluation of Liberal Guilt," *Novel: A Forum on Fiction* 25 (Winter 1992): 141–59, and are reprinted here with permission.

99 98 97 96 95 5 4 3 2 1

FOR MARY & ELIZABETH

CONTENTS

˚ACKNOWLEDGMENTS

I am deeply indebted to wise and patient mentors at the Graduate Center of the City University of New York: Irving Howe, Morris Dickstein, and Felicia Bonaparte.

Many thanks are in order, as well, to friends and family who encouraged me with critical reflections and emotional support: Ben C. Ollenburger, Wally Kroeker, Dale Suderman, Will Friesen, Gordon Zerbe, Raymond Cicetti, Carolyn Beauchamp, Peggy Samuels, Kenneth Itzkowitz, Jonathan Gross, Floyd Born, Bertha Toews, the late George L. Classen, and Mary Classen.

The Administration and Faculty Development Committee at Marietta College provided generous research time and financial support during the summers of 1993 and 1994. I am grateful to the National Endowment for the Humanities, and Jerome Christensen, for a memorable 1992 Summer Seminar addressing Romanticism and liberalism. David Binegar and Barbara McAtee provided invaluable technical assistance in the preparation of the manuscript. And special thanks are due Barbara Hanrahan, editor-in-chief at the University of North Carolina Press, and Ron Maner, managing editor, who saw this book through to completion.

My wife, Mary, and daughter, Elizabeth, have my deepest gratitude for their sustaining love and humor.

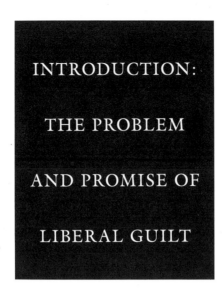

INTRODUCTION:

THE PROBLEM

AND PROMISE OF

LIBERAL GUILT

We more likely associate "liberal guilt" with rueful cocktail hour confessions than systematic or scholarly attention; the phrase invites expressions of wry self-deprecation or else righteous, contemptuous dismissal. Something Woody Allen has virtually made a career of, it provides great material for comedians. But to antiliberal critics—whether conservative, Marxist, or Nietzschean in orientation—it carries a bad whiff, and its emotional charge frequently overwhelms any residual intellectual freight.

Can we possibly approach this matter of liberal guilt soberly and with precision, without veering into comedy or polemics? And if we can, why would we want to? To the first question, I say yes. To the second, which is more complicated, I offer the beginnings of an explanation through the literary imagination in Dickens, Eliot, Gissing, Conrad, Forster, and H. G. Wells. Arising from a combination of historical developments that I shall detail shortly, liberal guilt gets thoroughly represented in Victorian and Edwardian fiction. And the novels considered in the chapters ahead constitute, finally, remarkable vehicles for investigating both the historical crises that stimulate this new sensibility, as well as the array of responses guilty liberals typically demonstrate.

Some readers might insist that liberal guilt is a topic more appropriately investigated by political scientists or psychotherapists. I suspect, however, that a greater proportion of my audience embraces the conviction that an eclectic approach to this kind of subject now weighs in not as optional but necessary. Even those of us who give mixed assent to poststructuralist developments in literary theory generally, have to be thankful that a mélange of approaches—new historicist, Marxist, Freudian, feminist—has restored context, every conceivable context, to literary study that had grown sterile under the proscriptions of the New Criticism. What makes now for truly "interdisciplinary" work may be debated. But that we need to rehistoricize texts if we want to understand them seems to me the characteristic stance of responsible practitioners of the critical methodologies enumerated above.

Adopting a historicist working methodology, we are compelled to approach liberal guilt by way of literary investigation simply because of the claims of the novelists themselves. Unlike us, the Victorians and Edwardians held enormously hopeful convictions about both the epistemological validity and the transformative possibilities of art. In short, they were Romantics. In his preface to *The Nigger of the Narcissus*, Conrad appeals, unapologetically and repeatedly, to the category of "truth" as it is discerned by the writer. And that question of truth is bound tightly to the larger question of human activity, of being. As Marlow tells Stein in chapter 20 of *Lord Jim*, "Strictly speaking, the question is not how to get cured, but how to live." Both Victorians and Edwardians refused to bracket aesthetic creation from the broader ethical and political claims they wished to make on their readers. Their expectations of what literature could do, particularly the novel, the dominant literary form of the time, were grandiose, and they made demands of it that sometimes seem almost embarrassing. Stein's response to Marlow, "How to be! *Ach*! How to be," summarizes the guiding question for his own creator's enterprise.

The scope of Conrad's ambitions as a writer seems overblown, even alien, to the sentiments of our more modest age, in which critics are more likely to make their reputations by announcing the death of the novel, perhaps even of literature itself.[1] But, paradoxically, Conrad's conscious integration of aesthetic and didactic aims seems at the present time to be gaining ground in the academy. Two major pressures have brought this about. The first is Marx. His dictum "The philosophers have only *interpreted* the world in various ways. The point is, to *change* it"[2] holds compelling force for many literature teachers today, who see themselves not merely as interpreters of texts, but also agents of social transformation. Second, and gaining ascendancy in current critical discussion, is American pragmatism, which reinforces linkage between thinking and doing and puts the query "What difference does it make?" at the center of intellectual life. These philosophical currents go far to explain why the old polarities of aesthetic and instrumental understandings of fiction have broken down and why debate in such mutually exclusive terms is no longer viable. These critical orientations also help rekindle an appreciation for the Victorian and Edwardian effort to integrate aesthetic and ethical aims.

Navigating the multiplying disciplinary pressures in an eclectic reading methodology is itself an act requiring skill and, at times, dogged insistence on not getting too distracted. The academic study of literature increasingly draws on the insights of virtually every discipline, and a whole new host of questions and possibilities simmers in, and between, the disciplines as we know them. Philosophers are rediscovering the pleasures of fiction, and some, like Richard Rorty, suggest stories rather than philosophy per se are more rewarding as an avenue for ethical discourse. Theologians in both Jewish and Christian traditions, tired of decades of historical-critical methodology, have embraced with considerable abandon literary-critical approaches to narrative. For their part, historians and scientists have grown increasingly self-conscious that to write "objectively" ineluctably necessitates reliance on literary conventions, tropes, and notions of narrative "story." Stephen Jay Gould observes, "Even the most distant and abstract subjects, like the formation of the universe or the principles of evolution, fall within the bounds of necessary narrative. Our images of evolution are caught in the web of tale telling. They involve progress, pageant; above all, ceaseless motion somewhere." [3] All phenomena are represented, are mediated, through narrative; archival data or statistics never come raw. Finally, if we turn to the therapists, we find an interesting phenomenon occurring in regard to the reputation of Freud. While his scientific authority (like Marx's) has suffered hard and maybe unanswerable knocks, virtually no one disputes his growing reputation as a literary genius in his own right. Colleagues in psychology are quick to tell me that the only people keeping his reputation alive these days are softheaded English professors. At least some English professors understand, however, that Freud the storyteller eclipsed Freud the medical scientist quite some time ago.

Not too surprisingly, critics who give themselves over to such broad, interdisciplinary reading become as interested in the making of human behavior as in the interpretation of the word. While "crossing" or "redrawing" disciplinary boundaries has become the catchphrase of current literary theory, resonant with connotations of brave guerrilla action, we do well to recognize that crossing different kinds of boundaries has always been taken for granted by our most distinguished older critics, those learned generalists of an especially high order: James, Arnold, Wilson, Trilling. James's phrase that literature must be a "criticism of life" carries renewed resonance today; restored is the perspective that literature gets encoded within, and not separate from, the languages of the larger world and culture. Literature, contrary to strict formalist doctrine, always requires study and knowledge of more than literature. But I want to also argue with certain poststructuralists that context is not reducible merely to other overlapping "texts." This mistake leads, once again, to suffocating theories of literary self-containment which, in the end, do not differ very much from those taught us by the New Critics. Books are more than responses to other books.

Yet another irony in the current poststructuralist critical scene needs to be mentioned given the ethical seriousness of the novels explored here. Contemporary focus in English departments on the trinity of gender, race, and class is relentlessly driven by a fundamental concern for justice. This engine moves the most exciting criticism today in the direction of advocacy and transformation. Yet most poststructuralists, in thrall to Nietzsche, have a great difficulty admitting that they are at heart moral critics, and many prefer to strike altogether the words "moral" or "ethical" from their working vocabularies. Why? Such terminology invokes too many associations with the company of naive foundationalists—or, worse, logocentric metaphysicians. This denial of the moral impulse leads to certain complications. The poststructuralist agenda—whether it be the new historicist concern about the workings of power camouflaged by rhetoric of "truth" or "virtue," the feminist exposure of millennia of patriarchal domination, or the Marxist unmasking of class hegemony—ultimately conveys in all its forms a crusade meant to right historical wrongs, to reinstate marginalized groups. The analogy to nineteenth-century reform movements is striking. Laurence Lockridge suggests that "advanced criticism need not propose a 'transcendence of the ethical' at all. Even dialectical transvaluation in Blake, Shelley, Marx, and Nietzsche yields yet another ethics—other ways of judging the obligations and moral values that obtain in the relatedness of individuals to themselves and to other people. The ethical can perhaps be contextualized by a broader critical horizon, but it need not and should not be transcended, condescended to, or made to wither away."[4]

Some poststructuralists, in spite of a discomfort with straightforwardly ethical categories, do reveal their basically moral—and I think teleological—intent; J. Hillis Miller's optimistic remark that "the millennium would come if all men and women became good readers in de Man's sense"[5] stands tall in this regard. I share Miller's hopefulness, while maybe not his certainty. And liberal guilt, I contend, deserves a thorough review if only because some of the greatest English novelists repeatedly return to it in their own quest for a millennium however understood.

Liberal guilt can be situated historically; some of the factors going into its making described; and its strengths, temptations, and foibles examined in turn. Liberal guilt has a distinct genesis, genealogy, and development. And while it is clear that liberal guilt arises in a particular milieu involving the thought of politicians, theologians, philosophers, and therapists, the synthesis occurs most completely in the novel, where the constellation of elements defining our discussion of liberal guilt reoccurs. These are the elements in that constellation:

(1) The breakup of theological certainty. The English novelists Dickens and Eliot follow the radical Romantics of the previous generation and typify Victorian liberalism's quiet dispensing of the theistic outlook. Thus anticipating God's death well in advance of Zarathustra's announcement, they can be said to reject Nietzsche by insisting on an ethic in the absence of deity. God dies; guilt thrives. As Gertrude Himmelfarb suggests, intellectual Victorians acknowledged God's death but at the same time such a loss reified their sense of guilt and duty.[6] Arthur Clennam and Daniel Deronda, inhabitants of a post-theistic world, are insistently driven by an urge to do good. Likewise, the central figures of the Edwardian novels considered here are interesting exactly because their ethical desire displaces theistic consciousness.[7] The prospect that all things are now possible does not carry a concomitant dose of freedom, but instead quite the opposite.

The moral terms in the new world are rendered more complex, and as the idea of God recedes, the consciousness of evil seems to grow. But it is evil conceived in a new way: not in terms of moralistic Victorian theology, wherein evil could be readily identified with the sinning individual, but rather in terms of the social organism. Here once again, Dickens and Eliot are deeply indebted to the Romantics' sophisticated sense of systemic and not merely individual wrong. Dickens's own development in this regard occurs between *Dombey and Son*, where the locus of moral activity is Dombey's heart, and the later novels, where Circumlocution and Chancery best embody the idea that evil has escaped its origins in the human heart and taken on a deadly life of its own. "The system! I am told, on all hands," cries Mr. Gridley in *Bleak House*, "it's the system. I mustn't look to individuals. It's the system."[8] Mr. Gridley's proto-Foucauldian complaint registers in equal measures recognition and protest. If in *Dombey* and *A Christmas Carol* individual conversion still stands as Dickens's hopeful response to evil, then we must admit that such optimism erodes later on. In *Little Dorrit* it is impossible to imagine that the conversions of all the Stiltstalkings and Barnacles can alter the malevolence of Circumlocution.

For the Edwardians, awareness of this distinctly systemic nature of evil focuses on two major aspects of English society, and these sociological aspects occupy center stage in the post-theistic liberal conscience:

(2) A simultaneous concern about and revulsion toward the class of urban poor. Of the writers to be considered, George Gissing, beginning with *Workers*

in the Dawn (1880) and ending with *The Private Papers of Henry Ryecroft* (1903), best typifies this concern. And the trajectory taken by Gissing's fiction demonstrates all too well the temptation of liberal guilt to proceed from a desire for involvement and activism to a fastidious withdrawal, a disengagement. Gissing tried to write this guilt about the poor out of his consciousness, but part of the uniqueness of his work is that the guilt never gets completely exorcized.

If Mayhew and Booth's works stand as the most encyclopedic journalistic efforts to represent the British lower classes,[9] Gissing's role is to engage most repeatedly, if not comprehensively, the plight of England's dispossessed within the tradition of British fiction. In this central aspect he resumes where Dickens leaves off. Yet this matter is also taken up by Forster in *Howards End*, with Leonard and Jackie Bast representing those on the brink of economic disaster. Fictional representation of the lower classes can be read in the context of a huge body of journalistic and sociological prose including not only Mayhew, the Parliamentary Blue Books, and Booth, but also Andrew Mearns's *Bitter Cry of Outcast London* (1883), William Booth's *In Darkest England, and the Way Out* (1891), C. F. G. Masterman's *From the Abyss* (1902), the writings of the Fabians, and Jack London's *People of the Abyss* (1903). The "abyss" motif itself becomes as common as the ideas of national decadence and degeneration current at the time.[10]

(3) The sense of breakdown in conditions at home is accompanied by despair and dismay about England's empire abroad. Liberal uneasiness involves not only England's domestic crisis of urban poverty, but also the global effects of imperialism. Clearly, long before the First World War, empire has become a hangnail of doubt on the British literary scene, torn at by both critics and advocates of England's world mastery.

The secondary literature about imperialism and British fiction is massive and proliferating and hardly needs one more encapsulation. The starting point for my treatment of imperialism is that Gissing, Conrad, Forster, and Wells all fix their sights on Kipling's jingoist and xenophobic imperial idea; in a sense, they are all planets attempting to spin out of Kipling's powerful gravity. And Kipling's role in the British literary tradition continues to grow more, rather than less, complicated. Martin Green, who besides Patrick Brantlinger has chronicled most comprehensively British fictional treatments of empire, argues that practically everybody writing in English since Kipling has written in reaction against him, even if they have not read him.[11] My claims for Kipling's influence are slightly less ambitious, but maybe more demonstrable, by locating within Edwardian fiction, especially Conrad's, a specific debt to Kipling. Direct allusions to him and his work situate the Edwardian liberal attitude toward empire and at the same time indicate Kipling's enormous influence.

The scenario grows even more complex when we actually bother to reread Kipling. His best work, as in some of the early stories, shows now and then a provocative ability to render in narrative the European from the perspective of the native "other," although this ability hardens with age into the more familiar emphasis on order and authority. The split in the young Kipling between sympathetic feelings for his native characters and the demands of imperial ideology suggests the imperial unease, the kinds of doubts about mastery we more commonly associate with Conrad or Forster. As it turns out, the language of "Kiplingese" is more difficult to summarize than normally thought.

Furthermore, if the Edwardian novelists use Kipling to define their anti-imperialist views, then most disturbing about these novels is a consistent pattern of acquiescence to the imperial dictate. Ponderevo, Wells's narrator in *Tono-Bungay*, ends up building high technology warships—a fact most critics prefer to understand metaphorically; Margaret Schlegel of *Howards End* marries the very "imperial type" she despises; and Jim becomes "Lord" Jim, the white emperor of Patusan, while elsewhere in Conrad, Marlow displays time and again an attitude of guilt, yet complicity, about imperial venturing. His ironic distance about his own activity does not prevent us from seeing he is a participant. Even Harvey Rolfe in Gissing's bestseller *The Whirlpool* (1897), despite his emphatic hatred of Kipling's music hall ditties, names his only son after Hugh Carnaby, an epitome of ravenous imperial appetite. Political scientists and historians may justifiably ask to what extent these novels articulate the degree of accommodation to empire that infects liberal politics in general, and the Liberal Party's politics of the milieu in particular. L. T. Hobhouse, one of the Edwardian era's more savvy political voices, gives some indication in his study *Liberalism* (1911): "Standing by national autonomy and international equality, Liberalism is necessarily in conflict with the Imperial idea as it is ordinarily presented. But this is not to say that it is indifferent to the interests of the Empire as a whole, to the sentiment of unity pervading its white population, to all the possibilities involved in the bare fact that a fourth part of the human race recognizes one flag and one supreme authority."[12] To put this in context, we need to consider with Ian Watt "that in the nineteenth century no real political alternative had been suggested to Western penetration of the other continents; the only practical issue was what form it should take."[13]

Gladstone himself, the greatest Liberal Party politician of the nineteenth century, a single-minded advocate for Irish Home Rule and vocal opponent of imperialistic policy, was to oversee the occupation of Egypt only a year after denouncing British adventurism and interventionism during his Midlothian campaign of 1879.[14]

Likewise, in considering the period's ideological horizon, we note to what extent racial ideas held sway even among progressive voices. J. A. Hobson, one of the leading Edwardian New Liberals, could direct this attack against empire builders, while at the same time share their racist underpinnings: "Even if imperialism can in some instances make good its claims to benefit certain lower races and to maintain good order in otherwise disordered regions, such gain may be purchased dearly by the damage done to democracy at home." [15] In 1899, one year after being elected Liberal opposition leader in the House of Commons, Campbell-Bannerman had argued against "jingoism," while simultaneously affirming Britain's right to protect and even to expand, if necessary, her empire.[16] The course of moderation he set was "to distinguish between two kinds of imperialism, the one 'false,' based on military power, the other 'true,' based on strict standards of national morality." [17] Given this species of reasoning, it comes as no surprise that the Liberals, having stepped up their anti-imperial rhetoric prior to the watershed 1906 elections, "did nothing to dismantle or reshape the Empire" once their landslide victory was achieved.[18] This double-minded attitude about empire prevented an alternate policy from emerging. While the liberals reviled the Kipling ethos, nonetheless they usually lived by its demands.

Can the Edwardian novelists' profound unease — and yet accommodation — to imperial dictates be read as parallel to the story of the Liberal Party's wavering imperial policy? To a degree, yes. The comparisons are apt; the same divisions inhabit the literature and the politics. Maybe nowhere are these divisions more apparent than in Conrad's *Lord Jim* and *Heart of Darkness*. If this makes the question of liberal guilt too simple — recognition of the enormous gap between liberal promises and liberal performance — then I would argue that this very ability to interrogate oneself, as Marlow does continually, defines in a crucial way the dialectic of the liberal mind. Here one of Trilling's more lucid passages proves helpful, and I explicitly connect it with my own effort to lay bare the workings of liberal guilt. In the interests of a liberal criticism, Trilling demands a no-holds-barred critique of liberalism. What Trilling demanded, and what we must continue to attempt (even if it means at certain points negation of Trilling himself), is the leavening of liberalism with attacks from both within and without.

It has for some time seemed to me that a criticism which has at heart the interests of liberalism might find its most useful work not in confirming liberalism in its sense of general rightness but rather in putting under some degree of pressure the liberal ideas and assumptions of the present time. If liberalism is, as I believe it to be, a large tendency rather than a concise body of doctrine, then, as that large tendency makes itself explicit, certain of its particular expressions are bound to be relatively weaker than others, and some even useless and mistaken. If this is so, then for liberalism to be aware of the weak or wrong expressions of itself would seem to be an advantage to the tendency as a whole.[19]

(4) A characteristic move made by guilty liberal protagonists in these novels is the retreat to the country house tradition. Such a move, more in keeping with the politics of a Carlyle or Disraeli which idealizes the bond between peasant and lord in the feudal order, over against the brutalizing effects of the new market economy, constitutes one of those "relatively weaker" or even "useless and mistaken" facets of liberal expression alluded to by Trilling. The Edwardian writers often invoke a passing order of civilization that, with great exaggeration, is invested with all the positive values seemingly lost in the present one. It may seem unfair to attach what has been an ongoing British obsession with a lost green world—Raymond Williams's *The Country and the City* (1973) most amply documents this—to a cultural malaise labeled liberal guilt. But the passions lodged in the country house tradition parallel in their ambiguity those held toward empire abroad and the abyss at home. Given the efforts of these writers to "see things whole" as Margaret Schlegel attempts to, a yearning for the aristocratic arrangement of the country house comes off at best nostalgic, at worst escapist.

Forster suggests in *Howards End* that the house with the wych-elms represents regenerative forces. There is a sense of vigorous folklore about the place, with pigs' teeth buried in tree trunks and the serene inhabiting spirit of Ruth Wilcox hovering over it all. Yet the fate of that house and its inhabitants seems singularly tenuous in view of suburbia's encroaching tide. Forster is not alone in this tenuous feeling, nor is he alone in his exploration of the house as indicative of a people's spiritual life. Gissing, Wells, Ford, Galsworthy, James—and even Conrad in his discussion of the country parsonage where Tuan Jim grew up—all use the country house as the primary symbol of the passing order of things. Notably, only Wells seems intent on shaking off such romanticism about the past, and he is only partly successful. For the longer we consider the disaster of the newly built house at Crest Hill and the proliferation of potent weapons and quack patent remedies under the two Ponderevos' guiding hands, the better that childhood country house of George Ponderevo's youth begins to look. Still, as a producer and product of his age, George Ponderevo strikes out beyond the grasp of liberal guilt into a realm we call postmodern. Such a vantage point affords few of the consolations served up by nostalgic doses of country living.

Nineteenth-Century Liberalism and Literary Intellectuals

In affirming liberalism as "a large tendency rather than a concise body of doctrine," Trilling shows his reluctance to trace, in even a cursory manner, some of the characteristics of that broad term he seeks to explain. Indeed, defining "liberalism" presents numerous difficulties, as contemporary scholarship repeatedly indicates. Political historian D. A. Hamer contends that nineteenth-century liberalism should be understood primarily as an incoherent set of often competing movements loosely grouped under one rubric, and that attempts to systematize the movements are likely to fail.[20] Another historian remarks that the Liberal Party taking shape in the 1860s was "less a party in the modern sense than a loose alliance of groups of many shades of political opinion and widely differing social background."[21] This tells us everything, and it tells us nothing. The same is largely true of Trilling's strategy in the passage quoted earlier, which I take to be an effort distinguishing liberalism conceived on one hand as cultural sensibility, and political Liberalism marked, on the other hand, with a capital "L." It is necessary, though, to mine a little more carefully than Trilling does some salient points of the tradition I am talking about, even if this means risking some truisms. For to understand liberal guilt we must be clear about what we mean by liberalism proper.

Philosophically understood, liberalism asserts the freedom of the individual over against any coercion of political and religious authority. This freedom is broadly conceived, including not only the right to free expression and thought, first articulated in Milton's *Areopagitica* (1644),[22] but also, as J. S. Mill would insist in his touchstone *On Liberty* (1859) over 200 years later, the liberty "of framing the plan of our life to suit our own character; of doing as we like . . . without impediment from our fellow-creatures, so long as what we do does not harm them."[23] Thus liberals, at least those of Mill's persuasion, assert freedom in a moral rather than amoral context. Finally, Mill argues for the liberty of "combination among individuals" to form voluntary associations without fear of interference.[24] The latter is a crucial point which communitarian critics, in their portrayal of liberalism as an ideology of atomistic individualism, usually forget. Brian Harrison summarizes the energies of nineteenth-century liberalism as having emerged from a combination of "evangelical theology, literary sensibility, industrial entrepreneurship, and Enlightenment rationalism"; the unleashed energies of the movement would boldly seek to remake fundamental social arrangements. "Emancipate blacks, women, and working men from the shackles of slavery, tradition, superstition, and drink, it was argued, and who could set a limit to their attainments? The very process of agitating helped to emancipate, by stirring up stagnant communities and encrusted habits of mind. Nineteenth-century liberalism was a bold and exhilarating experiment," Harrison concludes.[25] Other philosophical sources foundational to liberal thought can only be mentioned here in passing. Locke's constitutionalism, Bentham's utilitarianism, Smith's and Ricardo's laissez-faire market theory—these all go into classical liberalism's formula. Eugenio Biagini distills the essence of nineteenth-century liberal themes to be advocacy for "open government and the rule of law, for freedom from intervention both at home and abroad, and for individual liberty and community-centred democracy."[26]

However, we seriously deracinate liberalism if we conceive of it strictly as an aggregate of abstract ideas rather than an unfolding historical narrative. A number of historians argue that liberalism undergoes a clear reorientation in emphasis during the century, though they are not in agreement as to exactly when.[27] The most famous story of this transformation is John Stuart Mill's own: suckled on the mechanistic philosophy of Benthamist Utilitarianism, he recuperated his humanity, as well as liberalism's, by undergoing a personal conversion via Coleridge and Wordsworth. The results for his version of liberalism were profound: "what he came to value most," Isaiah Berlin contends, "was neither rationality nor contentment, but diversity, versatility . . . the unaccountable leap of individual genius, the spontaneity and uniqueness of a man, a group, a civilization."[28] We can safely say that if the literary spirit of Romanticism redeemed him, he returned the favor kindly by saving liberalism for literary intellectuals of his own generation and the next.

Mill's story, numerous historians argue, is indicative of the broader shift of the liberal paradigm during the nineteenth century. The initial version of liberalism, that of the Manchester School as well as the Enlightenment freethinkers, affirms the increase of personal liberty in the world as a response to diagnosed social and political ills. Liberalism of the second generation, including Mill, the Edwardian New Liberals, and liberal theorists of our own time, becomes more and more preoccupied with problems of cruelty and injustice in the world that are deterrents to liberty concretely realized.

These two goals—the first of increasing liberty, the second of decreasing cruelty—are at once complementary and contradictory, and it is precisely this conflict which the guilty liberal conscience continually seeks to alleviate. The second part of the liberal agenda correlates to that element of "conscience" embodied in writers as diverse as Milton and Isaiah Berlin.[29] Elaborating the difference between these two phases of liberalism, Ian Bradley says, "[James] Mill and other liberal theorists in the first half of the nineteenth century were primarily concerned with intellectual and civil liberty. In the second half a number of prominent thinkers extended the argument for liberty. . . . These New Liberals . . . saw that there were other evils apart from censorship, social pressure to conform. . . . poverty, illness, bad housing, and inadequate education, they argued, were just as much of a hindrance to individual self-fulfillment and the exercise of choice, and to free people from those particular constraints would require the positive use of public authority."[30] Edwardian writer A. V. Dicey, correlating these two phases of liberal thinking with the contours of major legislative reforms carried out in 1832 and 1867–84, respectively, perceived them as a contrast between middle-class individual interests on one hand and labor-class demands for collectivist guarantees on the other.[31] If capitalism unfettered was usually the answer for the Manchester School, the second generation of liberals came to view some constraints on unfettered capitalist enterprise as useful. "An economy which was increasingly dominated by the power of trusts, combines and the financial strength of the City of London," write Bullock and Shock, "could no longer be adequately diagnosed with the tools of Ricardian economics."[32]

Let me be clear that the late Victorian and Edwardian novelists considered in the pages to come should be read mostly in the context of this second wave of liberalism, one which, as Bullock and Shock put it, "is principally concerned with the effort to shake itself free from the preconceptions of the early 19th century."[33] At the same time, I would emphasize that the historic split, or transition, between these two "kinds" of liberalism hardly occurs in neat fashion. As far as literary intellectuals go, Shelley, Byron, and Hunt—the most consistently liberal Romantics—anticipate some of the concerns of this later phase of liberal thought in their awareness of unemployment, the dislocations brought about by new technology, and the evils of imperialism. And to nuance, or cloud, the picture even further, we should note that "pure" laissez faire liberalism was never actually operational, even in the early part of the century. The Factory Acts, beginning in 1802 and continuing through the 1830s and 1840s, found broad and diverse support among both Tory humanitarians and classical liberals, all of whom saw clearly the need for legitimate government intervention,[34] especially on behalf of child laborers.

The tone of the late Victorian and Edwardian liberal writers considered here—Dickens, Eliot, Gissing, Conrad, Forster, and Wells—no longer confirms the uplifting spirit of the early nineteenth-century reformer, who, as Brian Harrison argues, "gained optimism and energy from his belief that relatively straightforward issues of principle were involved; the advantage did not . . . seem to lie with experts and administrators. The reformer's intense consciousness of personal responsibility reflected the widespread conviction that an ordinary citizen can, by taking pains, transform the world; it was a philanthropic and reforming attitude that mirrored the thrusting entrepreneurship which was then producing such wonders in commerce and industry."[35] Harrison speaks primarily of the evangelical abolitionist cause, but argues that the same attitude of hopeful possibility would also permeate the women's movement, labor organizing, and temperance efforts sustained throughout the century on into the twentieth.[36] The novelists considered here represent sharply the erosion of such faith described by Harrison. While they have lost their belief in the efficacy of individual action to erase social misery and want (whether that misery be the kind dictated by poverty at home or adventurism abroad), they still retain—as good liberals ought—a strong allegiance to what Bullock and Shock call "the twin pillars of Liberal theory throughout its development": freedom and conscience.[37] For the late Victorians the pressure resulting from this disjunction will assume crisis proportions. "Consciousness of sin there might be among thinking people in the 1880s," Brian Harrison observes, "but as Beatrice Webb pointed out, it was less an affair of the individual conscience than a matter of collective class guilt. 'We have sinned against you grievously,' wrote Arnold Toynbee to the working classes, '. . . but if you will forgive us . . . we will devote our lives to your service.'"[38] In the later phase of Victorian liberal development, a registry of transgressions committed is much more the norm than sanguine promises of liberation.

Differentiating Liberal Guilt

Service is one of the few options the guilty liberal can exercise, as Toynbee's words, and Clennam's example at the conclusion of *Little Dorrit*, indicate. In the absence of a guiding metanarrative, there are few sustaining intellectual or spiritual consolations to be found. Borrowing Mannheim's terminology from *Ideology and Utopia*,[39] we can see that in Dickens's scheme of things, the great nineteenth-century forms of utopian thinking hold little attraction: neither the forward-looking utopias of Christianity (eternity) or socialism (the proletariat triumphant) nor the backward-looking utopia of an aristocratic feudal order desired by the most literate Tory brethren, Carlyle and Disraeli. Disraeli's work, particularly *Sybil, or The Two Nations* (1845), is of considerable interest, often coming close in sentiment to liberal guilt itself, with its careful rendering of the poor and sympathetic identification with Chartist demands. Yet as Raymond Williams suggests, the premises of both plot and character solidly sustain Disraeli's aristocratic and most antiliberal solution to the Two Nations: "Sybil, of course, is only theoretically 'the daughter of the People.' The actual process of the book is the discovery that she is a dispossessed aristocrat, and the marriage bells ring, not over the achievement of One Nation, but over the uniting of the properties of Marney and Mowbray, one agricultural, the other industrial: a marriage symbolical, indeed, of the political development which was the actual issue. The restored heiress stands, in the general picture, with Margaret Thornton's legacy, with Canada, and with the Horse-Riding."[40]

Still, although the union of Clennam and Little Dorrit poses a stark contrast to this, their humble response of service is one which can be made in the context of any number of ideological commitments, liberal or otherwise. So we are left with the remaining question of whether liberal guilt can be meaningfully distinguished from other kinds of guilt. I think it can. Put very simply, liberal guilt contrasts both its antecedent, Christian guilt, which is rooted in a theistic worldview, as well as modern guilt, which has become largely a psychological and subjective category understood in terms of a milieu dominated by therapeutic discourse.

The meaning of the term "guilt" itself undergoes radical transformation from Victorian times to the present. And vitally linked to this shift is the larger matter of why the novelists treated here found social crises of their time to be compelling material—and how the modernists' caustic criticism of this sociological imagination continues to skew our own assessment of much late Victorian and Edwardian fiction.

Between the nineteenth and twentieth centuries, "guilt" shifts in primary meaning from one of relatively objective description to one of subjective feeling or emotion. Nineteenth-century orthodoxy makes guilt to be, simply, a

breach of ethics. As the *Oxford English Dictionary* puts it in the primary meaning: "A failure of duty, delinquency: offence, crime, sin." Only in the fifth
recorded definition does the idea of a *feeling* of guilt get stated, and there
it is buried in parentheses: "The state (meriting condemnation and reproach
of conscience) of having wilfully committed crime or heinous moral offence;
criminality, great culpability." In our own time the priority of these two meanings has largely been reversed; one recent definition calls guilt "feelings of
culpability especially for imagined offenses or from a sense of inadequacy."[41]
The emotivist notion of feeling guilt—bearing no necessary relation to actual
behavior—begins to take precedence over the idea that guilt may actually serve
to indicate or deter transgression.

In short, translated from its moral context into a therapeutic one, guilt becomes not in any way descriptive of actual behavior but instead persists as a
symptom of what is now commonly labeled "low self-esteem." Thus it almost
always carries the pejorative connotation of mental unhealthiness. In the most
extreme manifestations of this view, guilt is something pathological, and not
useful, to personal development. This goes far beyond even Freud who, despite his misgivings about the damage guilt can do, maintained the necessary
linkage between civilization and the superego's repression of desire. Under an
older dispensation, Philip Rieff argues, "the unbreakable connection of self
with sacred order is best seen in the sense of guilt."[42] That connection is lost,
he says, in the very movement from a theological to a therapeutic worldview.
Implicit in Rieff's criticism of the Freudian and Nietzschean assaults on guilt
is the familiar idea that without a sense of sacred order, guilt evaporates and
we are plunged into moral chaos. Dostoyevsky has been here before. And yet
Rieff's account of this shift maybe indicates most clearly the profound break
between the Edwardian sensibility, which begs for some notion of moral limits
or controls, and the modernists' shrugging off such explicitly moral worries
as food for the fainthearted. Writes Rieff:

> Until the present culture rose to threaten its predecessor, our demand
> system could be specified by the kind of creedal hedges it raised around
> impulses of independence or autonomy from communal purpose. In the
> culture preceding our own, the order of therapy was embedded in a con-
> sensus of "shalt nots." The best never lacked binding convictions, for
> they were the most bound, mainly by what they should not do—or even
> think, or dream. "Thou shalt" precipitated a sequence of operative "shalt
> nots." . . . Individuals were trained, through ritual action, to express

fixed wants, although they could not count thereby upon commensu-
rate gratifications. The limitation of possibilities was the very design of
salvation.[43]

While the modernists found the eradication of "creedal hedges" to be one of
their central tasks, the Edwardians could not find in themselves a total loosen-
ing of restraints. Their voices register worry, particularly about the social
and economic conditions transforming England. Money and empire form the
matrix for their fiction. Their novels show a sense of collective guilt about
the very poor and the sins of empire and are packed with social and political
rumination. And this is exactly where Virginia Woolf's famous and damaging
assessment of them as mere vulgar "materialists"[44] needs to be reappraised.
The Edwardians cannot free themselves from topical social commentary, nor
can they find easy consolation in the varieties of energy, instinct, or physicality
pervading the fiction of a Lawrence, a Joyce, or a Hemingway. Quite the opposite, the Edwardians are far more likely to depict limitless energy and instinct
in destructive—and social and political—terms. Why? Simply because that is
how the increasingly swollen streams of power present themselves. Gissing
does not name by accident that libidinous, ever-hungry couple who triumph
in The Whirlpool the Carnabys. They are carnivores who devour. In short, if
the modernists found the freedom to say yes to life, the Edwardians felt themselves too troubled by historical circumstances to say yes with such facility. To
the Edwardians, yes was more likely to mean trouble; yes signified the absence
of boundaries still craved.

The imperial push represents the most naked, literal instance of this out-
ward expansion, this eradication of boundaries. Addressing that imperial
crisis, Jefferson Hunter considers these historical circumstances vital to the
formation of Edwardian fiction:

> It cannot be argued that Edwardian fiction was dramatically affected by
> any of these events—the Congo, the Boer War, or the election of 1906—
> that there was a consensus about imperialism among novelists, or even
> that novelists aligned themselves neatly in opposed camps. . . . The cer-
> tainty of a Buchan and a Chesterton was exceptional. A sense of vague
> disquiet, as in Wells's admission that when the Boer War came along,
> "something happened to quite a lot of us," was typical. In a few cases
> the disquiet, whatever its source, produced something one can only call
> a bad conscience about imperialism, and the bad conscience in turn pro-
> duced imaginative reactions—fictions which in altered or symbolic form
> admit guilt, reveal atrocities, express doubts.[45]

Trilling complains that the modernists were "indifferent" to matters of the liberal imagination.[46] He was right, but perhaps he overlooked the powerful expressions of liberal guilt—the shadow side of his "liberal imagination," if you will—to be found in the less-esteemed predecessors to the modernist masters. Quite clearly, the Edwardians had not yet grasped what Irving Howe calls the "terrible freedom"[47] of the modernist voice. Yet I would contend that the very cautions, doubts, and indecisions that mar their work ultimately may be read as a valuable defensive gesture against the charismatic, assured colors of authoritarian ideology permeating so much of the modernist canon.

Dickens and Eliot signal the birth of liberal guilt in the English novel. *Little Dorrit* (1855–57) and *Daniel Deronda* (1876), despite their differences, anticipate the death of God some time before Nietzsche's pronouncement while negating what Nietzsche would claim were absolute consequences. The sources both novelists draw on to fill the theistic void are Romantic in origin, for liberal guilt could emerge only after the heady visions of early liberal Romanticism had evaporated.

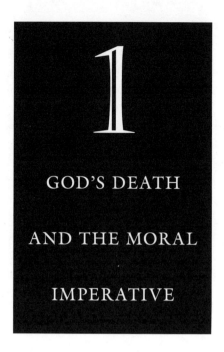

1

GOD'S DEATH

AND THE MORAL

IMPERATIVE

FORMATIVE BRITISH LIBERALISM

> The bad conscience is an illness,
> there is no doubt about that, but an illness
> as pregnancy is an illness.
> FRIEDRICH NIETZSCHE,
> *On the Genealogy of Morals*

We almost invariably associate the death of God with the name of Nietzsche, even though that death is presumed within the British Romantic tradition over half a century before the ringing pronouncement of *Zarathustra*. The English version of God's death is less dramatic and thus occupies a lesser place in intellectual history. But J. S. Mill provided the understated capstone to what had become standard doctrine for many liberal British intellectuals already in the 1850s, namely:

> The value, therefore, of religion to the individual, both in the past and present, as a source of personal satisfaction and of elevated feelings is not to be disputed. But it has still to be considered whether in order to obtain this good, it is necessary to travel beyond the boundaries of the world which we inhabit, or whether the idealization of our earthly life, the cultivation of a high conception of what it may be made, is

not capable of supplying a poetry, and, in the best sense of the word, a
religion equally fitted to exalt the feelings and . . . still be calculated to
ennoble the conduct than any belief respecting the unseen powers.[1]

Mill went one step further, arguing that not only was theistic affirmation unnecessary for doing ethics; it would likely prove harmful. He says, "There
is a very real evil consequent on ascribing a supernatural origin to the received maxims of morality. That origin consecrates the whole of them and
protects them from being discussed or criticized."[2] While the argument can be
mounted that nineteenth-century political Liberalism, at least, finds strongest
roots in the expressly religious sentiments of dissenting Nonconformity,[3] it is
quite clear that for literary intellectuals of liberal conviction, a post-theistic
outlook is more the norm, finding antecedent in the young British Romantics
including Shelley, Byron, Hunt, and Hazlitt. The story of liberal guilt is best
told if we recollect how the Romantics dispensed with God but sought to pre-
serve ethics—in fact, how they believed dispensing with God was crucial to
bringing in a new, better world order.

The Whitehead's famous maxim that Romanticism is spilt religion serves usefully here. Whereas for Nietzsche religion and all its residue could and should
be wiped away, the British Romantics writing in the early nineteenth century
show no intention of getting rid of the residue. Rather, they contend, Shelley
most cogently, that a radical ethic of freedom—from tyranny, cruelty, and
poverty—is attainable in human history rather than eternity, but that a preliminary step involves clearing away metaphysical baggage impeding the task.
For the Romantics, art necessitates political and ethical engagement; aesthetic
creation and ethical formation are one and the same process. Before delineating more fully why these writers desired such a transvaluation of metaphysics
into ethics, and how the Victorian intelligentsia inhabited but modified that
liberal legacy, it is useful for the sake of contrast to recall in some detail the
substance of Nietzsche's later continental argument.

Nietzsche aims his philosophical wrecking ball not only at belief in a personal deity, but also the essence of guilt ("debt," the German *Schuld*) and the
entire dualistic system of good and evil extending from Judaism to Christianity upon which such guilt is predicated. In the last years of his productive
life, 1887 and 1888, Nietzsche takes up the matter of theological orthodoxy
and psychological guilt with increased intensity. *On the Genealogy of Morals*
contains this prediction:

> History shows that the consciousness of being in debt to the deity did
> not by any means come to an end together with the organization of com-

munities on the basis of blood relationship. Even as mankind inherited the concepts "good and bad" from the tribal nobility . . . it also inherited, along with the tribal and family divinities, the burden of still unpaid debts and of the desire to be relieved of them. . . . The guilty feeling of indebtedness to the divinity continued to grow for several millennia— always in the same measure as the concept of God and the feeling for divinity increased on earth and was carried to the heights. . . .

The advent of the Christian God, as the maximum god attained so far, was therefore accompanied by the maximum feeling of guilty indebtedness on earth. Presuming we have gradually entered upon the *reverse* course, there is no small probability that with the irresistible decline of faith in the Christian God there is now also a considerable decline in mankind's feeling of guilt; indeed, the prospect cannot be dismissed that the complete and definitive victory of atheism might free mankind of this whole feeling of guilty indebtedness toward its origin, its *causa prima*. Atheism and a kind of *second innocence* belong together.[4]

In *Twilight of the Idols*, just a year away from debilitating illness, Nietzsche extends his critique of God and guilt, seeking demolition of the concept of free will itself. By doing so, Nietzsche takes to task once more the western theological tradition. But now he goes all the way. In targeting individual freedom and its concomitant—individual responsibility—Nietzsche lays waste not only to Christianity, but to the central tenet of secular Romantic liberalism itself:

The error of free will.—We no longer have any sympathy today with the concept of "free will": we know only too well what it is—the most infamous of all the arts of the theologian for making mankind "accountable" in his sense of the word, that is to say for *making mankind dependent on him*. . . . I give here only the psychology of making men accountable.— Everywhere accountability is sought, it is usually the instinct for *punishing and judging* which seeks it. . . . the doctrine of will has been invented essentially for the purpose of punishment, that is of *finding guilty*. The whole of the old-style psychology, the psychology of will, has as its precondition the desire of its authors, the priests at the head of the ancient communities, to create for themselves a *right* to ordain punishments—or their desire to create for God a right to do so. . . . Men were thought of as "free" so that they could become *guilty*: consequently, every action *had* to be thought of as willed, the origin of every action as lying in the consciousness (—whereby the most *fundamental* falsification . . . was made into the very principle of psychology). . . . Today, when we have started to move in the *reverse* direction, when we immoralists especially are trying with all our might to remove the concept of guilt and the concept of punishment from the world and to purge psychology, history, nature, the social institutions and sanctions of them, there is in our eyes no more radical opposition than that of the theologians, who continue to infect the innocence of becoming with "punishment" and "guilt" by means of the concept of the "moral world-order." Christianity is a hangman's metaphysics.[5]

Nietzsche's contention that "Men were thought of as free so that they could become guilty" summarizes most distinctly what will become the dilemma for Victorian writers, particularly novelists, who follow the Romantic belief that we as human agents are free to make or unmake our world, and that something called "God's will" no longer holds either terrors or consolations. Freedom does lead to guilt, especially when the world does not seem to improve noticeably despite our best efforts. But for the radical Romantics, guilt is not yet a problem, and the most intellectually daring of them, particularly Blake, Shelley, and Byron, all anticipate Nietzsche in their contention that orthodox theism upholds an entirely undesirable social order; in short, that for society to change, the given notion of God must go. Yet all the Romantics make individual free will central to their aesthetic and ideological project; in fact, faith in individual will and creativity is the single most important component of the Romantic ideology. Without it, there can be no Romanticism, nor, for that matter, any liberalism to speak of.

The coupling of post-theism with a renewed sense of ethical urgency is a persistent strategy for the younger Romantics; but Shelley gives it sharpest expression, and nowhere more so than in *The Mask of Anarchy*, written on the occasion of the Peterloo Massacre of 1819. The occasion of the poem became instantly famous. Peaceful protestors marching in Saint Peter's Field, Manchester, on behalf of parliamentary reform had been killed by drunken government cavalrymen and foot soldiers running amok through the crowd. Shelley seized upon the event to make plain what seemed to him the opposition between the interests of deity and the interests of the dispossessed and hungry. Arrayed against the innocents are the forces of God's side, those who uphold existing political and religious power, and who grovel before their master, Anarchy:

> Lawyers and priests, a motley crowd,
> To the earth their pale brows bowed;

> Like a bad prayer not over loud,
> Whispering—"Thou art Law and God."—
>
> (ll. 66–69)

Shelley's familiar first notoriety had come after his teenage collaboration with friend Thomas Hogg for writing *On the Necessity of Atheism*, a pamphlet which earned him prompt expulsion from Oxford in 1811. But the argument of that early tract addresses in rather dry fashion the absence of empirical philosophical proofs within theological orthodoxy and carries less impressive rhetorical weight than the explicitly moral arguments for post-theism in the mature poetry such as *The Mask*. There it becomes evident that Shelley's atheism is intended, in contradistinction to Nietzsche's, *not for the purpose of transcending ethics, but rather for making ethics possible*. And ironically, those ethics look remarkably like Christ's.[6] Shelley's Peterloo heroes, the innocent citizens passively taking the soldiers' blows until dead, enact exactly the kind of triumph of meekness, the slave morality, abhorred by Nietzsche. This is as close as Shelley ever came to articulating how his flirtation with pacifism could be shaped into a viable political strategy and movement:[7]

> And if then the tyrants dare
> Let them ride among you there,
> Slash, and stab, and maim, and hew,—
> What they like, that let them do.
>
> With folded arms and steady eyes,
> And little fear, and less surprise
> Look upon them as they slay
> Till their rage has died away.
>
> (ll. 340–47)

Abroad in Italy when he wrote the stanzas, Shelley sent the completed poem to his friend and promoter Leigh Hunt, then an influential man of letters and editor of the *Examiner*. Hunt refused to publish the poem for fear of libel charges and imprisonment, both of which he had already personally experienced in his career, and chose to wait instead until 1832, when the Reform Bill was safely passed, before bringing the poem to print.[8] By then the incendiary moment was long over; what had once seemed Jacobinical, and then radical, was now merely liberal.[9] Passage of the Reform Bill was solid evidence that much of the liberal social agenda for which Hunt and his friends had stuck their necks out was proceeding apace into legislative reality, and that the process would be hard to reverse. Hunt recollected many years later, "Almost every liberal measure that has since become a deed of the State—perhaps we might say, every one without exception, from Catholic Emancipation to the Anti-Corn Laws—did we advocate in the most trying times, when Toryism was at the height of its power, and when almost everybody, even its quondam friends, was trying to blow out the little taper of Reform, then kept alive by some half-dozen writers." [10] What should be kept in mind is that in 1819, the battered but still courageous movement which Peter Thorslev, Jr., calls "Post-Waterloo Liberalism" [11] was under severe attack. And it was branded as much for its religious and sexual unorthodoxies as for its politics. Had Hunt published Shelley's poem immediately, more likely than not he would have been charged with sedition and blasphemy.[12] The liberal intellectuals' insistence that justice resided not with, but against deity, and their willful severing of ethics from belief in God, simply appalled most of British society. Thorslev aptly summarizes both these liberals' Enlightenment belief and the hostility they faced:

> Moral (and political) imperatives frequently do, and ought always to precede and transcend all religious and metaphysical convictions. Pierre Bayle, the father of the Enlightenment . . . shocked the intellectual circles of Europe at the close of the seventeenth century by asserting that communities of atheists might be, and frequently have been, as morally behaved as communities of Catholics, or of Huguenots—Bayle's own persuasion. In our western democracies we take this assessment so much for granted (surely it is assumed by every card-carrying member of the ACLU), that it is a bit difficult to understand the consternation it caused all through the eighteenth century and beyond. In his *Reflections* Burke asserts more passionately than any of his other convictions his certainty that not only a belief in God, but indeed the institution of the church, is absolutely essential to any stability and order in society and the state— and by 1820 not only Coleridge and Wordsworth, but the vast majority of the British public were in wholehearted agreement.[13]

Shelley feeds such reactionary disapproval with his blanket assault on "GOD AND KING, AND LAW" (l. 37). Though his poem did not find print till after his death, the potent message was carried on meanwhile through other avenues. In 1822 the first number of the *Liberal*, a joint literary production financed by Byron and the late Shelley, edited by Hunt, and published by Leigh's brother John, appeared with Byron's poem *The Vision of Judgment* heading the contributions. While the first number made a profit, the magazine lasted only four issues.[14] Still, the *Liberal* proved to be one of the most influential failures in the history of English periodicals. Byron's poem, a mocking excoriation of the king, of Tory politics, and of orthodox state church belief embodied in the Lake Poets, defined starkly for the public what "liberal" could be taken to signify. "Byron's Magazine, or rather Hunt's, 'The Liberal' is arrived in Town," Carlyle wrote, "but they will not sell it—it is so full of Atheism and Radicalism and other noxious *isms*."[15] The *Courier*'s reviewer blasted the production even more thoroughly, contributing to the satanic mystique of the young Romantics:

> With a brain from heaven and a heart from hell—with a pen that can write as angels speak, and yet that riots in thoughts which fiends might envy—with the power to charm, instruct, and elevate—but with the ruling passion to provoke our loathing and deserve our scorn—this compound of rottenness and beauty— this unsexed Circe, who gems the poisoned cup he offers us, and exhorts our admiration of its rare and curious workmanship, while the Soul sickens at the draught within— seems to have lived only that the world might learn from his example, how worthless and how pernicious a thing is genius, when divorced from religion, from morals, and from humanity.[16]

But it was in large measure the imperative to sever individual conscience from religious creedalism that drove the early liberal political agenda, and on this point the young Romantics were to be vindicated as they were to be on so many others. Judith Shklar describes the historical divorce of religious affirmation from conscience, arguing that it constitutes the earliest formative phase of liberal political theory:

> Liberalism is a latecomer, since it has its origins in post-Reformation Europe. Its origins are in the terrible tension within Christianity between the demands of creedal orthodoxy and those of charity, between faith and morality. The cruelties of the religious wars had the effect of turning many Christians away from the public policies of the churches to a morality that saw toleration as an expression of Christian charity. One thinks of Sebastien Castellion among Calvinists, for example. Others, torn by conflicting spiritual impulses, became skeptics who put cruelty and fanaticism at the very head of the human vices; Montaigne is the most notable among them. In either case the individual, whether the bearer of a sacred conscience or the potential victim of cruelty, is to be protected against the incursions of public oppression.

> ... To insist that individuals must make their own choices about the
> most important matter in their lives—their religious beliefs—without
> interference from public authority, is to go very far indeed toward liber-
> alism. It is, I think, the core of its historical development, but it would be
> wrong to think of principled toleration as equivalent to political liberal-
> ism. . . . Nevertheless, liberalism's deepest grounding is in place from the
> first, in the conviction of the earliest defenders of toleration, born in hor-
> ror, that cruelty is an absolute evil, an offense against God or humanity.
> It is out of that tradition that the political liberalism of fear arose and
> continues amidst the terror of our time to have relevance.[17]

The stark simplicity of liberal theory—described here as the elimination of coercion from human life—finds frequent illustration in the liberal writing of the
early nineteenth century, and it is just as frequently condemned as subversive
by Tory power. Much of the liberal crusade focused on blatant examples of
institutionalized cruel practices, among them capital punishment for ridicu-
lously small offenses, the empire in India, and slavery, a matter on which
post-theistic liberals and the forces of Wesleyanism could agree. The campaign against flogging was particularly hard fought, because the practice was
so entrenched. Consider, for instance, the editorial from the *Stanford News* in
1810 by John Scott, entitled "One Thousand Lashes!!" Hunt was prosecuted
for libel because he dared reprint it in the *Examiner*.[18] The piece's rhetorical
strategy is to represent in graphic terms the procedure of military flogging and
to appeal to British popular sentiment for a change in the law that currently
enforces such inhumanity. This form of writing becomes increasingly common in the Victorian period, when moral crusades of every kind are vented in
the pages of popular periodicals to the end of effecting legislative and moral
"improvement"—Dickens's *Household Words* perhaps standing as the most
exhaustive compendium of the genre. And we should not underestimate the influence of that writing on the making of policy. Flogging, like numerous other
practices, eventually ceased largely because of the efforts of liberal writers.[19]
Again, like so much that was initially hailed as subversive and extreme, this
appeal of Scott's eventually found its way into mainstream consensus:

> Here alone, in this land of liberty, in this age of refinement—by a people
> who, with their usual consistency, have been in the habit of reproaching
> their neighbors with the cruelty of their punishment,—is still inflicted a
> species of *torture*, at least as exquisite as any that was ever devised by
> the infernal ingenuity of the Inquisitions.—No, as the Attorney-General
> justly says, Bonaparte does *not* treat his refractory troops in this manner;

there is not a man in his ranks whose back is seamed with the lacerating cat-o'-nine-tails—*his* soldiers have never yet been drawn up to view one of their comrades stripped naked,—his limbs tied with ropes to a triangular machine,—his back torn to the bone by the merciless cutting whipcord, applied by persons who relieve each other at short intervals, that they may bring the full unexhausted strength of a man to the work of scourging. Bonaparte's soldiers have never yet with tingling ears listened to the piercing screams of a human creature so tortured: they have never seen the blood oozing from his rent flesh;—they have never beheld a surgeon, with dubious look, pressing the agonized victim's pulse, and calmly calculating, to an odd blow, how far suffering may be extended. . . . In short, Bonaparte's soldiers cannot form any notion of that most heart-rending of all exhibitions on this side hell,—*an English military flogging.*[20]

It took some time for Victorian intellectuals to realize that building the good society was a considerably more complicated task than merely singling out specific kinds of vicious behavior or enacting appropriate legislation. Some Victorian liberals were more programmatic than others in their calls for legislative reform; while Dickens's *Household Words* focused on specific moral abuses without a clear political affiliation, Thornton Hunt and G. H. Lewes's *The Leader* called for reforms including "extension of the franchise, universal state education, and an enlightened economic policy to finance the reforms."[21] That kind of hopeful attitude about the power of popular opinion and legislative change had inspired Thornton Hunt's father Leigh, the solitary survivor of his Romantic generation, to write this testament to progress in 1835, speaking, as it were, on the cusp of Romantic-Victorian transition:

We have abolished inquisitions and the rack, burnings for religion, burnings for witchcraft, hangings for forgery (a great triumph in a commercial country), much of the punishment of death in some countries, all of it in others. Why not abolish war?[22]

We may readily characterize such a voice, as some do Shelley's, as that of an "ineffectual angel."[23] But Hunt's simplistic frame of mind reveals not so much his personal intellectual deficiencies, as it does the dominant reforming spirit and stance of early nineteenth-century liberalism. Hopefulness was possible for the Romantics because political solutions seemed to them within grasp. Such was the underlying and triumphant attitude of reformers in a variety of movements, which had overflowed the success of the evangelical abolitionist cause.[24] The post-Waterloo Enlightenment attitude among the young Romantics, while slightly different, was laced with equally sanguine sentiment: ethics would take care of themselves once various forms of "cant" and superstition had been cleared from human minds by the educating pen of poet and journalist; and by the same token, nationalist aspiration allowed to flourish free of imperial design would move international relations toward harmony.[25] Finally, conjoining these sensibilities was a third form of optimism which suggested that the problems of economic distribution—indeed of international warfare and strife—would inevitably work themselves out, given a free global economic marketplace allowed time and room enough to work. Thus argued philosopher Benjamin Constant on the Continent,[26] while in England a parallel case would be made by Bentham, the Manchester School, and Members of Parliament Richard Cobden and John Bright—who conceptualized Free Trade and the Peace Movement as inseparable pieces of progressive politics.[27] It is worth noting that this ideological formation, which we might designate liberal triumphalism, has had a heady but brief resurgence in recent times before being overtaken by powerful forces of nationalism and ethnic rivalry around the globe since the Cold War's end.

The liberals' most significant shortcoming was not that for which they are most often tagged: an overly benign view of human nature, the failure to anticipate human evil. Their poetry and prose is rife with representations of evil, embodied both in political institutions and powerful individuals. To thrive, cruelty requires both institutional practice and personal agency, and of this the Romantic writers were perfectly conscious. How else explain the repeated ad hominem attacks on tyrants such as Castlereagh, Wellington, and the king, or reactionaries such as Coleridge, Southey, and Wordsworth who had gone over to lend their poetic gift to the Tory cause? In fact, the liberal shortcoming did not lie in a naive view of human nature; rather, it inhered in a lack of ideological peripheral vision that persists even in our time but for which early liberals—as opposed to contemporary ones—perhaps need not be chastised. Today liberalism remains a hamstrung and ineffectual belief as long as it underestimates the two historical forces with which it is often associated and which frequently overshadow it: capitalism and nationalism. This raises historical and philosophical questions much too large for complete analysis here, quite deserving of another book. But it is sufficient for our immediate purposes to say that Victorian and Edwardian writers as diverse as Dickens, Gissing, Forster, and Wells recognize that liberal and capitalist systems of value do not easily merge: the endurance of poverty in London's streets will not be explained away. On this score, their voices loudly contradict the confidence of first generation classic liberal theory. The enduring visibility of the poor must be addressed specifically, in detail. This alteration of the liberal voice from confidence to despair, from prescription to guilt, might be read as a sign of liberalism's decline but also signals an enlargement and maturation of liberal concern.

The problem of nationalism appears in some ways more interesting, because both liberals and Marxists have historically misunderstood it. While the Marxist insistence that class is more important than nationality has proven simply wrong, liberals, for their part, have radically underestimated nationalism's potential virulence. Arguably, early formative liberalism gets tugged between two contending forces, Shelleyan idealistic nonviolence and Byronic nationalist militancy, with Byron prevailing almost from the start. Byron's career, ending in Missolonghi on behalf of the Greek revolutionary cause, remains one of the defining gestures of Romantic liberalism for many people the world over who have never read his poetry.[28] William St. Clair suggests that "by his death," Byron "unwittingly played a part in promoting nationalism to the position (long held by religion) of being the most divisive and destructive element in western civilization."[29] The claim is a little histrionic, but we do well to take care that Byron's superstar legacy be comprehensively understood, and not merely in terms of the literary production or sexual dynamism. The larger, final canvas is the nationalist one. "For good or ill," Carl Woodring observes, "nationalism has endured longer than some of the romantics' more specific enthusiasms."[30]

Though temperamentally opposed to violence and bloodshed, and antagonistic to the imperial policies of Castlereagh and Wellington, as well as the other great powers of the Grand Alliance, the liberal Romantics draw a firm distinction between imperialist warmongering on one hand and noble national freedom fighting on the other. A cornerstone of nineteenth-century nationalist sentiment, observes Michael Howard, was the belief that necessary, just wars of national independence would lead invariably to an international peaceful order of nations.[31] Although this liberal item of faith has thus far not found fulfillment, it has proven resilient and capable of numerous recyclings. And in this respect, we can take Byron's caustic lines about Wellington to be equally descriptive of his own mission to Missolonghi: "War's a brain-spattering, windpipe-slitting art, / Unless her cause by Right be sanctified" (*Don Juan* 9.4).

The consequences of such doctrine are not always anticipated. One of the choice ironies of the Philhellenes' support for the Greek revolution was the growing merger between the forces of secular Benthamism and those of

Wilberforce's evangelical Christianity.[32] Where that merger might lead is suggested through the activity of Bible distribution in Greece by Philhellenic enthusiasts of the revolution. Somewhat bemusedly, despite his iconoclasm about both Bentham and the missionaries, Byron had allowed himself to be one such carrier of bulk shipments of Bibles, which at first found a reluctant market among the Greeks. But by 1825 the thirst for the Scriptures in Greece had increased: paper was in short supply among the freedom fighters, who used it to roll gunpowder cartridges for their antiquated muskets.[33] The connection between Bibles and bullets, Christianity and military force, was to grow stronger, rather than weaker, throughout the rest of the century, although the marriage did not always take this literal a form. And the relationship between liberalism and the use of coercive violence would—as it still does—dog the liberal conscience.

The most important Victorian novelists, Charles Dickens and George Eliot, each illustrate in particular ways the radical Romantic inheritance. As T. A. Jackson observes of the generation of writers which included also Mill, Lewes, and Spencer, the starting point for them all was this: "There is no God; but that is a family secret!"[34] Post-theism among the Victorians, however, signifies not the certain promise of a more just ethical order, as it did for the Romantics, but rather more of a weight, an obligation to help bring that order into being. Hope turns to duty; utopian visions turn to guilt; the residue after the mopping up of spilt religion goes from sweet to sour. Dickens, like Shelley, vents his spleen with splendid outrage on lawyers and priests, but the impetus of his liberal doctrine in the 1850s will bog down in the mire of economics. George Eliot brings her genius to bear at the end of her career on the formation of evil as a joint production of individual will and imperial growth. But in a move rather reminiscent of Byron, she attempts to launch herself out of anomie in the last novel with a gesture of moral affirmation rooted in similarly nationalist enthusiasm, this time of Zionist variety. The solution is far less convincing than her brilliantly complex delineation of evil, Grandcourt.

It is best to begin with Dickens. When we meet Arthur Clennam, the protagonist at the center of *Little Dorrit*, we recognize the first fully developed case of liberal guilt in English literature. For him, as Nietzsche described it, the conscience formed in the brew of liberal ideas is going to be as debilitating as any illness. But if the illness of guilt is, in Nietzsche's phrase, like a "pregnancy" that can be gotten over, the price paid for the cure, at least in Clennam's case, seems high. Liberal guilt turns out to be something he has to live with, something impossible to purge.

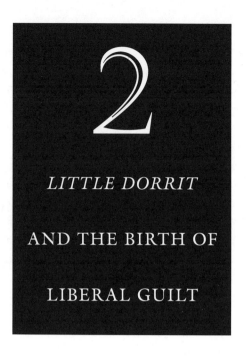

2

LITTLE DORRIT

AND THE BIRTH OF

LIBERAL GUILT

They have got rid of the Christian God, and now feel obliged to cling
all the more firmly to Christian morality: that is *English* consistency, let us
not blame it on little bluestockings *à la* Eliot. In England, in response to
every little emancipation from theology one has to reassert one's position
in a fear-inspiring manner as a moral fanatic. That is the *penance* one pays
there. — With us it is different. When one gives up Christian belief one
thereby deprives oneself of the *right* to Christian morality. For the latter
is absolutely *not* self-evident: one must make this point clear again and
again, in spite of English shallowpates. If one breaks out of it a
fundamental idea, the belief in God, one thereby breaks the whole thing
to pieces: one has nothing of any consequence left in one's hands. . . . If
the English really do believe they know, of their own accord, "intuitively,"
what is good and evil; if they consequently think they no longer have need
of Christianity as a guarantee of morality; that is merely the *consequence*
of the ascendancy of Christian evaluation and an expression of the
strength and *depth* of this ascendancy. . . . For the Englishman, morality
is not yet a problem.

FRIEDRICH NIETZSCHE,
Twilight of the Idols

Nietzsche's remark is merely one indication of the novel's meteoric literary ascendancy in England after Romanticism. And his specific singling out of "bluestockings *à la* Eliot" suggests how potent this army of scribblers had become: if not the most eloquent school of English moralizing, then certainly very influential. The end of the Napoleonic Wars, Alison Adburgham points out, found "no novelists of any note in London."[1] Yet only a short time later, exactly four years after Byron's death and four years before Scott's, a reviewer in the *Athenaeum* observes that one publisher's list for 1828 contains seventy-four novels, as compared to only four volumes of poetry.[2]

Apart from the rising quantity of novels published, however, there is also a shift underway in their subject matter. The genre during the 1830s was still much dominated by characters of the upper-class "silver fork" variety,[3] but increasing interest in the news itself followed the rapid spread of journalism given impetus by the Reform Bill of 1832. Kathryn Chittick argues that this decade marks "the periodical form of publication itself . . . revising the terms on which literature was produced. The intense political interest of the time meant that *news* in its regular bits and pieces was the most compelling reading and that, consequently, reading became a fragmentary experience."[4] And for a growing class of literate urban workers, she says, the newspaper and coffeehouse made reading accessible and affordable.

The great, grim novels of economic distress and misery written during this time, books which broaden drastically the novel's "social range"[5]—Dickens's *Oliver Twist* (1837), Disraeli's *Sybil* (1845), Gaskell's *Mary Barton* (1848)— must be read in the context of the news during the 1830s which was somber: a period beginning with wage riots, protests against high corn prices, and the wrecking of threshing machinery introduced in Kent. Violence subsequently swept much of rural England in 1830–31 resulting, as historians Royle and Walvin go on to say, in the "traditional" government response: "nineteen men hanged, 644 imprisoned, and 481 transported."[6] Reform in 1832, enfranchising a select group of middle-class men, did not adequately address working-class conditions, and discontent worsened in the economic depression between 1837 and 1842, which was by some historical accounts "the most severe . . . since the Industrial Revolution had begun."[7] The news was bad, but the public showed a strong desire to read more of it. And that this basic hunger for information would influence the writing of novels is made quite plain by an 1832 editorial in the *Edinburgh Review*, published several months before Sir Walter Scott's death. The piece praises Scott's fiction as proof of the formula meeting the appetite for both pleasure and "practicality"; his historical novels brilliantly exploit the public's demand for an entertainment loading the

yacht of frivolous escape with a cargo of respectable fact: "In consequence of
this newly-enlarged view of the principles on which fiction should be written,
we have, since the appearance of Waverley, seen the fruits of varied learning
and experience displayed in that agreeable form; and we have even received
from works of fiction what it would once have been thought preposterous to
expect—information. . . . We have learnt, too, how greatly the sphere of the
Novel may be extended, and how capable it is of becoming the vehicle almost
of every species of popular knowledge."[8]

One sign of the news' growing respectability was the increasing status and
influence of journalism as a profession. While the target of frequent and brutal repression during the Napoleonic Wars, the press now constituted a major
force in English life, with the ability to make parliamentary and royal con-
stituencies think twice about public policy decisions.[9] Not incidentally, both
Dickens and Eliot initiated their novelistic careers with journalism—Dickens
as a reporter for the *Mirror of Parliament* in 1831, and Eliot as assistant editor
for the progressive utilitarian organ, the *Westminster Review*, in 1852. It bears
repeating, I think, especially for our context in which the novel has been so
thoroughly academicized as a theoretical and disciplinary study, that novel
writing bears in many respects closer affinity to the work of the journalistic
press than to anything called "literature," even though writers of novels by the
end of the nineteenth century had self-consciously assumed a literary mantle.[10]
To the extent that the novel seeks the popular mass audience, this association
with the popular press cannot be underestimated.

The steady confluence of Christian moralizing and utilitarian yearning for
social improvement that imbued this mass audience often found expression
in the popular media of journalism and fiction. If the Romantic liberals' idea
of the good had employed (what was at least for the time) a trenchant analysis of institutional and political alignments of power, such analysis was often
hijacked in the 1820s and 1830s by an ascendant evangelicalism which took
individual virtue to be the primary, if not only, causal agent within the body
politic. Both Dissenting and secular forms of Radicalism begin with a shared
resentment against aristocratic privilege, but from there the differences multiply. Pam Morris, elaborating on the fusion of evangelical and utilitarian value
described by an earlier historian, G. M. Young, suggests the contours of the
mid-Victorian literate middle class:

> In the first stages of its struggle for hegemonic ascendancy, the middle
> class gained a sense of solidarity and identity by defining itself against the
> aristocracy. In opposition to aristocratic "vices" of paternalism, para-

sitism, indolence, and dissolute extravagance, the bourgeoisie asserted the moral virtues of enterprise, diligence, and thrifty sobriety. From the outset, these ideological claims were taken up and validated by two powerful discourses of "truth": the traditional "true" discourse of religion, expressed by the rising force of evangelicalism, and the potent new "true" discourse of empirical science, expressed by the Utilitarians. Thus reason and religion joined forces to insist on the divine and natural superiority of the middle class whose enterprise, energy, and industry had enriched the whole nation.[11]

The most unpleasant consequences of this ideological apparatus are too familiar. They became especially apparent in the growing effort by Victorian intellectuals to explain the haunting spectacle of urban poverty. Thus went the frequent hypothesis: crime, poverty, and prostitution are the natural outcome of individual depravity; conversely, righteous individuals are sure to prosper. The *Westminster Review* in 1849 ascribes the cause of poverty to these culprits: "indolence, unskilfulness, extravagence, drunkenness, dishonesty, and unpunctuality."[12]

Journalism and sociological discourse alike buttressed the predominant belief that the sufferings of the poor could be traced to individual defective will or desire. Anita Levy has documented how very often prominent Victorian sociologists identified the ultimate cause of poverty and misery not as working conditions, hours, or pay, but rather the loose morals of poor women who had no sense of sexual virtue; the harbor of vice in this paradigm is not simply the poor, but the poor woman, most specifically, the individual prostitute. Accompanying the growing use of scientific surveys and statistics to document the situation of the very poor, Levy contends, the interpretive analysis of numerous reports blames the victims of bad housing, overcrowding, and disease for their own "negligence and sexual misconduct."[13] One Victorian sociologist, Peter Gaskell, author of the 1836 study *Artisans and Machinery: The Moral and Physical Condition of the Manufacturing Population*, sees wages and unemployment as practically incidental to the crisis of working-class poverty. The focal issue, according to him, is "sluttishness" versus wifely virtue:

> Another misfortune of a very prominent character, attends upon the female division of the manufacturing population. This is, the entire want of instruction or example in learning the plainest elements of domestic economy; and this single circumstance goes far to explain many of the improvident bad habits which form a chief part of the curse upon their social condition. . . . Of all these essentials to the head of a household the

factory girl is utterly ignorant, and her arrangements, if arrangements they can be called, where every thing is left to chance, are characterized by sluttish waste, negligence, carelessness as to the quality of the food, and indifference as to the mode of cooking, and an absence of all that tidiness, cleanliness, and forethought which are requisite to a good housewife.[14]

However, if much of the sociological writing tended to reify Christian moralizing by blaming victims and eliding from the picture any account of social conditions or institutions, the best novels did not. The novels of the 1840s, Tillotson argues, begin to disturb their readers' peace, even "shock" them, precisely on account of the thoroughgoing documentation of class divisions, of the often miserable texture of life in cities and factories.[15] The best novelists turn middle-class moralizing inward; they force ethical self-reflection. Dickens and Eliot often embody this prophetic function, undermining rather than building on shibboleths. Their most radical effect is to impose upon their audience the necessity of enlarging its sense of social breakdown to encompass social and not merely individual terms of explanation. Consider, for instance, the subject of good housekeeping, which occupies Dickens considerably in *Bleak House* (1852–53), the first of his three great novels of the 1850s (the other two being *Hard Times* and *Little Dorrit*) to confront directly mid-Victorian ideology's most egregious claims. In that novel, Esther Summerson's housekeeping virtuosity, which Dickens treats with seriousness and not irony, proves ultimately no match for the entrenched collective evils of law and lawyers in Chancery, evils which only a more worldly, cynical narrative voice than Esther's can capably discern. Even more, the entropic world view of the novel's omniscient narrator, a view permeated by images of swirling fog, mud, decay, and rot, makes Esther's efforts seem all the more necessary, yet all the more pathetic. *Bleak House* subverts Victorian moral certainties just as surely as its picture of an interminably grinding lawsuit in Chancery represents the motion of a cosmological system moving inevitably from order to chaos, darkness, and death. If the second law of thermodynamics—first fully articulated in 1854 by Rudolf Clausius, a year after *Bleak House*'s book publication[16]—was unknown to Dickens, then his novel predicts with uncanny exactness its stark and terrible implications.

Eliot's novels take on similarly tragic proportions that give the lie to typical Victorian moral uplift. She brings us to a sense of profound sympathy for her victims—usually women—and not smugness about their shortcomings; moreover, manifestations of imperial power get represented as inextricable from expressions of male power. This becomes key to understanding Grandcourt in *Daniel Deronda*. Both Dickens and Eliot are moralists in that they want to apportion responsibility for wasted and tragic lives. But they reject standard Victorian moralism by their willingness to assign blame not only to individual profligacy, but also, and more aggressively so, to the powerful, the privileged, and the calloused who make the social rules; read here: middle-class agency, middle-class complicity. *Little Dorrit* (1855–57) and *Daniel Deronda* (1876) mark the beginnings of guilty liberal awareness in the English novel. And they also show that Nietzsche's assessment of one trend is accurate: the post-theistic world picture makes the English more rather than less obsessed with the moral life.

Arthur Clennam

Dickens finished writing *Little Dorrit* only two years before Darwin's *Origin of Species* (1859), the book which dramatically punctured — if the assertion of the law of entropy had not done so already — time-honored notions of super-natural agency, teleology, providential order, and meaning. Though this has become so standard a piece of intellectual doctrine in the twentieth century as to be taken for granted, it is critical to remember that the repercussions of Darwin's shattering work were felt by British intellectuals, particularly novel-ists, all the way from the 1850s through the Edwardian period. And although none of the shocks resulting from these scientific revelations are made explicit in *Little Dorrit*, Dickens's central protagonist of that novel, Arthur Clennam, perfectly captures the metaphysical doubt that afflicts most Victorian intellec-tuals.

Having lived abroad for many years, an expatriate, the returned native Clennam finds the city of London appalling. Entitled "Home," chapter 3 is actually the novel's starting place:

> It was a Sunday evening in London, gloomy, close, and stale. Madden-ing church bells of all degrees of dissonance, sharp and flat, cracked and clear, fast and slow, made the brick-and-mortar echoes hideous. Melancholy streets, in a penitential garb of soot, steeped the souls of the people who were condemned to look at them out of windows, in dire despondency. In every thoroughfare, up almost every alley, and down almost every turning, some doleful bell was throbbing, jerking, tolling, as if the Plague were in the city and the dead-carts were going round.

Everything was bolted and barred that could by possibility furnish relief to an overworked people. No pictures, no unfamiliar animals, no
rare plants or flowers, no natural or artificial wonders of the ancient
world—all *taboo* with that enlightened strictness, that the ugly South Sea
gods in the British Museum might have supposed themselves at home
again. Nothing to see but streets, streets, streets. Nothing to breathe,
but streets, streets, streets. Nothing to change the brooding mind, or
raise it up. Nothing for the spent toiler to do, but to compare the monotony of his seventh day with the monotony of his six days, think what
a weary life he led, and make the best of it—or the worst, according to
the probabilities.[17]

If this rather unsubtly establishes for the reader connections between God,
religion, plague, and death [18]—in Clennam's or at the very least Dickens's own
mind—then what follows immediately sets up the conditions of the great crisis
to which doubting Clennam will be forced to respond, specifically later when
he meets the Dorrits. Sitting "in the window of a coffeehouse in Ludgate Hill,"
Clennam contemplates the city.

Fifty thousand lairs surrounded him where people lived so unwhole-
somely that fair water put into their crowded rooms on Saturday night,
would be corrupt on Sunday morning; albeit my lord, their county member, was amazed that they failed to sleep in company with their butcher's
meat. Miles of close wells and pits of houses, where the inhabitants
gasped for air, stretched far away towards every point of the compass.
Through the heart of the town a deadly sewer ebbed and flowed, in the
place of a fine fresh river. What secular want could the million or so
of human beings whose daily labour, six days in the week, lay among
these Arcadian objects, from the sweet sameness of which they had no
escape between the cradle and the grave—what secular want could they
possibly have upon their seventh day? Clearly they could want nothing
but a stringent policeman. (68)

The first guilty liberal hero in English fiction, Clennam compensates for his
lost faith with a hyperactive sense of duty toward the less fortunate. He will
define his self-worth entirely in terms of that duty, one getting snarled in his
apprehension of familial crime. But it is the psychology of guilt, and not the
typically labyrinthine plot whereby Clennam discovers dark family secrets,
that makes the book interesting. As a psychological study Clennam is the most
fully developed of Dickens's characters; in fact he is one of the few who could

be fitted into the canvas of an Eliot novel without ripping the fabric. He represents something quite new and complicated in the work of an artist associated too often with only caricature.

Before plumbing the depths of Clennam's liberal guilt more fully, other interesting parallels between Dickens's novel and Eliot's work, particularly *Daniel Deronda*, bear mentioning besides the common exploration of how the moral life takes shape in the absence of God. If Clennam foresees the extreme expression of guilt without crime of Kafka's work—notably Joseph K. in *The Trial*—then Eliot's Grandcourt must be viewed as the exact inverse: a figure absolutely without remorse, a creature for whom guilt has no meaning. And if Clennam represents a fundamental artistic experiment for Dickens, the same can be said of Eliot's Grandcourt, a character who explodes the Comtean positivist intellectual scaffolding which Eliot had painstakingly built around the edifice of her shattered religious faith. For that positivism, which maintained that the growth of intelligence is necessarily accompanied by an increase in moral sympathy,[19] is flatly denied by the character of Grandcourt. He poses, as several critics have observed, a radically new force in Eliot's work, and his very name, suggestive of the huge estates he possesses as well as the dominant imperial imagery with which he is always associated, implies the evil he embodies must be interpreted beyond a merely personal level, must be perceived in its broadest sense as a comprehensive indictment of all of English society.[20]

Like the Circumlocution Office and Merdle's financial empire in which Clennam gets entrapped, Grandcourt represents a heart of darkness in English society, which has been created wholly by that society, and is the very affirmation of its highest values. The way different segments of society affirm Grandcourt's steady accumulation of power as necessary, just, and admirable—from Gascoigne, to Sir Hugo Mallinger, and even to Gwendolen herself—is only one indication that a new explanation of evil becomes necessary. For calling Grandcourt a villain is pitifully inadequate to describing him. Aesthetically, this in part explains why the figure of the villain can function only in the context of comedy or melodrama; villainy as a serious moral category no longer contains convincing explanatory value.

Thus the stock villain Rigaud-Blandois of *Little Dorrit* is patently unconvincing as a threatening individual menace. Rather, he points continually to the "society" that made him, just as Conrad's most notable villains, James Wait of *The Nigger of the Narcissus* and Gentleman Brown in *Lord Jim*, do.[21] We cannot be too surprised that as these novelists' understanding of evil grows to include collective, institutional constructs as well as the strictly personal, the stock figure of the Victorian villain becomes proportionately hollowed out, weightless. The villain begins to appear as a signal of a rotting social order, not its source. Thus Rigaud suggests, " 'I have been treated and respected as a gentleman universally. If you try to prejudice me by making out that I have lived by my wits—how do your lawyers live—your politicians—your intriguers—your men of the Exchange?' " (48).

Although both novelists reveal a more comprehensive vision of evil that far transcends conventional Victorian wisdom, they both also propose in fictional form characters whose natures seem messianic and salvific, characters whose outlines unmistakably suggest that agnosticism has not yet eclipsed the need or possibility of quasi-religious consolation. This consolation, though translated into secular terms—Daniel Deronda as political leader of his people, seeking nationhood; Little Dorrit as a secular pilgrim who holds service higher than martyrdom [22]—still retains the bold outline of messianic goodness. Irving Howe has objected to calling Dorrit a Christ figure, arguing that "she has no designs on the world . . . either to transform it or to transcend it." [23] This contradicts Trilling's influential judgment that she represents "the Beatrice of the *Comedy*, the Paraclete in female form," [24] but both critics are right: while it is true that Little Dorrit acts as rescuer of Clennam, who has fallen almost irredeemably into the Marshalsea prison's Slough of Despond, the novel scarcely requires transcendent categories to be understood. The terms of its vision are Clennam's—bleak, secular, modern:

> The shadow of a supposed act of injustice, which had hung over him since his father's death, was so vague and formless that it might be the result of a reality widely remote from his idea of it. But, if his apprehensions should prove to be well founded, he was ready at any moment to lay down all he had, and begin the world anew. As the fierce dark teaching of his childhood had never sunk into his heart, so that first article in his code of morals was, that he must begin, in practical humility, with looking well to his feet on Earth, and that he could never mount on wings of words to Heaven. Duty on earth, restitution on earth, action on earth; these first, as the first steep steps upward. (368)

The subdued ending of the novel, with its downward motion of the protagonists into the "roaring streets" of London, suggests no heavenward glance at all. On the other hand, Amy Dorrit's goodness stretches the credulity of most readers today. Too much virtue concentrated in one character, despite the skepticism of Clennam-Dickens's narrative voice, periodically threatens to catapult the novel out of the realm of fiction into the clouds of numinous revelation.

In the end, it is not illuminating enough to say Amy is a Christ figure. Rather, her significance, like Deronda's, inheres in her combination of absolute goodness and intelligence. If these two are messiahs of sorts, then they are some of the last in English fiction who wed mind and heart, the last who are neither idiots nor holy fools. Amy Dorrit's shadow, the retarded Maggy, is premonition of the kind of Christ figures to come, particularly in twentieth-century fiction.[25]

That both Deronda and Amy are only partial successes in literary terms, while Circumlocution and Grandcourt rank among their creators' greatest literary triumphs, also suggests things to come, especially when we read the Edwardian novels treated in subsequent chapters. The Edwardian novelists cannot create likenesses of Amy or Deronda; the type is no longer conceivable. Nor can the later Victorian and Edwardian writers claim the high prophetic moral ground held with such confidence by Dickens and Eliot. Who, after Dickens, can open an appeal to the reader with the words, "Verily, verily" (844)? Who, after Eliot, can plausibly claim for the novelist the explicit vocation of homiletical instruction, as Eliot does in her "Leaves from a Note-Book": "But man or woman who publishes writings inevitably assumes the office of teacher or influencer of the public mind. Let him protest as he will that he only seeks to amuse, and has no pretension to do more than while away an hour of leisure or weariness—'the idle singer of an empty day'—he can no more escape influencing the moral taste, and with it the action of the intelligence, than a setter of fashions in furniture and dress can fill the shops with his designs and leave the garniture of persons and houses unaffected by his industry. . . . And bad literature of the sort called amusing is spiritual gin."[26] Though she lost her Evangelicalism, Eliot never lost her sense of evangelical mission.

But the certitude upon which Eliot builds her novels, her homiletic, has begun to fray in her final novel. Robert M. Adams describes the deterioration of the Religion of Humanity in her late work: "And yet, when so many streams of thought and feeling pour down into the same basin, one is bound to feel that 'the religion of humanity' is becoming something of an intellectual and spiritual sink. It is a sink into which the loftiest feelings drain away when they have no prospect of becoming anything more than good intentions, yet retain too much nostalgic appeal to be discarded altogether. The religion of man—speaking broadly and with occasional exceptions excepted—tends to be Apollonian, rational, progressive, cosmopolitan, and benevolent."[27] In Eliot's late phase, we find confirmation of Nietzsche's prediction that ethics become necessarily problematic in a theistic vacuum. Neither Dickens nor Eliot enjoyed the benefits of a Nietzschean retrospective window on their own work, but nevertheless, in both *Little Dorrit* and *Daniel Deronda* the plausibility of an Apollonian picture is severely tried. "George Eliot not only recognized the epistemological atheism logically entailed in her rejection of Christianity," William Myers observes, "but in the final phase of her career deliberately and self-consciously invaded the territory of violence, ambiguity, and radical doubt into which Nietzsche and Freud were later to make their pioneering expeditions. Her world was thus every bit as dangerous and amorally structured as theirs." [28] Grandcourt very certainly suggests this terrain, although as we shall see, Eliot did not venture there quite so willingly as Myers supposes.

The Dilemma of Ethical Bookkeeping

In *The Genealogy of Morals* (1887), Nietzsche argues that the word *Schulde*, "guilt," originates in the material concept of debts, *Schulden*.[29] Citing this etymological connection between money exchange and moral conscience, he suggests the infliction of pain became the primary mode for getting moral satisfaction, and he outlines what we can practically take as the blueprint for Mrs. Clennam's psychology:

> For an unconscionably long time culprits were not punished because they were felt to be responsible for their actions; not, that is, on the assumption that only the guilty were to be punished; rather, they were punished the way parents still punish their children, out of rage at some damage suffered, which the doer must pay for. Yet this rage was both moderated and modified by the notion that for every damage there could somehow be found an equivalent, by which that damage might be compensated—if necessary in the pain of the doer. To the question how did that ancient, deep-rooted, still firmly established notion of an equivalency between damage and pain arise, the answer is, briefly: it arose in the contractual relation between creditor and debtor, which is as old as the notion of "legal subjects" itself and which in its turn points back to the basic practices of purchase, sale, barter, and trade.[30]

Guilt and punishment are conceptualized from the first in terms of an economic exchange system. The fundamental principle of bookkeeping—that all debits and credits must ultimately balance—establishes the norm for handling the guilt commodity. In Mrs. Clennam, Dickens created a being who makes no distinction whatsoever between her moral and financial entries, and her self-imprisonment is, in her view, the self-inflicted pain meant to balance out the pain she knows she has dealt to others: first, the suppression of the will entitling Little Dorrit to a legacy, and second, the casting out of the illegitimate son Arthur. The second action she perceives as justifiable in light of the pain she has suffered for being forced to marry his father. Pain suffered, as Nietzsche observes, demands equal infliction of pain on someone else, and the target for that infliction of pain finally does not matter—just so long as the requisite damage is done to balance the books overall. When Mrs. Clennam tells Amy Dorrit that she treated Arthur harshly in his childhood, "For his good. Not for the satisfaction of my injury" (859), she is both lying and self-deceived.

Precisely because of his familiarity with this exchange system of pain—and to a considerable extent his imbibing of its rules—Arthur begins to wonder immediately upon returning to England whether his family owes someone something. He knows that feeling already in the coffeehouse on Sunday morning, but it hits him with huge force when he visits Mrs. Clennam. Living practically entombed in her chamber, she tells him, "The world has narrowed to these dimensions" (73). He immediately suspects that this masochism, in her perverse system of accounting, must point to a correspondent evil inflicted elsewhere. Later Mrs. Clennam confirms this, snarling at Flintwinch with terse finality, "Let me suffer" (228). Punishment, even self-imposed, must always be associated with crime, as Arthur recollects, reentering the house for the first time in twenty years: "There was the old cellaret with nothing in it, lined with lead, like a sort of coffin in compartments; there was the old dark closet, also with nothing in it, of which he had been many a time the sole contents, in days of punishment" (72). Through the labyrinth Arthur follows Flintwinch to his stepmother's lair, "up the staircase, which was panelled off into spaces like so many mourning tablets, into a dim bed-chamber, the floor of which had gradually so sunk and settled, that the fire-place was in a dell. On a black bier-like sofa in this hollow, propped up behind with one great angular black bolster like the block at a state execution in the good old times, sat his mother in a widow's dress" (73). The motion takes us through successive claustrophobic enclosures, one within another, as if through the protective outer chambers and then actual wrappers of a mummy until at last Mrs. Clennam, appropriately motionless like an embalmed corpse, is reached within the innermost confine. This is Dickens at his gothic best.

Now Clennam has been called by one critic "perhaps the first notably passive hero in English fiction,"[31] but what occurs on his subsequent visit to this chamber of "old dark horrors" (75) reveals, on the contrary, his activist courage. He displays the same combative spirit later while he navigates the equally daunting corridors of Circumlocution. "Is it possible, mother," he asks, ". . . that he [father] had unhappily wronged any one, and made no reparation?" (87). Then Clennam goes directly to the accusation: " 'In grasping at money and in driving hard bargains—I have begun, and I must speak of such things now, mother—some one may have been grievously deceived, injured, ruined. You were the moving power of all this machinery before my birth; your stronger spirit has been infused into all my father's dealings for more than two score years' " (88).

"You were the moving power." There is a hint of irony in this unwavering condemnation of a mother who has become both physically and emotionally frozen, but the speech contains nothing passive about it. If Arthur pleads for an opportunity to expiate his own guilt for suspected wrongdoing, he nonetheless seems unafraid to point out that the crimes were his parents', not his. "The transgressions of the parents," as Mrs. Clennam points out later, "are visited on their offspring" (859). But though Clennam is more than willing to assume responsibility of reparation for parental crime, he requires also that those crimes be named. He wants the itemized, line-by-line descriptive account, the one his mother recoils from giving. The accounting must explain both Mrs. Clennam's self-imposed imprisonment and her hiring of Amy. Mrs. Clennam's bookkeeping system shows itself merely as a column of sums, one that fudges itemization; she misremembers purposely, always to her own favor; and thus the claim of personal suffering ultimately becomes the blanket justification for tyranny. Clennam would agree with Dickens's assessment of the stepmother: "Thus she was always balancing her bargains with the Majesty of heaven, posting up the entries to her credit, strictly keeping her set-off, and claiming her due. She was only remarkable in this, for the force and emphasis with which she did it. Thousands upon thousands do it, according to their varying manner, every day" (89).

This can be interpreted as a cynical comment on moral bookkeeping of any kind, but another reading inheres as well. It suggests that Mrs. Clennam, like most of us, tends to cheat on one side of the ledger: the accounts-receivable side. Arthur himself practices a strict system of moral bookkeeping, done without any repository of metaphysical justifications. What is that system? To what extent has Mrs. Clennam's twisted mind invaded his? As Janet Larson observes, Arthur "may have rejected his mother's otherworldly doctrine, but emotionally much of 'the fierce dark teaching of his childhood' *has* 'sunk into his heart.' " [32]

What about Arthur's own crimes, apart from the parental ones? George

Holoch argues that when Arthur chooses imprisonment in Marshalsea, having grossly mismanaged the public funds invested in the Doyce-Meagles-Clennam business concern, his choice resembles his stepmother's self-imposed imprisonment, "but it is made morally acceptable by his refusal to judge anyone but himself."[33] This is true. But Arthur is no believer in the phrase that titled the first few numbers of this novel's serialization: "Nobody's Fault." He holds responsible other human beings for their acts, including his stepmother, Rigaud, and Miss Wade, in appropriate situations. He can judge others because he can judge himself. Moral accountability, in many ways similar to the kind practiced by his mother, but more principled and more honest, is not negated by Arthur, but conscientiously observed.

Thus in dismissing Mrs. Clennam's perverted idea of accountability we err if we dismiss the notion of accountability altogether. Only by unraveling the respective moral codes of Clennam and his stepmother can we get on the track toward understanding the novel. Here Holoch observes that Arthur's "moral and intellectual development" lies in "his assumption of responsibility and his recognition of connections that do not depend on the kind of moral bookkeeping represented by his mother, even though he shares certain basic moral assumptions with her."[34] But what exactly are those assumptions? And what kind of bookkeeping, if not his stepmother's kind?

Clearly, Arthur's basic impulse, at least initially, is not masochistic like hers. We are mistaken to conflate entirely his goal of righting an economic wrong with self-punishment, although that has been argued. Janet Larson asserts that from the outset "the danger for Clennam is more than Calvinism perverted. . . . it is renunciation coupled with the loss of any transcendent faith"; moreover, "Arthur now pursues a self-denial motivated by no religious idea at all."[35] The latter claim cannot be questioned, but the first makes too blanket an assertion for masochism by skipping over the entire middle of the novel. That middle reveals a man who, in spite of what theologians would call a crisis of faith and what therapists describe as midlife crisis, has the wherewithal to find an interest in Pet Meagles, inspires Daniel Doyce not to give up hope in himself and his invention, joins a creative business partnership, willfully combats the intransigent forces of Circumlocution, and sets Pancks on the trail to discover the source of the Dorrit family's misfortune. This is neither passive, nor masochistic. Contrary to our general perception of him, Clennam would seem throughout much of this narrative to be if not a dynamo, then at least very energetic. He takes up the cause of the Dorrit family based on suspicions of familial Clennam crime, but that action is more in keeping with a notion of just compensation, not renunciation of self. There is a dif-

ference. Furthermore, it is not his involvement with the Dorrits that initiates
Clennam's eventual state of passive renunciation, but rather his speculative
and disastrous gambling of stockholders' funds in the Merdle financial empire.
This precipitates the pathos of Clennam we know too well: the broken man
slowly committing suicide in Marshalsea before Amy Dorrit's forgiveness and
love can reverse the process.

Still, there is no contesting that, eventually, his surrender to passivity and
embrace of imprisonment parallels at least in certain points Mrs. Clennam's
own. Arthur shows himself as bound up in the pain exchange system of guilt
and suffering as she. Having discovered the entire capital of the partnership
to be lost in the Merdle disaster—and we must not forget that the corporation has gone public and thousands of shareholders' investments besides the
partnership's own have evaporated—Clennam both confesses his personal responsibility for the loss, to the extent of publishing his role in the London
newspapers, exonerating his partners of any responsibility (780–83), and expresses the wish to atone for his mismanagement by pledging to work off his
debt to the company if it survives bankruptcy, "at as small a salary as he could
live upon" (782). Of course, such reparation is but an intention. No possibility
exists of ever balancing the actual monetary losses. This leaves Clennam with
the only recourse he knows, surrender to the punishment of debtors' prison.
In the moral exchange system, only death, like that chosen by Merdle, can be
viewed as equal to the crime. Clennam, like his stepmother, chooses the more
painful option of a living death. Unlike her, however—and this is the largest
irony—he fully embodies a spirit of penance and confession, and unlike her
he can also accept the forgiveness offered by Amy. Void of faith, Clennam
nonetheless executes all the moves of the sinner finding grace. Mrs. Clennam,
on the other hand, has inverted faith perfectly, rationalizing every personal
wrongdoing both on the basis of self-torture and as the visitation of God's
wrath on sinners: "I have been an instrument of severity against sin" (860).
She knows nothing of confession and atonement; she speaks a language exclusively of pride and pain. Clennam has no use for her doctrine of Original
Sin, and the perverted use to which she puts it is the principal reason why.

The most practical consequence of Mrs. Clennam's idea of universal Original Sin—we might usefully entitle it "Everybody's Fault"—is that its impact
on personal moral responsibility is no different from that of Circumlocution's
motto, "Nobody's Fault." The consequences of either position are identical.
In this intersection we begin to grasp exactly what the hero Clennam cannot
abide. As only one example, the Byronic Miss Wade—on the surface so different from the Bible-quoting Mrs. Clennam—writes Clennam a wrenching

personal account of injustice suffered at the hands of an oppressive patriarchy, but only to the purpose of justifying her own selfish use of Tattycoram. She is not so much interested in liberating Tattycoram from the suffocating power of Mr. Meagles as she is drawing a companion into her net of ressentiment and rage. There can be no doubt that the world has been unfair to Miss Wade, Dickens indicates, but her understanding of pain suffered, just like Mrs. Clennam's, mutates rapidly into rationalizations for inflicting pain on others. Tattycoram is led to exchange one form of dependency for another. Likewise Rigaud sees his behavior as perfectly sound: calling everyone a scoundrel works to legitimate, he thinks, his own corruption.

By far the most threatening incarnation of this threat, however, to Clennam's system of personal accountability, is the Office of Circumlocution, which with Chancery in *Bleak House* ranks as Dickens's most profound exploration of evil. J. Hillis Miller remarks, "*Little Dorrit* creates a disquieting sense of the selfish indifference diffused everywhere in things and people. By making certain characters vessels for the concentration of this guilt, it allays our terror and gives us something concrete to hate and fear. Mrs. Clennam, Merdle, Blandois, and Casby are materializations of this undefined evil, but in *Little Dorrit*, nevertheless, evil exceeds any particularization of it and we are left at the end with an undefined and unpurged sense of menace." [36]

The portrayal of Stiltstalkings and Barnacles as the principal families inhabiting Circumlocution's many chambers, as the class of paper pushers parasitically feeding on the body politic, is hardly meant to suggest that evil can be traced to certain families, groups, or classes—although clannish nepotism is part of the bureaucratic mess. Rather, the family names become pegs upon which the attributes of an entire society's inverted sense of value can be humorously pinned. Whenever Circumlocution's efficacy gets called into question, a mere summation of the sheer volume of paperwork generated is sufficient to cow Parliament (571–72). All of England is complicit. I previously noted how the stock figure of the villain, the ideological cipher for evil understood as individual will, becomes emptied out as a more complex understanding of evil takes shape in the late Victorian novel. On this level, Dickens's representation of Circumlocution—a monstrous maze of bureaucracy having no source, no head, no real origin—uncannily anticipates Foucault's depiction of the workings of power. In a well-known passage of *Power/Knowledge*, Foucault explains,

> power is not to be taken to be a phenomenon of one individual's consolidated and homogenous domination over others, or that of one group

or class over others. What, by contrast, should always be kept in mind is that power, if we do not take too distant a view of it, is not that which makes the difference between those who exclusively possess and retain it, and those who do not have it and submit to it. Power must be analysed as something which circulates, or rather as something which only functions in the form of a chain. It is never localised here or there, never in anybody's hands, never appropriated as a commodity or piece of wealth. Power is employed and exercised through a net-like organisation. And not only do individuals circulate between its threads; they are always in the position of simultaneously undergoing and exercising this power. They are not only its inert or consenting target; they are always also the elements of its articulation. In other words, individuals are the vehicles of power, not its points of application.[37]

This describes a system without agency, causality, or source; a grid in which power remains ineffable and indefinable but always present. Power here "circulates" like invisible microbes through individuals, rather than accruing to them like so many chips at a casino cashier's window. If we apply this idea of power in an analysis of Circumlocution, the implications are clear. The evil of that growth cannot be identified with any particular act or individual, as might be suggested by most theologies; nor can that evil be identified with one powerful class actively oppressing powerless classes, as in standard Marxist thinking. Power does not filter from the top down, argues Foucault; in fact it might be supposed that the very categories of "oppressor" and "oppressed" get voided of meaning; the binary set, like others, is seen as deconstructing itself. Plainly put, Circumlocution is nobody's fault, and by its operative mode would deny moral indignation of any sort. Hence, the successive Barnacles' dismay that Clennam calls them into some kind of accountability. Clennam's quest for information in the case of William Dorrit strikes them not only as an imposition, but also as a touchingly naive quest for a source: "Ecod, sir, . . . he said he wanted to know, you know! Pervaded our department—without an appointment—and said he wanted to know!" one of the young Barnacles comments (251–52).

Against the disease of Circumlocution, Dickens projects one man whose integrity remains untouched: Daniel Doyce. He represents individual creative genius at war with a society no longer able to recognize or celebrate talent. Doyce carries himself and his affairs with "a certain honest rugged order" (311). The records of his operation are couched in words "always plain and directed straight to the purpose" (311) that contrast with Orwellian simplicity the doublespeak of the most prominent Parliamentary Barnacle, Lord Decimus, a man known for "trotting, with the complacency of an idiotic elephant, among howling labyrinths of sentences which he seemed to take for high roads, and never so much as wanted to get out of" (458). Doyce becomes an especially lonely figure when Dickens describes how Meagles, anxious to have his daughter marry a young friend of the Barnacles named Gowan, begins to succumb to the national disease: "As a mere flask of the golden water in the tale became a full fountain when it was poured out, so Mr Meagles seemed to feel that this small spice of Barnacle imparted to his table the flavour of the whole family-tree. In its presence, his frank, fine, genuine qualities paled; he was not so easy, he was not so natural, he was striving after something that did not belong to him, he was not himself. What a strange peculiarity on the part of Mr Meagles, and where should we find another such case!" (252).

The case anticipated here is Clennam's own. He will succumb to the other pernicious evil that has swept through society like a fever: the Merdle investment house. Clennam's decision to sink his firm's—and thousands of stockholders'—capital into the gold-plated but, in the end, stinking Merdle investment house is maybe the best example of Foucault's familiar argument that "individuals . . . are always in the position of simultaneously undergoing and exercising this power. They are not only its inert or consenting target; they are always also the elements of its articulation." The crash in the novel is suggestive of the Roaring 1920s and the 1980s; and in it, Clennam like so many others is both a doer and a victim.

Clennam's acknowledgment of his error, however, ultimately strikes a blow against the idea that collective guilt erases all need for individual accountability. Like Mrs. Clennam's idea of Original Sin, such sophistry can too easily level distinctions between greater and lesser degrees of moral responsibility. To the same extent, both Nobody's Fault and Everybody's Fault make moral judgment and action impossible. Clennam's lawyer Ruggs represents another facet of Circumlocution in attempting to dissuade Clennam from public disclosure. Ruggs's greatest fear is that little investors might get the idea that certain individual financiers, like Clennam, actually bear some responsibility for fiscal mismanagement. But Clennam is unwilling to hide behind specious reasoning of this sort and clings to ancient ideas of individual guilt, need for reparation, and punishment, as well as the notion that individuals with relatively more power must assume a proportionately larger burden of moral responsibility. There is, Clennam asserts against the attorney, a time and place to distinguish agents and victims of evil. He owns his agency. This, rather significantly, corresponds to one of the primary challenges mounted against Foucault's theory of power. Charles Taylor argues:

> There are all sorts of ways in which power can be inscribed in a situation in which both dominators and dominated are caught up. The first may see himself largely as the agent of the demands of the larger context; the second may see the demands on him as emanating from the nature of things. Nevertheless, the notion of power or domination requires some notion of constraint imposed on someone by a process in some way related to human agency. Otherwise, the term loses all meaning. "Power" in the way Foucault sees it, closely linked to "domination," does not require a clearly demarcated perpetrator, but it requires a victim. It cannot be a "victimless crime," so to speak. Perhaps the victims also exercise it, also victimize others. But power needs targets. Something must be imposed on someone, if there is to be domination. Perhaps that person is also helping to impose it on himself, but then there must be an element of fraud, illusion, false pretences involved in this. Otherwise, it is not clear that the imposition is in any sense an exercise of domination.[38]

The salvation of Clennam finally depends not only on his recognition of Little Dorrit's love, but also, as Ross Dabney has observed, on the renunciatory gesture toward money that is carried through in Amy's burning of the codicil: her entitlement to a portion of the Clennam estate.[39] The burning of the codicil implicitly acknowledges the totality of a society immersed in the corruption of money, an immersion given greater emphasis only in the giant dirt piles of *Our Mutual Friend*.

This final renunciatory gesture is oddly conjoined with Doyce's semi-miraculous financial rescue and restoration of Clennam to the partnership. But the renunciation overshadows the rescue and confirms Clennam's deepest, earliest instinct: "I have seen so little happiness come of money" (88). It also signals a diminishing of the social optimism that Dickens, earlier in his career, had associated with moral conversion. If Clennam does the right thing and is rewarded for it, there is now no thrill nor efficacy left in the formula. In Dickens's work of the 1840s, particularly *Dombey and Son* and *A Christmas Carol*, Dennis Walder argues, individual conversion of central protagonists, particularly rich protagonists, supposedly cures social ills. Walder suggests Dickens's thesis in those two books is that "the salvation of a grasping, self-centred and materialistic society depends upon a conversion of the individual from sterile mammonism to love, innocence and generous fellow-feeling."[40]

At the conclusion of both these earlier books, financial empires are left intact, to be righteously administered by newly converted men. In his sparring with T. A. Jackson's *Dickens the Radical,* Orwell was to take roughly this same line of moral argument. He claims, for instance, in a famous passage, that the whole gist of Dickens's reformist attitude in *Hard Times* "is that capitalists ought to be kind, not that workers ought to be rebellious. Bounderby is a bullying windbag and Gradgrind has been morally blinded, but if they were better men, the system would work well enough—that, all through, is the implication. And so far as social criticism goes, one can never extract much more from Dickens than this, unless one deliberately reads meanings into him. His whole 'message' is one that at first glance looks like an enormous platitude: If men would behave decently the world would be decent." [41]

This is more applicable to Dickens's early novels. Clennam finds relative peace at the end of *Little Dorrit*, but it is the peace of personal relations, not of any kind of uplifting prospects for social or economic justice. His conversion, maybe the best psychological portrayal of one that we get in Dickens, does not carry with it any corresponding belief in a more decent world. In this novel individual moral conversion seems about as adequate to combating Circumlocution as Esther Summerson's basket of keys does in prevailing against Chancery.

We may also ask whether Doyce's reinstatement of Arthur in the partnership fully dispenses with the "universal economic guilt" [42] undergirding Arthur's initial probe into his family's financial improprieties. What are we to do with that guilt's "pervasiveness," [43] which finds partial expiation in Amy's burning of the codicil? One thing is certain: that same disquiet reverberates through Gissing's early heroes, Conrad's Marlow, Forster's Schlegel sisters, and even Wells's Ponderevo. To put it another way: on any map of liberal guilt, it looms as the terrain's largest feature.

It is an Indian critic speaking autobiographically, Badri Raina, who provides us with maybe the sharpest insight into the mind of Dickens in the 1850s. Raina recalls coming of age a century later in what was once England's most valuable colony:

A special trauma was reserved for those of us who grew up semiprivileged but radical in the decade after independence: we discovered that we had become supereducated and well-to-do (in contrast to eight out of ten Indians who were illiterate and living below thinkable levels of subsistence). Soon, the egalitarian jargon we mouthed deceived nobody, not even ourselves. . . . It was in the context of this sort of introspection

that Dickens acquired for me over the years the force of a kindred recognition. Of the major intelligences engaged with the Victorian scene,
Dickens, placed as he was, seemed the most closely to approximate the
ambition, the self-doubt, and the guilt of many of us in India, who . . .
had begun well but ended well-to-do.[44]

Victorian orthodoxy would have concluded this final phrase of Raina's, "*and
ended well-to-do.*" Raina's use of the coordinator "but" signals most inci-
sively the continued impact today of Dickens's tortured economic reflections.
If formative liberalism asked questions primarily about political liberty, a half
century later the road of liberal reflection, at least for Dickens, leads directly
into the question of economic relations. Dickens responds to the question not
with a theoretical set of answers, but rather with an offering of guilt through
his most unlikely hero, Arthur Clennam.

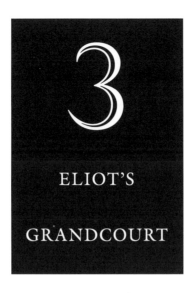

ELIOT'S GRANDCOURT

NATURE, NATION, AND EMPIRE

> The clearer our conceptions in science and art become, the more they
> will assimilate themselves to the conceptions of duty in conduct, and will
> invite the same sort of language in dealing with them.
>
> MATTHEW ARNOLD,
> *Literature and Dogma*

> The foundation of morality must needs lie in the constitution of nature.
>
> THOMAS HUXLEY,
> *Nineteenth Century: A Monthly Review*, May 1877

No discussion of *Daniel Deronda* (1876) can avoid the cracks and strains, the
basic intellectual dividedness, afflicting George Eliot's enormously ambitious,
final novel. Like Dickens, she is a liberal who shows the way concentrated
power can turn to tyranny and destroy individual lives; hers is, in Judith
Shklar's terminology, more effectively a "liberalism of fear" than of hope. Like
Dickens, in her final novel she does not hold back from castigating the values
of the English middle class, of which she is most definitely a member. And like
Dickens, she discovers economic relations to be the most critical, most vexing
problem for any liberal affirmation.

Both novelists illustrate a basic aspect of liberalism's evolution in the nineteenth century. Questions about liberty and rights, primary for the Romantics,
now get taken up increasingly within the larger context of political economy.

The matter of personal freedom cannot be prized apart from questions of class; the issue of rights becomes moot if attempts are made to lift it out of the lived reality of economic relations. The most convincing argument of Eliot's novel is that great concentrations of power and wealth, embodied in the character of Grandcourt, are rotting England from the inside out. But that must be qualified, because in the imperial terms by which Grandcourt is repeatedly represented, "inside" and "outside" England no longer signify. What is England? Nation, or empire? To call the novel a "Condition of England" novel begs that question.

As if this is not complicated enough, Eliot attempts to posit over against England's national decadence a salutary form of nationalism — Zionism — that can be fulfilled, at least according to Mordecai, through the affirmation of pure racial Jewish identity.[1] Nationalist, imperialist, and ethnic ideologies zigzag crazily through this book like so many loose threads, but the real problem begins when Eliot attempts to weave out of them a pattern of moral uplift and affirmation. The situation Eliot leaves us with, bad imperial behavior on one hand, and Zionist nationalist purity and idealism on the other, seems if not downright disturbing from our late twentieth-century vantage point, then certainly crude. We now know all too well that nationalist and ethnic enthusiasms of any kind, especially when mixed together, are volatile, and often disastrously so, posing as many problems for liberal values as imperialism itself.

Eliot's search for a moral-political affirmation, and her answer, embodied in Mordecai and Deronda, replicates almost exactly the nationalist, specifically the Philhellenic, enthusiasm for the Greek revolutionary movement that we find in earlier Romantic liberalism. Most remarkably, both forms of nationalism are inextricably bound up in appeals to ethnicity, and appeals to religion, in spite of their proponents' allegedly secular Enlightenment belief. Shelley's famous cry in the introduction to *Hellas*, the most resounding cultural defense of the revolutionary movement, "We are all Greeks," is well known; less familiar perhaps is his argument, resonant of holy war, that pits pagan Turks against Christian Greeks: "The English permit their own oppressors to act according to their natural sympathy with the Turkish tyrant, and to brand upon their name the indelible blot of an alliance with the enemies of domestic happiness, of Christianity and civilization."[2] Interesting words, these, coming from an atheist. For his part, Hunt was to reprint from the *Times*, immediately following his appeal for a Greek subscription (*Examiner*, 7 October 1821), this analysis of the righteous Greek cause:

The publicist cannot deny his right of revolt; the Christian cannot impugn the zeal which elevates the banner of the cross. The Turk won the soil by his sword—conquest is his only title. The conquered owe him no allegiance; and his claims to obedience cease, when he has no longer the power to command. The Turk, fanaticized in the tenets of a religion hostile to European civilization, is the general enemy of European society; and the hand which is raised to strike down the crescent, is a hand raised in favour of European freedom and morality.

The Christian community cannot, therefore, be indifferent to the appeal which is made by the civilized Greeks for aid and succour.[3]

Finally, what is most fascinating about the liberal Romantics' affirmation of the Greek cause is their understanding that the business of making Greece back into a nation will necessarily incorporate elements not only of religious, but also blatantly ethnic, division. One problem with Eliot's Zionism, as with liberal Romantic nationalism generally, is its hopefulness that the enterprise can be accomplished without a protracted mess. But the potential ugliness of ethnic feuding is brought home matter-of-factly by Hunt's 7 October editorial in the *Examiner*, even if he fails there to envision how incredibly long the historical legs of such conflict may be. This passage on the Greeks' consolidation of power seems especially ironic, considering the enduring role of Balkan strife in this century: "With their admitted capacities for improvement, and under a national government, which would allow them to develop their powers, they would soon obtain a decided ascendancy over the Albanians, and other half barbarous tribes, and would be able to extend their dominion over Attica, Boetia, and Thessaly, the only districts beyond the isthmus where the Greeks are numerous."[4]

Bernard Semmel's effort to explain Eliot's nationalist argument in *Daniel Deronda* as being a species of "nonaggressive cultural nationalism"[5] is especially problematic when we consider that her case for Zionist nationhood in *Impressions of Theophrastus Such*, her last published work, puts the entire enterprise within the context of successful Greek and Italian revolutionary upheaval. It is one thing to argue that these were liberal nationalist movements, which they were—quite another to claim for them the status of "nonaggressive." To succeed, nationalism of whatever stripe must necessarily be aggressive. George Eliot, like Shelley, wants to envision the birth of a nation without violence, achieved through intellect, a nation whose cultural legacy will eventually spill out to enrich the entire world community. This is a uto-

pian Romantic dream. It is also signally dangerous. One nation's destiny—
provided it is the right nation—goes the argument, can translate into a cultural cornucopia on a global scale. For the liberal Romantics, this vision was
of the Greeks and Italians; for Eliot, the Jews. These instances each suggest
the liberal propensity to underestimate the violent political ramifications of
nationalism and ethnicity dressed up in the clothes of cultural beneficence.
After all, that was exactly how England marketed its own global imperial
destiny. And that, of course, has not proven the worst case.

Henleigh Grandcourt

Still, any triumphalism in this novel, however articulately argued, must be
read against the towering figure of Henleigh Grandcourt. And because on an
aesthetic level he succeeds in capturing our attention so completely, we can
wonder whether that success holds proportionately shattering implications for
Eliot's progressive, Comtean worldview. I think it does.

Most critics of the novel have been content to follow the terms initially
imposed on it by Henry James, whose exercise in wit, "*Daniel Deronda*: A
Conversation,"[6] excoriated the Jewish element and characters as mawkish,
aesthetic failures, and praised the rendering of Gwendolen and her husband.
This dual critical division of the book was further enhanced when F. R. Leavis
chose to distinguish between the novel's "good half" and "bad half,"[7] and
suggested that James himself tried to match the "good half" about Gwendolen
in *The Portrait of a Lady*, and fell short. All of which is to say how magnificent
a novel this is, in spite of its flaws.

Yet critical appraisals of the novel which follow the path forged by James
and Leavis tend to ignore precisely what is distinctly new in the book. Three—
not two—characters demand our attention, but in the terms set by James and
Leavis, the person of Grandcourt tends to be left out of the equation. Gordon
Haight's biography of Eliot (1968) contains background discussion of the
"originals" in *Daniel Deronda*, but there is no mention of Grandcourt.[8] Ruby
Redinger asserts that "Gwendolen embodies the inner forces of egoism, hostility, and aggressiveness that George Eliot had long feared would master her;
and Daniel is the incarnation of counteracting ideals."[9] Another critic assesses
accurately that Grandcourt is "the only major character whom George Eliot
made totally unsympathetic,"[10] but does not seem to realize how profoundly
important that observation is.

Frequently when Grandcourt does receive attention, there is an effort to flatten his character into a typological mold, an attempt to categorize him with other members of his species in the Eliot menagerie so as to deprive him of unique force. Calvin Bedient's irreverent catalog of Eliot's favorite characters exemplifies this tendency:

> *The typical characters.* The Repentant Egoist: like Janet, the individual who, having rebelled against his lot, burns in the fire of his rebellion until he learns, anew, the meaning of love, reverence, and submission. Hetty Sorrel, Arthur Donnithorne, Maggie Tulliver, Godfrey Cass, Silas Marner, Romola, Bulstrode, Esther Lyon, and Gwendolen Harleth are later examples of the type. Then the Unrepentant Egoist: the hardened, irretrievable sinner who "deservedly" meets with misery or death. In the novels, Dunsey Cass, Tito Melema, Lawyer Jermyn, Raffles, Grandcourt, and Mirah Lapidoth's father are among those who follow Dempster to a dark end. . . . Then the Confessor: the moral physician who . . . serves also as a model of the altruistic uses of suffering.[11]

In the latter category Bedient predictably includes among others Felix Holt, Dorothea Brooke, Dinah Morris, and Deronda himself. Where the schema breaks down, however, is by including Grandcourt in a class with Mirah Lapidoth's father. The disparity in scale of evil is too profound to make such a comparison. Moreover, while both Deronda and Gwendolen illustrate aspects of Eliot's theory of moral education—the search for a higher form of community that can instill values, and the submission of wayward egotism to community's binding necessity—Grandcourt simply does not fit. He is a disturbance in Eliot's universe which eludes naming.

That Grandcourt is something special within Eliot's work was first noted by U. C. Knoepflmacher, who observes him to be the only protagonist in her novels to "approximate pure evil," someone who, unlike villains such as Tito or Bulstrode or Raffles, cannot be "rationally explained in terms of . . . background or psychological make-up."[12] Irving Howe elaborates on this to say that in her depiction of him, Eliot moved away from the familiar moral territory of her earlier successes and into an unfamiliar and terrifying realm: "the relationship between Gwendolen and Henleigh Grandcourt . . . is not just the anatomy of a bad marriage, nor even the terror felt by a young woman trapped by an overmastering husband. It is *a system of dehumanized personal relations*, and thereby more than personal relations; it is the barbarism that civilization lightly coats and readily becomes."[13] This apprehension of Grandcourt's centrality to the novel is still the exceptional view, however. Badri Raina summarizes the critical problem:

New writing on *Daniel Deronda* every passing year confirms the feeling that critical comment on Grandcourt falls short of the extraordinary and unusual power of his creation. One is aware of a disturbing hiatus. Do we adequately meet the quality of our felt emotional and aesthetic response to Grandcourt by counting him merely as one among the long list of egoists in George Eliot? Some readers of *Daniel Deronda sense* Grandcourt as a construct to be in a class apart from Casaubon, Harold Transome, Lydgate, Tito and the others, and are yet unable quite to *account* for that sense. Egoism seems too puerile—and as it turns out, inaccurate— a tag to put on Grandcourt, when we remember that, after all, Klesmer is equally an egoist and perhaps Deronda as well.[14]

Eliot's creation of Grandcourt demonstrates, I think, to what extent she was revising, either consciously or unconsciously, her long-held positivist convictions. For Grandcourt overturns the benign Comtean doctrine that moral perception necessarily translates into moral development. Gwendolen Harleth herself is the last protagonist in a long line of Eliot heroines who live out this developmental paradigm, one which Eliot had explained early in her career:

It may be doubted, whether a mind which has no susceptibility to the pleasure of changing its point of view, of mastering a remote form of thought, of perceiving identity of nature under variety of manifestation— a perception which resembles an expansion of one's own being, a pre- existence in the past—can possess the flexibility, the ready sympathy, or the tolerance, which characterizes a truly philosophical culture. Now and then . . . we meet with a nature that combines the faculty for amassing minute erudition with the largeness of view necessary to give it a practical bearing . . . a profound belief in the progressive character of human development . . . a wonderful intuition of the mental conditions of past ages with an ardent participation in the most advanced ideas and hopeful efforts of the present.[15]

This coalesces an outline for the characters of Gwendolen and Deronda both but also intimations of the liberal imagination espoused by Arnold, and later, Trilling. The linkage between imagination and "sympathy," between keenness of intellect and high-minded ethics, however, is the very point at which Grandcourt upsets the formula laid down by Eliot twenty-five years earlier. Robert McCarron observes that "the interdependence of sympathy and understanding forms the cardinal basis of all Eliot's moral thought," but in the case of Grandcourt "insightfulness does not quicken his moral sense. Rather, because his awareness of the other's inner life vitally enhances the piquancy of his dominance, Grandcourt's . . . imagination is the principal means by which he enacts and gratifies his lust for mastery." [16] Understanding another's pain does not necessarily include a corresponding ready sympathy, as Grandcourt's refined sadism so explicitly bears out. His demand that Gwendolen wear the diamond earrings, formerly belonging to his mistress Lydia Glasher, is based precisely on an understanding that Gwendolen will find wearing them pure torture. The famous recurrent equestrian imagery, as well, of Grandcourt as the rider and Gwendolen the horse who has been mounted and broken, can hardly be missed. Gwendolen is likened to "a young race horse," [17] "a high mettled racer" (134), and although she loves to "mount the chariot and drive the plunging horses herself" (173), Grandcourt's droll comment to her at their first meeting that "I run a horse now and then" (147) portends their marriage relations to come. Gwendolen is very shortly "brought to kneel down like a horse under training for the arena" (365), she "answered to the rein" (482), and finally like "a wounded animal" (495) she is dominated by "bit and bridle" (741). Eliot's authorial comment on Gwendolen's wedding day intrudes: "she had the brilliancy of strong excitement, which will sometimes come even from pain" (401). Eliot abandons all subtlety here, for taken in combination with the grid of equestrian imagery, the passage easily suggests boots, whips, and sadomasochism. McCarron does not exaggerate in pointing to the undercurrent of sexual sadism running beneath this brutal language.[18]

Grandcourt achieves mastery not merely by superior strength. In her most explicit commentary on his power, Eliot amplifies a horrific reptilian and phallic imagery with the express acknowledgement of his moral intelligence:

> Already, in seven short weeks, which seemed half her life, her husband had gained a mastery which she could no more resist than she could have resisted the benumbing effect from the touch of a torpedo. Gwendolen's will had seemed imperious in its small girlish sway; but it was the will of a creature with a large discourse of imaginative fears: a shadow would have been enough to relax its hold. And she had found a will like that of a crab, or a boa-constrictor which goes on pinching or crushing without alarm at thunder. Not that Grandcourt was without calculation of the intangible effects which were the chief means of mastery; *indeed he had a surprising acuteness in detecting that situation of feeling in Gwendolen which made her proud and rebellious spirit dumb and helpless before him.* (477–78, my italics)

Sally Shuttlesworth attempts to show how this animal imagery used to describe Grandcourt—he is also likened to "a handsome lizard" (174), an "alli-
gator" (195), and a "serpent" (831)—ultimately points to his "low position
within the evolutionary scale," and to qualities of "vacillation" and unpre-
dictability which contrast Deronda's "directed energy."[19] But in her effort to
situate Eliot's book within a biological and evolutionary intellectual framework, Shuttlesworth overlooks entirely the more obvious mythic and symbolic meanings that accrue to Eliot's choice of reptilian imagery. Elsewhere
Shuttlesworth argues that Grandcourt's dismissal of the "Jamaican negro" as
"a beastly sort of baptist Caliban" (376) demonstrates the limited imaginative perceptions of the ruling class.[20] Grandcourt can stand accused of many
things, but limited intelligence or perception are not among them.

Yet as McCarron demonstrates, Grandcourt poses a singular dilemma for
Eliot's positivism. By book 6, "Revelations," Eliot feels compelled to alter
her commentary on him, downgrading at once his intelligence and imagination, and attempting, as it were, to bring him to rein under her own familiar
comforting doctrine of the moral imagination. We are suddenly presented,
arbitrarily, with a Grandcourt unsure of his power and dull in his perceptions:

> His object was to engage all his wife's egoism on the same side as his
> own, and in his employment of Lush he did not intend an insult to her:
> she ought to understand that he was the only possible envoy. Grand-
> court's view of things was considerably fenced in by his general sense,
> that what suited him, others must put up with. There is no escaping the
> fact that want of sympathy condemns us to a corresponding stupidity.
> Mephistopheles thrown upon real life, and obliged to manage his own
> plots, would inevitably make blunders. (658)

> He conceived that she did not love him. . . . But what lay quite away
> from his conception was, that she could have any special repulsion for
> him personally. (734)

This quite contradicts what Eliot has shown us previously about Grandcourt,
a man whose "understanding of the other," McCarron observes, "is far from
limited; he comprehends the nature of his victims and exploits that knowledge of their weaknesses."[21] By the book's conclusion, in order to maintain
the integrity of her moral theory, Eliot has attempted, but not successfully, to
reshape his character of intelligent malevolence into the more familiar grain of
the "befuddled villains" who inhabit her earlier novels.[22] Hints of the split between Eliot's moral theorizing and Grandcourt's subversion of it are already

apparent early in the book, as in the epigraph to chapter 21: "Of a truth, knowledge is power, but it is a power reined by scruple, having a conscience of what must be and what may be" (268). Eliot the philosopher wants desperately to insure Deronda's later sermon that "our life becomes more spiritual by capacity of thought" (802). But to do so, Eliot the novelist must violate the plausibility, the aesthetic portrayal, of Grandcourt. Perhaps nowhere is D. H. Lawrence's maxim to trust the tale, not the teller, better taken to heart.

The newness of Grandcourt in Eliot's fiction raises profound philosophical and social questions, and her wavering as she handles his character suggests an author in troubled transition from earlier unshakeable assumptions. Myers's claim that she "not only recognized the epistemological atheism entailed in her rejection of Christianity," that she "in the final phase of her career deliberately and self-consciously invaded the territory of violence, ambiguity, and radical doubt,"[23] can be taken as overstatement, but a very useful one. While I am concerned with the ways in which Grandcourt's depiction anticipates later Edwardian critiques of plutocracy's almost unlimited power, the philosophical questions that intersect in his character are just as important. Those questions are appropriately raised because few authors before or since Eliot have sought so obsessively, and so cerebrally, to integrate their philosophical reading into finished fictional narrative. Moreover, although some critics are somewhat dismissive of efforts to place Grandcourt within the social and political framework of late Victorian aristocracy,[24] it seems more than coincidental that Eliot's philosophic reappraisal of human nature should combine with her most explicit attack on Victorian society—specifically, on that class known as gentlemen. Part of the greatness of *Daniel Deronda* lies in the way it escapes its ideological matrix, the way it eludes critical efforts to summarize Eliot's perception of self and society. For instance, Calvin Bedient confidently asserts Eliot's "characteristic subject is the necessary submission of individuals to their own society. . . . any society is preferable to the explosive egoism of the individual. Society's function is to contain man, and it is not for the individual to complain."[25] But this argument can hardly account for the novel's depiction of a debased aristocracy which forces submission upon its subjects. Gwendolen's tragedy is not her virtually untameable ego, but her inability to perceive that the glittering society she wishes to enter by way of marriage is exactly the thing out to destroy her. Likewise, Grandcourt's flawless functioning within his milieu, the public perception of him as a representative great man, shows all too well that a comfortable fit between an individual and his society may indeed enforce, contrary to Bedient's argument, the most profound collective evil imaginable. In Eliot's earlier rural novels, we can agree that social harmony is in itself a goal to be attained; but in *Daniel Deronda* this question gets complicated by the much larger one: society *to what end*?[26]

We have seen the degree to which Grandcourt roils the placid Comtean waters of Eliot's universe, as well as Eliot's own mixed reactions and efforts to control the disturbance. But did the writing of this book have a measurable impact on her Comtean beliefs themselves? Her reliance on Comte can no longer be in question. T. R. Wright acknowledges modern skepticism about such a tendency—"That a novelist as intelligent as George Eliot should have been a keen student of a philosopher as open to ridicule as Auguste Comte is not easy to accept"[27]—but goes on to document from Eliot's late notebooks and letters her continuing debt to the positivist philosopher. In the case of her final novel, argues Wright, "Eliot was obeying a specific injunction of Comte's: 'Catholicism owes a debt of gratitude to Judaism which it has never paid; Positivism alone can discharge it, as the systematic organ of the gratitude of the Great Being to all her servants collective as well as individual' [Comte, *Polity*, III]. George Eliot wrote to Harriet Beecher Stowe that her intention in writing *Daniel Deronda* was to help pay this debt."[28] Comtean positivism was preferable to Darwinism because it affirmed, in continuity with Eliot's earliest biblicism, this sense of teleological purposiveness. For a time, it is true, British writers including Arnold and Huxley had attempted to ground a benevolent moral theory in Darwin's nature,[29] but Spencer's Social Darwinist views quickly eclipsed such efforts, leading Huxley to reverse himself completely in 1893 with this declaration: "Let us understand, once for all, that the ethical progress of society depends, not on imitating the cosmic process, still less in running away from it, but in combating it."[30] Perhaps Grandcourt, depicted in repeatedly zoological terms, is also suggestive of Eliot's reluctance to ground ethics in any natural order of things. Comte's moral affirmations, more in line with a historical schema, even eschatology (the march of history conceptualized in terms of theology, then metaphysics, then positivistic science), than with any essentialist notion of nature, also held considerable attraction because they were not discontinuous either with Christianity's moral affirmations or its confidence about history's direction. If, however, Eliot continued to believe in a world moving toward moral order in proportion to a corresponding growth in intellectual enlightenment, this Comtean idea would have to contend with her reading of another philosopher during the period prior to writing *Daniel Deronda*: Arthur Schopenhauer.

Eliot was familiar with Schopenhauer's work already in the 1850s, but as Raina points out, she read his *Die Welt als Wille und Vorstellung* in 1872, "which is to say *after* all the other novels and *before Deronda*."[31] There are two principal points at which Schopenhauer's masterwork collides with Eliot's Religion of Humanity, and the combined result seems to have much to do with the molding of Grandcourt. At the broadest level, Schopenhauer attacks the primacy of intellect over will, inverting the relationship: "all philosophers before me, from the first to the last, place the true and real inner nature or kernel of man in the *knowing* consciousness. Accordingly, they have conceived and explained the I . . . as primarily and essentially *knowing*, in fact *thinking*, and only in consequence of this, secondarily and derivatively, as *willing*. This extremely old, universal, and fundamental error . . . must first of all be set aside. . . . My philosophy alone . . . puts man's real inner nature not in consciousness, but in the will."[32] Grandcourt's intelligence, his knowingness of what transpires in his victims' heads, might be seen as one distinct possibility of this subordination of mind to the mood of the will. If we observe Grandcourt rather than listen to Deronda, there can no longer be sanguine confidence that our lives become "more spiritual by capacity of thought" (802). The hypothetical basis for Grandcourt is established. Even more, Schopenhauer, in his specific delineation of this fearful type, practically provides Eliot with a detailed plan for making this character:

> There finally results even that delight at the suffering of another which has not sprung from egoism, but is disinterested; this is *wickedness* proper, and rises to the pitch of cruelty . . . when at last all wishes are exhausted, the pressure of will remains, even without any recognizable motive, and makes itself known with terrible pain as a feeling of the most frightful desolation and emptiness . . . he tries to mitigate his suffering [unconsciously] by the sight of another's and at the same time recognizes this as an expression of his power. The suffering of another becomes an end in itself; it is a spectacle over which he gloats. . . . Neros and Domitians . . . The thirst for revenge is closely related to wickedness. It repays evil with evil disinterestedly, not as a means but as an end, in order to gloat over the offender's affliction caused by the avenger himself.[33]

Granting the gains and losses invariably occurring in translation, the dark predilections for the "disinterestedness" described here are notable, especially when read against the supreme value placed on "disinterestedness" by Arnold. Yet Grandcourt is not merely a disinterested player at life, much like one of the gamblers described in *Daniel Deronda*'s opening scene—"Not his the gambler's passion that nullifies appetite, but a well-fed leisure, which in the intervals of winning money in business and spending it showily, sees no better resource than winning money in play and spending it yet more showily" (37)—

but he also shares the "affliction" of these leisured gamblers in whom, as Schopenhauer might say, "all wishes are exhausted": boredom. Eliot describes their faces in terms of "a certain uniform negativeness of expression which had the effect of a mask — as if they had all eaten of some root that for the time compelled the brains of each to the same narrow monotony of action" (37).

For Grandcourt that monotonous action has become the infliction of pain, be it to his dogs, his horses, his mistress, or his wife. Gwendolen will shortly discover just what his eyes, which "expressed nothing but indifference" (145) at their first meeting, signify. Even more suggestive, however, is her initial impression of his deathly bearing: "it was perhaps not possible for a breathing man wide awake to look less animated" (145). When we recall Eliot's judgment on the opening casino scene with its atmosphere of "dull, gas-poisoned absorption" (37), the connection becomes unmistakable. Later, Deronda will comment, "I think what we call the dulness of things is a disease in ourselves" (464).

Grandcourt's Making: The Colonial Background

The tone established by that opening scene as well as Grandcourt's languid mannerisms both suggest another force in the confluence of evils that shape him. While Grandcourt delights chiefly in mastery, both personal and political, his individual style seems more attuned to the Decadent Nineties. William Myers suggests Eliot was responding to "A new spirit of brutal faithlessness . . . based on the urbanities of aestheticism and political agnosticism and the will to violence in men and nations. The threat came jointly, as it were, from Pater and Bismarck, nor was it less dangerous for being capable of concealment behind the impeccable manners of an English gentleman." [34] Alasdair MacIntyre pinpoints even more specifically Grandcourt's brand of aestheticism, tying it closely to a specific culmination of class and power. He identifies James's *Portrait of a Lady* as the primary treatment of this "particular kind of rich person at one particular time and place." [35] A strong Schopenhauerian twist can be felt in these characteristics, but MacIntyre also emphasizes what kind of historical conditions make the traits possible:

> It will in fact turn out that *The Portrait of a Lady* has a key place within a long tradition of moral commentary, earlier members of which are Diderot's *Le Neveu de Rameau* and Kierkegaard's *Enten-Eller*. The unifying preoccupation of that tradition is the condition of those who see in the

social world nothing but a meeting place for individual wills, each with its own set of attitudes and preferences and who understand that world solely as an arena for the achievement of their own satisfaction, who interpret reality as a series of opportunities for their enjoyment and for whom the last enemy is boredom. The younger Rameau, Kierkegaard's "A" and Ralph Touchett put this aesthetic attitude to work in very different environments, but the attitude is recognisably the same and even the environments have something in common. They are environments in which the problem of enjoyment arises in the context of leisure, in which large sums of money have created some social distance from the necessity of work. . . . The rich aesthete with a plethora of means searches restlessly for ends on which he may employ them.[36]

Aestheticism may denote Grandcourt's personal style but cannot hide the essential aim both he and his society take for granted: the ever increasing concentration of power. If the equestrian imagery conveys Grandcourt's mastery of Gwendolen in the personal realm, then repeated use of another word— "empire"—carries Eliot's comment on the gentry's power into an explicitly political sphere. Once again the novel exceeds the limitations we usually associate with Eliot. Eagleton's attack on her for the "nostalgic organicism of . . . historically backdated rural fiction"[37] does not apply to this book. Furthermore, Eagleton's charge that Felix Holt's "'progressive' political critique is no more than the idealist protest of traditionalist values against the political itself,"[38] while it may find ready targets in Deronda's and Mordecai's nationalist messianism, does not describe Eliot's project in Grandcourt.

That exposure antedates what a whole host of Edwardian New Liberals, including Masterman, J. A. Hobson, and L. T. Hobhouse, were attempting to do during the first decade of the twentieth century by writing broadsides against England's plutocratic elite. In representing Grandcourt the way she does, Eliot also seems intent on drawing clear connections between the landed gentry's power at home and its colonial interests abroad, a connection later novelists sometimes obscure by their portrayal of imperial types as issuing primarily from the "new" middle classes, and not the ranks of the landed gentry. Both Gissing and Forster are apt to represent the imperialist class as hungry new fortune hunters rather than long-settled English aristocrats. Conrad's "flabby devils" out for quick profit in *Heart of Darkness* and Wells's nouveau riche Teddy and George in *Tono-Bungay* also suggest the type. Gissing and Forster are both too much enamored of an idealized nostalgia for country living (Eagleton's charge pertains more appropriately to them, I think) to be able to subject it to very frank economic scrutiny or to show the gentry in any kind of compromised colonial position. In this respect, at least, Eliot shows herself truly of a radical mind.

She peppers her narrative with allusions to empire, subtly preparing the way for interpreting that acme of imperial rule himself, Gwendolen's husband. Early we are told that Gwendolen "had no notion how her maternal grandfather got the fortune inherited by his two daughters; but he had been a West Indian—which seemed to exclude further question" (52). The limitations of Gwendolen's education are brought home when Eliot pronounces, "She had no permanent consciousness . . . any more than it had occurred to her to inquire into the conditions of colonial property and banking" (94). Likewise Rex, we are informed, "had not studied the character of our colonial possessions" (117). Surely these are odd grounds on which to berate adolescent ignorance, but such revelations of cultural illiteracy are significant when we realize Gwendolen confidently believes she is the worldly intellectual equal to the older men of the community. Their notions of empire reveal the modesty and pathos of her own: "With human ears and eyes about her, she had always hitherto recovered her confidence, and felt the possibility of winning empire" (95). Buoyant that Grandcourt will be her "slave" (127), she willingly undergoes the process of becoming his "proud slave" who "has been proud to be bought first" (133), signaling how profoundly she has imbibed the very ideology that enslaves her, for she is the colony about to be colonized, even more, about to be crushed by the "empire of fear" (479).

In this context, Grandcourt's comments about the "Jamaican negro" being "a beastly sort of baptist Caliban" (376) confirm his imperialist will. These words also allude directly to the bloody pacification of the Jamaica colony in 1865 by the island's Governor Edward Eyre, under whose orders nearly 500 Jamaican blacks had been massacred, an equal number flogged, imprisoned or tortured, and martial law imposed—actions which Eyre would claim kept order and saved 13,000 white British subjects.[39] The uprising at Morant Bay and Eyre's ruthless suppression of it became instant headlines in England, neatly dividing Nonconformist radicals and patriotic imperialists. The literary community did not stay aloof. Lending Eyre and the ethos of imperial law and order their solid support were Carlyle, Ruskin, and Tennyson; Dickens allowed his name to be attached to the movement but stayed distant.[40] Meanwhile, J. S. Mill, Huxley, and Spencer angrily denounced the massacre and the government's refusal to prosecute. Eyre was removed from the governorship, but a grand jury in 1868 refused to indict him on charges of murder. Majority popular opinion, Bernard Semmel suggests, established in this instance a strong precedent for future policy justifying imperial ends with whatever bloody means were necessary.[41]

In her correspondence, Eliot is silent on the Eyre controversy. But she undoubtedly had it firmly in mind when writing this famous passage about Grandcourt and Gwendolen's marriage, in which all the allusive threads to equestrian domination, personal empire, and colonial tyranny are drawn skillfully together: "Every slow sentence of that speech had a terrific mastery in it for Gwendolen's nature. . . . He knew the force of his own words. If this white-handed man with the perpendicular profile had been sent to govern a difficult colony, he might have won reputation among his contemporaries. He had certain ability, would have understood that it was safer to exterminate than to cajole superseded proprietors, and would not have flinched from making things safe in that way" (655). Eliot's use of the word "proprietors" here is interesting. The talk of "extermination" almost certainly suggests they are black not white (ironically, it was precisely those white fears of extermination at the hands of the black majority, reminiscent of the Haitian revolution, that fueled much British popular sentiment for Eyre's defense), and we can suppose Eliot knew that many of the victims of the massacre were small farmers — "proprietors" —whose numbers had proliferated in the hills after slavery's abolition. These blacks, who preferred to scrape out an existence on their own patches of ground rather than work for mostly absent British landowners, were frequently converts of the Nonconformist Wesleyan and Baptist missions in the colony. Finally, the irregular trial and execution of George Gordon, a mulatto Baptist member of the Jamaican House of Assembly who stood accused of fomenting the rebellion, became a central issue in the Nonconformist case against former Governor Eyre.[42]

Eliot's description of Grandcourt forms a wry comment on the popular sentiment favoring use of British imperial force regardless of constitutional principle or justice, the rule of the strong man over the rule of law. Writing a quarter of a century later, J. A. Hobson would remark about the men who formed Britain's policy in South Africa: "The most momentous lesson of the war is its revelation of the methods by which a knot of men, financiers and politicians, can capture the mind of a nation, arouse its passion, and impose its policy."[43] Eliot's perception of evil in *Daniel Deronda* has not hardened yet into such a ruling-elite conspiracy theory of history, but there abound hints of grave concern about excessively concentrated power. Commenting on one of Deronda's reveries, Eliot says, "he was in another sort of contemplative mood perhaps more common in the young men of our day—that of questioning whether it were worth while to take part in the battle of the world: I mean, of course, the young men in whom the unproductive labour of questioning is sustained by three or five per cent on capital which somebody else has battled for" (225). Eliot's musings about the distribution of resources and labor might well have been prodded by government inquiries into those questions concurrent with her composition of *Daniel Deronda*. One parliamentary investigation in 1874 revealed that one-fourth of the kingdom's total surface was owned by 1,200 people; half the land by only 7,400.[44] "The radicals regarded the landed aristocracy," one historian observes, "as the section of society most hopelessly corrupted by unchecked power, excessive authority and influence, and the lack of exertion and daily labour."[45]

These drastic inequities of power and wealth are exactly what trouble Hyacinth Robinson in *The Princess Casamassima*, and there the burden of almost Marxist consciousness is jolted directly toward the possibility of class war. Eliot, like Dickens, sustains a darker view than James does of unhampered accretions of power, but she suggests a fictional solution to the crisis, dampening and deflecting revolutionary possibility. If Dickens gives Clennam a soulmate to help navigate London's "roaring streets," Eliot's solution to the condition of England is to escape England altogether, in the form of Mordecai's messianic Zionism.

That flight, however, leaves Grandcourt's centrality to this novel all the more, rather than less, troublesome. This is especially acute if we subscribe to Bernard Semmel's recent argument that the novel affirms primarily a notion of organic cultural "inheritance."[46] Semmel's case seems solid—until we realize he has abstained from commentary on Grandcourt, whose existence absolutely undermines those received notions of cultural inheritance guiding the English aristocracy. Like Dickens's portrayal of Circumlocution as a web of social forces, Eliot's rendition of Grandcourt suggests she apprehends evil to be something more insidious than a merely wicked, even purely wicked, human individual. Grandcourt's power will outlast his death. After all, such is the aim of the aristocratic institutions of inheritance themselves.

Eliot shows us Grandcourt's peers endorsing his every action as logical, right, and proper for a gentleman. Mr. Gascoigne, the rector, speaks for the entire social order when he urges his niece to marry Hugo Mallinger's wealthy heir:

> This match with Grandcourt presented itself to him as a sort of public affair; perhaps there were ways in which it might even strengthen the Establishment. To the Rector, whose father . . . had risen to be a provincial corn-dealer, aristocratic heirship resembled regal heirship in

excepting its possessor from the ordinary standard of moral judgments, Grandcourt, the almost certain baronet, the probable peer, was to be ranged with public personages, and was a match to be accepted on broad general grounds national and ecclesiastical. (176, 177)

"Gwendolen, . . . you hold your fortune in your own hands—a fortune such as rarely happens to a girl in your circumstances—a fortune which almost takes the question out of the range of mere personal feeling, and makes your acceptance of it a duty. If Providence offers you power and position—especially when unclogged by any conditions that are repugnant to you—your course is one of responsibility." (178, 179)

Thus grasping for maximum power and position describes the essence of Reverend Gascoigne's gospel. It is the gospel of Grandcourt's Britain, constituting the seamless fabric of institutions "national and ecclesiastical." When Eliot inspects those lesser wills that fold into Grandcourt's greater power, she identifies how power, emanating it would seem from a central subjectivity, is in fact created by the collective assent of a people who accede legitimacy to the ruling idea. This accounts for much of Grandcourt's strangely absent, passive exterior manner; he remains a set of perfect gentlemanly gestures awaiting fulfillment by his peers' and subjects' idea of him. As Foucault suggests,

We should try to grasp subjection in its material instance as a constitution of subjects. This would be the exact opposite of Hobbes' project in *Leviathan*, and of that, I believe, of all jurists for whom the problem is the distillation of a single will—or rather, the constitution of a unitary, singular body animated by the spirit of sovereignty—from the particular wills of a multiplicity of individuals. Think of the scheme of Leviathan: insofar as he is a fabricated man, Leviathan is no other than the amalgamation of a certain number of separate individualities, who find themselves reunited by the complex of elements that go to compose the State; but at the heart of the State, or rather, at its head, there exists something which constitutes it as such, and this is sovereignty, which Hobbes says is precisely the spirit of Leviathan. Well, rather than worry about the problem of the central spirit, I believe that we must attempt to study the myriad of bodies which are constituted as peripheral *subjects* as a result of the effects of power.[47]

This practically describes Eliot's project in *Daniel Deronda*. Grandcourt's terrible force of will becomes represented as an accretion of collective assent, and not merely the individual manifestation of a single consciousness. Grandcourt's death confirms that the power—of which he is the most manifest evidence—will go on unchanged, because he is quite clearly not its sole source. In a wry passage Eliot describes Gascoigne's reaction to news that the will cuts Gwendolen out and gives the inheritance to the illegitimate son: "Female morality is likely to suffer from this marked advantage and prominence being given to illegitimate offspring" (826). Rather than perceive the victimization of both Lydia Glasher and Gwendolen Harleth, the minister shifts the burden of ethical wrongdoing off of Grandcourt and his lawyers and onto the generalized female body. To the very end, Eliot foregrounds Gascoigne's inability to denounce Grandcourt's vileness: he "did not . . . lower himself by expressing any indignation on merely personal grounds, but behaved like a man of the world who had become a conscientious clergyman" (826). Subjects like Gascoigne, Eliot indicates, will faithfully uphold the rotten system. Indeed as Foucault observes, these "peripheral subjects" make the power possible. Our fascination with Lush, or Lydia Glasher, or even Gwendolen, persists because of the way they feed the power and are crushed by it in the same moment.

Eliot and Evil: Reconstructing Victorian Liberalism

A recurrent charge against liberal humanism is that it maintains a shallowly optimistic view of human behavior and has no understanding of evil. In the absence of God, goes the argument, evil likewise is deprived of ontology and becomes fully explained as "really a failure of intelligence, imagination, or sympathy."[48] This commonplace criticism of liberal theory still persists; as a caricature it has had a lasting impact. And it has an important bearing on how we read the mature works of Eliot and Dickens, and the Edwardians who followed them.

Such a conception of liberalism was initially articulated late in the Edwardian period by some of the influential voices staking out the turf for literary modernism. And it has had the damaging result of implicating an entire generation of writers as hopelessly naive. T. E. Hulme, the originator of Pound's poetic theories and most of T. S. Eliot's political and theological ones,[49] trumpeted in the pages of A. R. Orage's influential New Age the doctrine of Original Sin, as if the previous generation had grown Pollyannish about badness. Orage himself—a minor figure whose role in making and breaking literary reputations then looms increasingly large now—proposed in 1911 that Liberalism understood as both a political and cultural agenda[50] should be abandoned. Orage focused on what he saw as the two tenets, and flaws, of Liberal belief:

(1) society's capability for "indefinite progress," and (2) the "perfectibility" of the human individual.[51]

These charges stuck, although they were specious. As any examination of serious liberal writing of the period will show, from Masterman's journalism to Hobhouse's sociology to Forster's fiction, the overriding concern is one of English society's rapid devolution and degeneration. The attack on human perfectibility might be interpreted as a thrust against architects of social planning who, like H. G. Wells and the Webbs, to name just some, in their worst moments imagined that such planning would make issues of individual human conduct and collective institutional organization moot.

Unfortunately, or perhaps willfully, writers like Hulme and Orage did not take a closer look at both late Victorian novelists and much of the Edwardian fiction being written by their contemporaries. Had they done so, the force of their cry and their claim to newness might have been more muted. Nonetheless the vitriol against liberalism has left a considerable impact, if only because greater lights such as T. S. Eliot and Pound borrowed and then intensified the vitriol. Eliot gave credence, for example, to Hulme's sweeping thesis that nineteenth-century "romanticism" needed to be cleared away by the hard shattering gaze of "classicism." Eliot adopts wholesale Hulme's virtually synonymous usage of romanticism and liberalism, as well as the necessity of a "reactionary" spirit to sweep out that alliance's "democratic" spirit. Eliot calls Hulme "the forerunner of a new attitude of mind, which should be the twentieth-century mind, if the twentieth century is to have a mind of its own. Hulme is classical, reactionary, and revolutionary; he is the antipodes of the eclectic, tolerant, and democratic mind of the end of the last century."[52] The main targets of the young modernists' attacks were the Big Three Edwardian novelists: Wells, Bennett, and Galsworthy. But the modernist take on literary history leaves out far too much in the development of the nineteenth-century novel to be very reliable. Most pointedly, when we consider the grasp and comprehension of evil as something overwhelmingly systemic and complex in Dickens's and Eliot's late books, Hulme's announcement of Original Sin as the insight that will purge literature and liberalism of democratic softness begins to appear not just a little inadequate and simpleminded. In fact we can argue that these novelists' understanding of social forces, and their ability to give them fictional embodiment, complicates the question of moral responsibility and guilt far beyond the traditional boundaries of assent or dissent to prescriptive orthodoxy—the very prescriptiveness Hulme wished to revive. Dickens and Eliot both take on the prescriptive orthodoxies of their generation, going against the grain in making the possibility of redemption—however that term is now understood and by whatever means it is to be achieved — infinitely more difficult.

George Gissing, deeply influenced by both Dickens and Eliot, especially at the start of his career, takes these questions into new terrain, bringing into sharper focus both the broken will of England's poor and the larger will to power of an imperial nation. Yet the question of how the individual is to live in the midst of these forces remains central in each book; can one live, ask Gissing's intellectuals, both gracefully and responsibly in the midst of such a society? An attitude of pessimism and passivity creeps into Gissing's books, even as he energetically details the new inhabitants of his London: from that creature of the abyss, Slimy, to the commercial sliminess of men like Jasper Milvain. Gissing can avail himself of neither the comic relief of Dickens nor the stubbornly Comtean faith of Eliot. For Gissing, even more than for them, humanity's unleashed will presents the liberal imagination with more horrors than it does possibilities. That is why, in Gissing's world, the solution to liberal guilt becomes the surrender of will itself.

GEORGE GISSING

THE APOLOGETICS OF
DISENGAGEMENT

"You have hardened your heart with theory.
Guard yourself, Rhoda!"
GEORGE GISSING,
The Odd Women

He cannot understand that I can enjoy the study of things
which I yet condemn.
The Diary of George Gissing

George Gissing returns to the problem of the displaced intellectual more often
and more obsessively in his voluminous body of work than any other novelist of the nineteenth century. That sense of displacement, however, embodied
in countless protagonists, achieves sharpest resolution in the author himself.
Thus any criticism of Gissing's body of work is hard pressed not to engage the
biographical record. His career encompasses all the phases of liberal guilt: an
explicitly theological trauma; a continual mulling over the twin social crises
of urban poverty and the spirit of nationalist imperial violence; and finally, the
conscious retreat to pastoral in a state of intellectual exhaustion. The withdrawal to the country garden literally means the desire to stop thinking—
because the Gissing intellectual typically can find no respite to the force of his
guilt. Gissing and his brood of characters are all sons—and in some instances
daughters—of Clennam.

Numerous Gissing novels develop one or more of these ideas. Some suggest
with special lucidity the liberal mind's struggle, its effort for a form of secular

salvation. Gissing is the least stellar of the novelists considered here, and by far
the least read. But as a bridge figure between the Victorians and Edwardians
he exercises considerable influence; and his output provides a virtual catalog
for the dominant interests of Edwardian writers and journalists.

In the English novel, the intellectual as a marginal type appears as early
as Charlotte Brontë's *Villette* (1853). George Eliot develops a similar figure:
Will Ladislaw, Felix Holt, and Daniel Deronda must find some arena for the
application of their considerable gifts. And in Eliot they usually do achieve a
measure of integration with their society, either through love, or discovery of
a vocation, or both. Deronda, as much visionary as intellectual, must attempt
to achieve it through the commitment to create a new society entirely. In this
emerging crowd of intellectuals, Clennam is maybe the most somber: for him,
liberal guilt contributes toward mental illness. And in a way Gissing's characters, his heirs, are merely Clennam pushed to further extremities. No Paraclete
comes to their aid, nor, as in *Daniel Deronda*, does any form of messianism
offset the grimness of their vision. The means for translating thinking into
doing are ever elusive in Gissing. Eliot's heroes can move from alienation to
vocation, but in Gissing the hero must perpetually wander the margins.

This may sound familiar to contemporary intellectuals, especially those
who teach the humanities within the academy. Gissing's heroes are prototypi-
cal for modern liberal guilt. Recognizing their powerlessness and inefficacy,
they nevertheless feel compelled to define themselves in socially useful terms—
that is to say, by adopting some oppositional stance to existing cultural formations. Gissing's work has special contemporary resonance. If we ask how the
establishment of aesthetic standards has been eclipsed within the discipline
by the more urgent task of unmasking ideological representations, if we continue to wrestle with the opposition between cultural commentary and active
transformational agency within culture, then consideration of Gissing's work
is illuminating.

Ironically, Gissing himself was initially destined for academic greatness,
but his university career was cut short by a liaison with a young prostitute
named Nell Harrison. The relationship seems to have been the result of part
attraction and part compassion. Caught stealing money in a coatroom—he
was allegedly giving Nell money to keep her off the streets—the star pupil was
kicked out of school in 1879.[1] Sent to America by his family, he began writing
short stories, first for newspapers in Chicago and then in upstate New York.
During one period he claims to have survived by eating nothing but peanuts.[2]
The would-be scholar was forced, by default, into a second career of novel

writing. Austin Harrison, a contemporary, offered this assessment of Gissing in 1906, three years after his death:

> To understand and even to sympathise fully with him one must remem-
> ber that all his hopes and ambitions had been shattered at the most
> impressionist period of his life; that he had been shipwrecked, as it were,
> at the outset of his progress in the world; and that, as a consequence, the
> youth had been transformed into a hard and bitter man. By nature he
> was made for the life of . . . cultured leisure and repose. Constitutionally
> he was an idealist, a dreamer, an impressionist, a scholar. In other cir-
> cumstances he might have been a university don, a famous scholar, have
> amassed learning and fame. He worshipped the old, the dusty volumes
> of dead languages; vellum and parchment. I have seen him take up a
> worm-eaten copy of an old chronicle or Greek author and caress it as
> a child will stroke the coat of some fond animal. A library was to him
> a garden of roses; he loved books as women love flowers: emotionally,
> instinctively. He had a Grecian love for all beauty.[3]

One of the strongest, earliest paradoxes of Gissing's writing career is the tension between this love of beauty and the actual novelistic output between 1880 and 1899, which painfully underlines the ugly squalor of lower-class existence—and initially earned him the reputation of an unsavory realism. Yet Gissing himself accurately pinpointed his true fictional purpose in 1895: the profiling of displaced intellectuals. That displacement practically always en-tails poverty: "My books deal with people of many social strata. There are the vile working class, the aspiring and capable working class, the vile lower-middle, the aspiring and capable lower-middle, and a few representatives of the upper-middle class. . . . But what I desire to insist upon is this: that the most characteristic, the most important part of my work is that which deals with a class of young men distinctive of our time—well-educated, fairly bred, but *without money*."[4]

Arthur Golding of *Workers in the Dawn* (1880) and Osmond Waymark of *The Unclassed* (1884) are the two earliest examples of the type, but even in the later fiction, where Gissing's intellectuals have risen on the economic scale, their psychological profile, like Hardy's Jude and James's Hyacinth Robinson, is perpetually that of the resentful outsider looking up the social ladder and finding himself unwelcome. Piers Otway of *The Crown of Life* (1899) and the narrator of the memoir-novel *The Private Papers of Henry Ryecroft* (1903) are always embarrassed by their backgrounds. The painful class consciousness permeating Gissing's fiction is as ubiquitous as in Dickens; but for Gissing the damage was done at school, not in a blacking factory. In a diary entry of 1890 Gissing complains, "It is first-class people who know me, whilst I myself am always compelled to associate with the second-class."[5] Later in that decade, when Gissing had attained the status in England of a major novelist, he became acquainted with Thomas Hardy, and his remarks about the older man after a visit of just a few days indicate an unchanged class snobbery: "I perceive that he has a good deal of coarseness in his nature—the coarseness explained by humble origin. He did an odd thing at breakfast—jumped up and killed a wasp with the flat of a table-knife! He seems to me to be a trifle spoilt by success; he runs far too much after titled people, and, in general, the kind of society in which he is least qualified to shine."[6]

Gissing's own resentments shine transparently here, especially when we consider how many of his heroes are obsessed with their "humble origins." A year later, after meeting radical activist Harold Frederic, Gissing expressed "disappointment": "Frederic I had classed with Henry James; I found a burly man with hands like a blacksmith's, talking roughly."[7] Gissing was an unregenerate Pip to the end, in spite of being one of Dickens's most perceptive readers. Rarely could he view the follies of class with humor rather than bitterness. One exception is Morley Roberts's anecdote about the time he was asked by "a lady . . . what his experience was in the management of butlers." Gissing replied thoughtfully "that he always strictly refrained from having anything to do with men servants, as he much preferred a smart-looking young maid."[8]

Gissing's fiction is seldom lightened with such playfulness, although heavy hints of the misogyny find their way in. Nell, whom he married upon his return from America, died of alcoholism and syphilis in 1888; and his marriage in 1890 to his second wife, Edith Underwood, a union equally impulsive, ended in recrimination and separation. Gissing charged her with child abuse prior to her committal to an insane asylum, which she never left. While it is true that these somber facts—all perhaps contributing to Gissing's untimely death at the age of forty-six—often threaten to overwhelm the commentary about Gissing's work, it is equally true, as John Halperin observes, that Gissing's fiction is virtually incomprehensible if not understood biographically.[9] His writing output, given even the best of circumstances, would seem gargantuan: roughly twenty novels, several volumes of short stories, what is the first major critical work on Dickens, as well as several posthumous novels. This averages better than a book a year beginning in 1880. *New Grub Street* (1891) has been most consistently praised, but my attention falls elsewhere here on some other works which highlight the full trajectory of liberal guilt in his fictional development. In the early novels a loss of faith and an awareness of the anguished condition of London's poor are treated as part of the same existential condition. Gissing's study of the abyss, anticipating the interest of later Edwardian writers and journalists, begins with his apprentice novel *Workers in the Dawn* (1880) and is capped by *The Nether World* (1889). Later, perhaps reflecting his own relatively more stable economic position, Gissing turns his attention to the appetites of a prosperous middle class that in its own way exhibits a savagery as ferocious as that in the East End. However, these comfortable suburbanites fight not over little scraps, but rather pieces of the Empire itself. This interest culminates in the popular and critical success of *The Whirlpool* (1897).

In his later years Gissing assumes the posture of a liberal tired out from the struggle. With increasing frequency he lapses into a comforting vision of country living, of the pastoral ideal embodied in the British country house. But is his moral indignation, his liberal guilt, exhaustively spent? *The Private Papers of Henry Ryecroft* (1903) answers that question in the form of a thinly veneered fictional testament of Gissing's final ruminations about the moral life.

The Representation of Poverty: Early Gissing

The most cogent criticism of Gissing's first novel was conveyed by Frederic Harrison's wife. Harrison, the intellectual positivist who launched Gissing's career by introducing him to key figures of literary London, made this note in a postscript to Gissing in July 1880: "P.S. — To show you that I do not write in any unfriendly way I will repeat to you these criticisms or remarks made on the book by my wife, whose judgment in fiction I trust far more than my own. 1. There is enough stuff in the book to make six novels. 2. The finer type of London workman has never been so truly drawn. 3. Where are the 'Workers in the Dawn'?" [10]

Mrs. Harrison's first observation is most astute. The tale begins with the narrator inviting us along on a guided tour of London's slums, street markets, and gin palaces ("Walk with me, reader, into Whitecross Street."). It promises, and delivers, considerably more naturalistic detail of these kinds of neighborhoods than we ever get in Dickens. But it also seeks, in its three-volume "triple-decker" immensity, to convey the intellectual pilgrimages of its main characters, Arthur Golding and Helen Norman, whose lives crisscross in a meandering plot ending with Arthur's suicide at Niagara Falls. What is interesting, as Mrs. Harrison further notes, is that the lower classes are observed from the outside in set passages such as the beginning, but no major protagonist comes from the class of the dawn workers, except Carrie, a prostitute Arthur marries in a mental haze compounded of lust and the urge to rescue. Like Hyacinth Robinson of *The Princess Casamassima*, the orphaned Arthur is exceptional by virtue of his upper-class birth, and finds himself torn in the dilemma between exercising his social conscience and pursuing his artistic gift. If James was able to resolve such a dilemma with one book, Gissing's career represents, as Jacob Korg observes, the recurrent grappling with that question, resulting often in a damaging "conflict of intentions" in his work.[11] At the same time, however, Gissing's treatment of that dilemma, extending through his entire professional life, might also suggest he takes it more seriously than James did.

Gissing's own uncertainty is profound about his artistic aims in *Workers*. Privately, he admitted, "The book in the first place is not a novel in the generally-accepted sense of the word, but a very strong . . . attack upon certain features of our present religious and social life which to *me* appear highly condemnable. First and foremost, I attack the criminal negligence of governments which spend their time over matters of relatively no importance to the neglect of the terrible social evils which should have been long since sternly grappled with. Herein I am a mouthpiece of the advanced Radical party."[12] But shortly afterwards, Korg notes, Gissing protested of a review in the *Athenaeum* that its writer viewed the novel "as if it were a mere polemical pamphlet, and not a *work of art*, as which, of course, I desire it to be judged."[13]

The plot turns largely on Arthur's unhappiness between marriage to Carrie, and longing for the truer intellectual companionship of Helen Norman. Meanwhile, many pages are devoted to cataloging an entire range of ideological intellectual positions open to young Arthur. Granted, those ideological positions are represented by characters. Mr. Tollady, his early mentor, tells him to "be a successor to Hogarth"[14] by painting the squalor of the slums. Helen Norman, the good angel, says with Shelleyan confidence that art carries its own seeds of social change. The proletarian conscience of Mark Noble demands full-time commitment to the workingmen's self-help league, while the embittered Mr. Pether advocates all-out class war against the rich. The epicureans, Gresham the famous artist, and Helen's father—a lukewarm clergyman able to leave his parish on account of a legacy—complete the overly busy picture. Later in his career, Gissing was to pinpoint one of the weaknesses of the book this way, in remarking on one of Mrs. Humphry Ward's novels: "Her method is *precisely* what mine was when I wrote 'Workers in the Dawn.' Of course she has a mature mind, and wide knowledge; but artistically I believe she is at the very point I had reached, after study of George Eliot, some ten years ago. Her books are enormously long, and she develops with great labour the intellectual advance of every character." [15] Gissing's debt to George Eliot is strong; indeed in this novel Helen Norman practically mirrors Eliot's own intellectual journey. Helen moves through a phase of piety, to doubt, to reading Strauss's *Life of Jesus*, to studying abroad with the higher critics in Tübingen, to an encounter with Darwin's *Origin of Species*, and then through the influence of Schopenhauer, Comte, and Shelley to a version of her own Religion of Humanity. "What can a woman do in the world?" (328) she asks, echoing Dorothea Brooke. A secular saint, she chooses to work among the poor in spite of lost faith; as with Arthur, her primary drive lies in seeking both intellectual foundations for, and the practical means of, exercising the moral life. "If *Workers* can be said to be 'about' one thing," remarks Gillian Tindall, "it is about the desire to *do good* on the part of the main characters." [16]

Gissing's reliance on Eliot displayed itself again a few months after publication of *Workers*. Commissioned by editor John Morley of the *Pall Mall Gazette* to write a series of articles on German socialism, Gissing wrote this warning toward the conclusion of the series: "How far are the theories of scientific Socialism really grasped by the masses of German revolutionists? It needs little special inquiry to convince one that the vast majority are only following a vaguely luminous ideal of material comfort. . . . Let us suppose that the socialist State was proclaimed tomorrow; how many workingmen would be found possessed of that self-reliance, self-control, self-respect which such a society inevitably presupposes?" [17] Felix Holt's "Address to Working Men" does not say it any more emphatically; and Gissing's latching onto Eliot's most conservative strain of thought demonstrates how short-lived his embrace of radicalism was to be. However, if Eliot moves in her final novel toward recognition of defectiveness within Britain's social and political structure even as she emphatically retains more traditional notions of individual virtue, Gissing's focus on individual moral character at the expense of his social critique takes on increasingly dogmatic force in his career. More simply, if Eliot moves to a broader liberalism in *Daniel Deronda*, Gissing explicitly entrenches Victorian moralism and class snobbery as he grows older.

In the early 1880s Gissing was also rapidly moving away from the positivist orbit. In an unpublished essay of 1882, "The Hope of Pessimism," Gissing rejects the Comteans as unrealistically sanguine about human nature, and suggests that only Schopenhauerian renunciation of the will remains as a viable answer to the rampant forms of egotism endorsed by both Social Darwinists and "Christianity in its modern form of optimistic protestantism." [18] For Gissing, that was a nightmare coalition of forces. The implications of this essay, a systematic philosophical statement of belief that he was not to repeat again, are profound for the remaining novels of the poor classes that Gissing wrote through the rest of the decade. Social reform—that buoyant hope of the Romantic liberals, and slightly less buoyant hope of Dickens—gets exposed itself as a form of egotism in *The Unclassed* (1884), *Demos* (1886), and *Thyrza* (1887). In all its guises—philanthropy, socialist experimentation, and education—reform according to Gissing can be cast as activity carried out more for the psychological benefits of the reformers than for any positive outcome accruing to the supposed beneficiaries of such activism.

The ripest development of that bleak idea occurs in Gissing's final novel of this phase, *The Nether World* (1889). Yet that novel succeeds artistically in a way its predecessors do not. By this time Gissing has learned to pare away much—although not all—of the excessive authorial commentary that marred his apprentice work. Korg observes that *Workers* relies on an "unsettling" combination of "careful observations with interpolations of sarcasm, indignation, sympathy, and revulsion"; Dickensian scene mixes with Eliotish authorial intrusion.[19] We can add to this Gissing's own use of naturalistic detail, even though he had not read Zola at the time of writing *Workers*,[20] and later expressed less than enthusiastic attitudes toward naturalism itself.[21] Gissing's growth as a novelist involved unlearning lessons—or better, learning when to skillfully appropriate lessons learned maybe too well from Dickens and Eliot. The best parts of his early work, such as the Victorian striptease in *Workers*—in which two women wearing flesh-colored body stockings enact Eve's offer of the apple to Adam, writhing under a tavern gaslight to the accompaniment of a hand organ (3:358-59)—or the terrifying characterization of the homeless man Slimy in *The Unclassed*, inhabit a naturalistic realm impossible in either Dickens or Eliot. Indeed, such powerful writing, contrary to Gissing's increasingly overt reviling of the lower classes, reinforces our awareness that underneath his revulsion remains an attitude of sympathy and even advocacy. "Partisanship," Terry Eagleton observes, ". . . is inherent in reality itself: it emerges in a method of treating social reality rather than in a subjective attitude towards it."[22] Gissing's best work about the very poor transcends his increasing repugnance and moralizing about them. When the central protagonist in *The Unclassed*, writer Osmond Waymark, declares he "no longer has a spark of social enthusiasm,"[23] his friend Casti shrewdly observes, "Yet the old direction still shows itself in your choice of subjects. Granting that this is pure art, it is a kind of art only possible to an age in which the social question is predominant" (212).

For Gissing that "social question" was never to be abstract. In late 1888 he received a message that his wife Nell was dead. Gissing went with Morley Roberts to her lodging and recorded this entry in his diary:

> She lay on the bed covered with a sheet. I looked long, long at her face, but could not recognize it. It is more than three years, I think, since I saw her, and she had changed horribly. Her teeth all remained, white and perfect as formerly. . . . Came home to a bad, wretched night. In nothing am I to blame; I did my utmost; again and again I had her back to me. Fate was too strong. But as I stood beside that bed, I felt that my life henceforth had a firmer purpose. Henceforth I never cease to bear testimony against the accursed social order that brings about things of this kind. I feel that she will help me more in her death than she balked me during her life. Poor, poor thing! [24]

Immediately after, Gissing began writing *The Nether World*, completing it in less than five months.[25]

That novel is Gissing's final frenzied and exhaustively documented assault on the indignity of poverty. But once again it aborts as futile any possible course of action meant to alleviate economic disadvantage. In a chapter entitled "The Soup Kitchen," Gissing captures the mutual aggressions that tear down human dignity between do-gooders and charity's recipients:

> But the present year saw a change in the constitution of the committee: two or three philanthropic ladies of great conscientiousness began to inquire busily into the working of the soup-kitchen, and they soon found reason to be altogether dissatisfied with Mr. and Mrs. Batterby. No, no; these managers were of too coarse a type; they spoke grossly; what possibility of their exerting a humanising influence on the people to whom they dispensed soup? Soup and refinement must be disseminated at one and the same time, over the same counter. Mr. and Mrs. Batterby were dismissed, and quite a new order of things began. Not only were the ladies zealous for a high ideal in the matter of soup-distributing, they also aimed at practical economy in the use of funds. Having engaged a cook after their own hearts, and acting upon the advice of competent physiologists, they proceeded to make a "stock" out of sheep's and bullocks' heads; moreover, they ordered their peas from the City, thus getting them at two shillings a sack less than the price formerly paid by the Batterbys. . . . But, alas! these things could not be done secretly; the story leaked out; Shooter's Gardens and vicinity broke into the most excited feeling. I need not tell you that the nether world will consume—

when others supply it—nothing but the very finest quality of food, that the heads of sheep and bullocks are peculiarly offensive to its stomach, that a saving effected on sacks of peas outrages its dearest sensibilities. What was the result? Shooter's Gardens, convinced of the fraud practised upon them, nobly brought back their quarts of soup to the kitchen, and with proud independence of language demanded to have their money returned. On being met with a refusal, they . . . emptied the soup on to the floor, and went away with heads exalted.[26]

Gissing's characters are portrayed in a language crackling with Dickensian vitality but which eschews any sentimental or romantic notions about their hidden humanity.[27] Clem Peckover, in the same book, is a buxom sixteen-year-old working girl who executes her tyrannical acts with fierce joy: "The frankness of Clem's brutality," observes the narrator, "went far towards redeeming her character" (6). Like Hardy's Arabella, or even James's Millicent Henning, she exults in her sheer animal strength and health. Against her, the more mousy characters of Jane Snowdon or Pennyloaf Candy can only be pitied. There is a scoundrel lawyer, Scawthorne, much in the Dickens vein; a paternally benevolent patriarch, Michael Snowdon, whose dreams of philanthropy imposed as iron duty on his niece Jane are exposed as tyrannical selfishness; an ambitious but poor aspiring actress, Clara Hewett, whose career is destroyed when a rival in the touring company tosses acid on her face; and a whole minor host of drunks and wife beaters, whose lives are chronicled in both domestic detail and panoramic sweep. Gissing's scenes range from the interiors of slum dwellings to the halls of the Crystal Palace, where characters such as Jack Bartley and Bob Hewett carouse and riot during their off hours. The mechanistic plot intricacies—maybe also suggestive of late Dickens—revolve around Jane Snowdon's discovery of her family lineage and subsequent battle over a legacy.

At the book's hub, however, stands Sidney Kirkwood, a skilled craftsman surviving on a miserable wage, who recognizes he is a good man leading a hopelessly blighted life among London's wretched. There is little he can do but ache for the injustices of this world: "with all his feeling there blended that reflective bitterness which is the sad privilege of such as he" (166). After marrying the disfigured actress, Clara, Kirkwood seems to enact even more intensively than Clennam the passive center upon which life's crimes get etched. And the conclusion of *The Nether World* reads as a somber tribute to Dickens's great finale of *Little Dorrit*. Kirkwood and Jane coincidentally meet at the cemetery on the first anniversary of Michael Snowdon's death:

In each life little for congratulation. He with the ambitions of his youth frustrated; neither an artist, nor a leader of men in the battle for justice. She, no saviour of society by the force of a superb example; no daughter of the people, holding wealth in trust for the people's needs. Yet to both was their work given. Unmarked, unencouraged save by their love of uprightness and mercy, they stood by the side of those more hapless, brought some comfort to hearts less courageous than their own. . . . Sorrow certainly awaited them, perchance defeat in even the humble aims that they had set themselves; but at least their lives would remain a protest against those brute forces of society which fill with wreck the abysses of the nether world. (392)

The particularities in his characters' lives give Gissing's book a distinction lacking in later chronicles of the abyss, which too often deteriorate into raw statistical overkill or the glibness of generalities. Gissing renders hell with detail; the power of his description, conveyed in the lives of individuals such as Kirkwood, Pennyloaf, or Clara, is often missing in subsequent versions of the netherworld theme where the abyss is summarily glimpsed as a collective and disgusting "they." In Wells's *Time Machine* (1895) the underground working class of Morlocks is distinctly subhuman. By the time of Masterman's *From the Abyss: Of Its Inhabitants by One of Them* (1902), the force of that promising subtitle (at last, a first-person account, we are led to believe) is undercut by passages that treat the abyss's inhabitants not as human, but as furry, invasive vermin: "They have poured in as dense black masses from the eastern railways; they have streamed across the bridges from the marshes and desolate places beyond the river; they have been hurried up in incredible number through tubes sunk in the bowels of the earth, emerging like rats from a drain, blinking in the sunshine."[28] Repeated use of "they," and use of the adjective "black," among other things, clearly show this is not "by one of them." To the kinds of subconscious fears revealed in this passage can be added Asa Briggs's observation that in the Victorian literature of the slums, a repeated analogy is made between the savagery of East Londoners and that of "darkest Africa"; for instance, one report, by the London Diocesan Building Society in 1865, described the East End to be "as unexplored as Timbuctoo."[29] Briggs warns that these analogies "reveal not 'the truth' about the East End but rather the deep gulf in experience and values between observers and observed in the late nineteenth century."[30] This is where Gissing's experience living a less-than-privileged life, as opposed to theorizing about it, becomes valuable; the novels resonate in their particularity, over against most late Victorian and Edwardian studies that we can say are written more "from above" than "from below." This is not to say that living and writing "from below" does not create its own set of resentments and concurrent textual distortions. It does. But the particularities of the novels emerge out of Gissing's lived experience; not out of some kind of categorical argument or theory.

Categorical thinking, however, mars some of the perceptions of Gissing's novel itself. Take for instance this assessment by Fredric Jameson:

> *The Nether World* cannot be said to be a proletarian novel, in spite of the nominal occupations—die-sinking, the manufacturing of jewelry or artificial flowers—of some of its characters. Its conceptual and organizational framework is not that of social class but rather that very different nineteenth-century ideological concept which is the notion of "the people," as a kind of general grouping of the poor and "underprivileged" of all kinds, from which one can recoil in revulsion, but to which one can also, as in some political populisms, nostalgically "return" as to some telluric source of strength. Gissing's own relationship to "the people" is a unique combination of revulsion and fascination.[31]

Such a notion of "the people" seems more applicable to Dickens, whose rousing favoritism on behalf of social underdogs frequently prevents him from bluntly appraising the vitiating effects of poverty on human character. In fact, far more often in Gissing those vitiating effects make the possibility of good lower-class character very difficult indeed. John Halperin notes of one of Gissing's descriptions of poor people in *The Nether World*, "These are not the innocent, dewy-eyed, lovable, playful progeny of Dickens's poor. The feeling expressed in these passages is quite clear: poverty *never* brings human nobility to the surface. Gissing did not equate poverty with virtue, as Dickens, in his most sentimental moods, was prone to do."[32] The exaggerations of both Jameson's remarks about "the people" and Halperin's observation to just the opposite effect are indicative of the urge to generalize Gissing's depictions of lower-class character into a single overarching aesthetic judgment. John Goode perhaps best sums up the novel when he suggests Gissing employs set pieces such as the Bank Holiday riot at the Crystal Palace (or the soup kitchen episode quoted earlier) in "*describing* the working class"—contrasted to his technique in most of the novel of "*presenting* human lives."[33] Yet even Goode seems uneasy that different modes of representation should inhabit the same book. Delivering a tight-lipped reproof that the two methods of presentation are incompatible, he insists that only one of them, "presenting lives" as opposed to "describing the working class," is valid. This begins to sound precious. Gissing uses multiple modes of presentation in the same way a director uses close-ups and long-range panoramic shots in a film. And the multiple modes of presentation themselves work to prevent the kind of damaging monolithic assessments of the abyss noted earlier.

To return to Jameson's remarks: it is indeed true that Gissing is simultaneously attracted and repelled by the working class. No one disputes this. The larger question is why Gissing demonstrates such ambivalence. Korg uses a different pairing of words to say the same thing: "The poor, evoking in Gissing a curious blend of guilt and indignation, called forth his strongest powers."[34] Where Jameson's attempt to circumscribe Gissing's work within his terminology of the "proletarian novel" falls short is exactly in that genre's inability to admit that individual differences of character may need to be given the same weight as social theories. And class analysis, unlike novelistic method, seldom grants that kind of weight to the particularity of individuals. In our earlier reflections on Foucault in the context of Dickens's Circumlocution, we noted how the individual is lost sight of exactly in the effort to explain power strictly as the product of circulating, impersonal social energy. By analogy to the world of physics, we might say that in the paradox of wave versus particle theories of light, the particle side of the equation gets entirely negated. The result is theoretical distortion.

Gissing pays attention to both particles and waves. Note that he distinguishes between "vile" and "aspiring and worthy" members of the same class; there are good people such as Thyrza and Gilbert Grail and Kirkwood, but then there are always also the Bob Hewetts. Perhaps Jameson is unwilling to admit Gissing's analysis to be about class at all because Gissing is not categorical enough, monolithic enough, or maybe because Gissing still employs a vocabulary of individual ethical accountability, a vocabulary for which Jameson's theoretical muse has no place. Fiction does indeed come permeated with ideology, and as Jameson so convincingly suggests in the larger thesis of The Political Unconscious, comes with an implicit and subconscious political content. But it is equally true that the most interesting novels are irreducible to a single reading exactly because they will not be bent to the ideological design of any single hegemonic theory.

Working-class novels, however, seem to be subjugated repeatedly to such narrow readings. For another instance, Esther Waters, George Moore's masterpiece contemporaneous with Gissing's work, must withstand the same kind of criticism, the kind that sacrifices textual complexity on account of theoretical schemata. One critic, P. J. Keating, objects to what might be called literary miscegenation:

By the time he came to write *Esther Waters*, Moore's early enthusiasm for Zola was on the wane and other influences are apparent. We thus have the odd situation that the only English working-class novel of this period that can be said to be profoundly influenced by French naturalism belongs in many ways to a purely English tradition. . . . The central fault of *Esther Waters* lies . . . in the character of the heroine. On the one hand Moore presents her as the victim of forces she is unable to combat (the naturalistic tradition), and on the other, he allows her qualities of moral strength that enable her eventually to survive (the English tradition).[35]

The attitude of horror expressed here toward the mingling of French and English traditions is more than a little ridiculous; it seems akin to childhood fears that one's meat and vegetables might come into contact on the plate. An alternate—and liberal—view would be that the resulting eclecticism in the novel charges it with resilience and inherent truth: the commonplace and commonsense apprehension that both environmental limitations and inner resources of strength contain explanatory value. This is exactly what makes Esther Waters memorable. The same can be said of Sidney Kirkwood or Clara Hewett in *The Nether World*, although their heightened awareness of the circumscribing power of poverty adds additional pathos to their situation. Kirkwood recognizes his own entrapment and yet will survive with a measure of dignity. This is so not merely because Gissing asserts it at the book's conclusion, but because Kirkwood as a distinct character demonstrates it.

The Nether World is Gissing's last novel specifically written with the "problem" of the lower classes in mind. David Grylls argues that with its completion Gissing "had over-exercised his social conscience to the point of emotional exhaustion" and, furthermore, that if in terms of didactic purpose the novels of the underclass purportedly show every avenue of social reform—revolution, philanthropy, self-help—to be ineffectual, they actually demonstrate that "social concern is psychologically unsatisfying."[36] The phase of Gissing's work culminating in *The Nether World* seems to reach a point of impasse beyond which little more can be said. John Goode reads the vicious circle of Gissing's thought this way:

The lower classes, at their worst, are dehumanised by toil and poverty, and become savages, rogues or brutes. These characteristics are actually bred by poverty, and thus in a world of poverty they are strong enough to overwhelm any human qualities which may exist there. Since they are also qualities which are totally individualistic, there is no possibility of communal effort in a world dominated by them. Neither can there be any hope of amelioration through individual virtues, because these virtues are always overwhelmed by the dehumanised vices. In short, the only hope for the amelioration of the working classes is an improvement in moral standards, and there can be no improvement, because the economic forces to which they are committed predetermines their low moral quality.[37]

True in its way, this diminishes and even ignores the accomplishment of realized individual character in *The Nether World*, as well as the subdued—admittedly, very subdued—tinge of hope in its ending: if not happiness, a tiny measure of dignity. Goode's summary also demonstrates the recurrent temptation to read Gissing as little more than a proponent for a set of philosophical attitudes—in his case, antireformist ones.

That Gissing kept returning in successive novels to the problem of the urban poor is a tribute to his underlying compassion in spite of the increasingly reactionary message. Gissing's kind of compassion, however, based on the denial of every mode of social reform, can be justifiably attacked as a form of moral self-congratulation lacking in any substance. Samuel Hynes makes that judgment about Gissing's contemporary, Masterman. "Right feeling," Hynes says in reference to Masterman's frequent declamations about the plight of the poor, is to be faulted when it goes unaccompanied by a concern for justice or a proposed solution to the problem.[38] Yet at the same time we are right in asking how or whether such solutions can ever be worked out in fictional terms. Is *Daniel Deronda* a model? Furthermore, as Virginia Woolf was to ask, are such solutions, even if they exist, capable of successful mediation through fiction? Novels tend on the whole to work better when they depict ideologies at war rather than when they espouse a single ideology; this perhaps explains the difference in quality between novels like *The Brothers Karamazov* and *Beyond Freedom and Dignity*. In the case of typical proletarian fiction, Upton Sinclair's novel *The Jungle* gives exemplary weight to this argument. Sinclair's book breaks down exactly at the point where it takes up the burden of a solution to the brutal social and economic milieu of turn-of-the-century meatpacking Chicago. Only as long as it focuses on the social conditions inciting guilt and indignation in its audience does it succeed as art. Proceeding further to the altar call of socialist salvation, it collapses in a heap of prescriptive verbiage.

Gissing's distancing from the subject matter of England's poor, which came after much struggle, was never quite complete. Even in his final testament of hermetic disengagement, *The Private Papers of Henry Ryecroft*, he feels compelled to justify morally, against the suffering of the masses, the supposedly well earned aesthetic pleasures of "an author at grass." But the need to justify oneself shows how impossible it was for Gissing to ever wholeheartedly submit to a strictly aestheticist sensibility.

Money, Masculinity, and Empire: Gissing in the 1890s

Before his final retreat to pastoral, however, Gissing turned his attention in his middle phase to issues of imperial conquest. This is a natural extension of dismay at the plight of the local poor; it is that same dismay carried to a global level. In the story of empire, guilty liberals read a similar narrative of oppression crying out for redress. Thus Gissing begins to focus his attention on the middle classes' hunger for power, which extends to global dominance. Numerous matters perplex and motivate this middle class: Gissing engages the spiritual meanness of suburban living (*In the Year of Jubilee*); women's liberation and women's perspectives more generally (*The Odd Women*); and finally, the connection between middle-class financial rapacity and the spread of the British empire itself, the collusion if you will, between capitalist and nationalist interests. In *The Whirlpool* (1897), which begins and ends with reflections on the power of Kipling's jingoism, all these concerns are successfully united into what is probably, apart from *New Grub Street*, Gissing's finest novel. For these reasons it deserves extended attention.

A recurrent problem dogs Gissing's fiction: the disjunction between his plots, usually pertaining to the love interests of hero or heroine and the social commentary made explicit by means of direct authorial voice. This defective integration is especially apparent in Gissing's most explicitly anti-imperialist and pro-pacifist novel, *The Crown of Life* (1899). There, Piers Otway's rise in social status through marriage has absolutely nothing to do with the anti-imperialist rhetoric suffusing the book. But in *The Whirlpool*, Gissing grasped the full implications of the imperial metaphor. The novel succeeds as a study of the imperial appetite at work in career, in marriage, in business enterprise, and in national politics. This unrelenting emphasis on egotistic savagery—like the mechanism of the marketplace determining both the literary output and domestic arrangements in *New Grub Street*—releases Gissing's full powers.

Harvey and Alma Rolfe's unraveling marriage occupies the center of attention, but their friends Hugh and Sibyl Carnaby set the carnivorous tone for most of the novel's action. They are characters bred for the express purpose to consume and destroy; like Fitzgerald's Tom and Daisy Buchanan, they are people who break things, who are users. Whether overseeing gold mining operations in south Africa, starting new manufacturing ventures at home, or indulging in extravagant safaris when on the verge of bankruptcy, they take for granted the creed espoused by the ruined actress Clara in *The Nether World*: "We have to fight, to fight for everything, and the weak get beaten" (207). This is rudimentary but effective Spencerian doctrine. For the Carnabys, the basic duty of upstanding citizens is to avoid being one of the weak.

Gissing had registered the emerging dominance of Social Darwinism in "The Hope of Pessimism" essay more than fifteen years earlier. There he conceded that any affirmation of life would acknowledge egotistical self-interest as the operative principle. Against the realpolitiks of the Social Darwinists he could only reiterate a Schopenhauerian renunciation, a surrender in place of a response, and the force of this renunciation—if that is not an oxymoron—is repeated over and over through the various displaced intellectuals inhabiting his novels. Harvey Rolfe, the principal character of *The Whirlpool*, exemplifies this position. His attitude toward power is an extremely complicated one. In ways reminiscent of Rupert and Gerald's relationship in *Women in Love*, Harvey maintains an extremely close relationship with Hugh Carnaby, who possesses all the qualities that Rolfe seems to despise. Rolfe repeatedly invokes Kipling, with ambiguous effect, and critics are still not sure whether these allusions are straightforwardly cynical or otherwise. And in spite of his avowed inclinations to gentleness, he asserts marital dominance over Alma, after initially professing his faith in equality, individual independence, and the aspirations of the "New Woman." If we try to take these aspects of Harvey's behavior one at a time, in doing so we discover that domestic household tyranny, and the national brand of imperialism carried out under the British flag, mirror each other. The pattern of mastery, as George Eliot so brilliantly shows in *Daniel Deronda*, is of one piece. Politics can hardly be divided between domestic and public life.

The male-bonding scene that initiates the story is standard in Rider Haggard but uncharacteristic for Gissing. The menfolk sit drinking whiskey in Hugh Carnaby's den, surrounded by mounted animal heads bagged on expeditions in Africa and Asia. The conversation drifts from complaints about the difficulty in finding good servants to the increasing restrictions on male freedom that come with marriage and family. Rolfe's reactionary mood is interesting to recall in light of events later in the book. On the law of natural selection, he muses:

> "A widower with two young children and no income—imagine the position. Of course, he ought to be able to get rid of them in some legitimate

way—state institution—anything you like that answers to reason. . . .
People talk such sentimental rubbish about children. I would have the
parents know nothing about them till they're ten or twelve years old.
They're a burden, a hindrance, a perpetual source of worry and misery.
Most wives are sacrificed to the next generation—an outrageous ab-
surdity. People snivel over the deaths of babies; I see nothing to grieve
about. If a child dies, why, the probabilities are it *ought* to die; if it lives,
it lives, and you get survival of the fittest." [39]

On the necessity of national self-righteousness and "natural" aggression:

"If I had a son . . . I think I'd make a fighting man of him, or try to. At all
events, he should go out somewhere, and beat the big British drum, one
way or another. I believe it's our only hope. We're rotting at home—some
of us sunk in barbarism, some coddling themselves in over-refinement.
What's the use of preaching peace and civilisation, when we know that
England's just beginning her big fight—the fight that will put all history
into the shade! We have to lead the world; it's our destiny; and we must
do it by breaking heads. That's the nature of the human animal, and will
be for ages to come." (14)

Finally, on the inferiority of women: "Wherever I go, it's the same cry: domestic life is played out. There isn't a servant to be had—unless you're a Duke and
breed them on your own estate. All ordinary housekeepers are at the mercy of
the filth and insolence of a draggle-tailed, novelette-reading feminine democracy. Before very long we shall train an army of men-servants, and send the
women to the devil" (15).

The misogyny shifts to talk of Africa and "Nigger-hunting," which Carnaby
asserts to be "a superior big game" (16). Harvey then expostulates Britain's
global intentions: "I was looking at a map . . . the other day, and it amused me.
Who believes for a moment that England will remain satisfied with bits here
and there? We have to swallow the whole, of course. We shall go on fighting
and annexing, until—until the decline and fall of the British Empire. . . . Some
of us are so overcivilised that it makes a reaction of wholesale barbarism in
the rest. We shall fight like blazes in the twentieth century. It's the only thing
that keeps Englishmen sound" (16).

To what degree does cynicism embody resistance, and to what degree surrender? That opposite interpretations persist in readings of *The Whirlpool*
indicates the extent of the critical problem. And the difficulty for interpreting
that ending and these opening speeches, with their explicit echoes of Kipling's

nationalist sentiment, is not made easier in light of Harvey and Alma's on-going domestic crisis through most of the book. That crisis elaborates on the home front the same issues of coercion and power.

At the outset of their marriage, Harvey and Alma give at least lip service to respect for one another's independence, as well as to the shared belief that they must escape the mad maelstrom of London living. But two problems inter-vene: boredom and children. Alma's desire for a professional music career takes the two of them back into the vortex, and meanwhile the upbringing of their son Hugh occupies more and more of Harvey's time. It is a famil-iar contemporary dilemma. The brash bachelor who had once said he would prefer to see his children when they were ten or twelve years old discovers a tenderness within himself as a father that is rather surprising; he "could not see too much of the little boy" (383). At the same time, however, the finan-cial demands of running a bigger household in London begin to crimp his independent income, and he is sucked into the necessity of actively seeking business ventures to enlarge his capital. Accustomed to independent wealth, he takes the ignominious plunge into the working world. Work, however, makes Harvey feel physically nauseous: "He picked up financial newspapers at rail-way bookstalls, and in private struggled to comprehend their jargon. . . . At the Metropolitan Club . . . he talked with men who were at home in City matters, and indirectly tried to get hints from them. He felt like one who meddles with something forbidden—who pries, shamefaced, into the secrets of an odious vice. To study the money-market gave him a headache. He had to go for a country-walk, to bathe and change his clothes, before he was at ease again" (208). Harvey seeks the illusory solution of "the country walk" as his wife's professional career occupies more of her time. Likewise Carnaby, distressed with his wife's extravagant living, "preferred to stay down at Coventry with his partner Mackintosh, living roughly, smoking his pipe and drinking his whisky in the company of men who had at least a savour of sturdy manhood" (184). Drums and bear grease cannot be far off. Stark oppositions define Giss-ing's gender categories: if the city holds wayward wives in its grip, husbands must desperately retreat to the country where they can make a last stand for manliness.

Two good country people moored in ancient traditions, Basil Morton and his wife, ultimately provide impetus for Harvey to reassert "manhood" in his crumbling marriage. Morton, a corn merchant, is the paragon of the country gentleman. "He lived by trade, but trade did not affect his life" (323). Here we find Gissing's first rule of mammon: one must have plenty of it, to begin with, not to be touched by its filthiness, and the filthiness comes in the getting.

Morton has a fine old house, garden, and library loaded with treasured books. Minus a wife, he would be the perfect understudy for Ryecroft.

But his wife, foremost among his possessions, is the perfect mother that Alma is not: "she conceived her duty as wife and mother after the old fashion, and was so fortunate as to find no obstacle in circumstance" (324). Asking Mrs. Morton's advice about his own marital difficulties, Harvey requests her opinion about the interference between Alma's professional career and household duties. He knows full well what he is about to hear. Mrs. Morton begins with "a commonplace—that a married woman would, of course, be guided by her husband's wish." This dialogue ensues, bearing out the connection for Mrs. Morton between the domestic and divine chains of command:

> "You think that equivalent to reason and the will of God?" said Harvey jocosely.
> "If we need appeal to solemn sanction."
> Rolfe was reminded, not unpleasantly, that he spoke with a woman to whom "the will of God" was something more than a facetious phrase.
> (337)

Consciously free from religious dogma himself, Harvey finds Mrs. Morton's expressions of godliness more than welcome, much as the freethinking Ryecroft in *The Private Papers* will find his housekeeper's piety delightful because it undergirds her pliant obedience. Harvey takes the Morton doctrine conveniently to heart, throwing over every feminist idea he has up to this point endorsed. Quarreling with him upon his return home, Alma asks, "Are we talking on equal terms, or is it master and servant?" Harvey insists,

> "Husband and wife, Alma, that's all."
> "With a new meaning in the words."
> "No, a very old one." (354–55)

Already somewhat numbed by the relative failure of her musical debut, Alma submits to the idea of replicating the Mortons' gender roles. But her efforts to run a household prove as futile as those to succeed professionally. In one scene, where she attempts to command unruly servants, Gissing's intrusive voice breaks in, asserting the connection between hierarchy and male authority: "No one could better have illustrated the crucial difficulty of the servant-question, which lies in the fact that women seldom can rule, and all but invariably dislike to be ruled by, their own sex; a difficulty which increases with the breaking-up of social distinctions" (366). In passages like these Gissing's novel crumbles into increasingly bitter and brittle polemic. A short time later, Harvey intervenes to say that servants, like disobedient colonies, must be kept down: "Nothing will keep them and their like in subordination but a jingling of the purse. . . . For the sake of quietness we must exalt ourselves" (367). Alma's inability to manage servants is mirrored in numerous other ways to prove Harvey's, and Gissing's, thesis about women who leave their traditional role: she cannot drive a buggy without letting the horses get out of control; her efforts to succeed in the music business inevitably compromise her sexually with the likes of Dymes and Cyrus Redgrave and coincide with her refusal to be a good mother; she becomes nervously hysterical—that staple feminine malady of the nineteenth century; she turns to drugs; and, finally, she commits suicide. There may be tragedy here, but it is compromised by our sense that Gissing has stacked the deck so heavily against Alma that the novel's equilibrium as a study of modern marriage is totally lost. Gissing's treatment of her is rivaled only by his negative portrayal of Mutimer, the leader of the socialist experiment in *Demos*.[40]

Perhaps Alma's death is meant to confirm the Social Darwinist principles Rolfe articulates early in the book: weakness takes certain individuals out of the game early. As if to reinforce this idea, Gissing contrasts to Alma the woman named Sibyl, a remorseless survivor who manages almost always to get what she wants. If we look ahead at *Ryecroft*, it becomes apparent Gissing continued to think at length about her as the most emphatic embodiment of the New Woman:

Midway in my long walk yesterday, I lunched at a wayside inn. On the table lay a copy of a popular magazine. Glancing at this miscellany, I found an article, by a woman, on "Lion Hunting," and in this article I came upon a passage which seemed worth copying.

"As I woke my husband, the lion—which was then about forty yards off—charged straight towards us, and with my .303 I hit him full in the chest, as we afterwards discovered, tearing his windpipe to pieces and breaking his spine. He charged a second time, and the next shot hit him through the shoulder, tearing his heart to ribbons."

It would interest me to look upon this heroine of gun and pen. She is presumably quite a young woman; probably, when at home, a graceful figure in drawing rooms. . . . She would give one a very good idea of the matron of old Rome who had her seat in the amphitheatre. Many of those ladies, in private life, must have been bright and gracious, highbred and full of agreeable sentiment; they talked of art and letters; they could drop a tear over Lesbia's sparrow; at the same time, they were con-

noisseurs in torn windpipes, shattered spines and viscera rent open. . . .
Of course her style has been formed by her favourite reading. . . . If not
so already, this will soon, I daresay, be the typical Englishwoman. . . .
Such women should breed a remarkable race. (44–46)

Sibyl seems the understudy for a more famous character of the same type:
Hemingway's Mrs. Macomber. Like Coriolanus's imperial mother Volumnia,
these are the sturdy mothers of conquering nations, women who affirm the
law of life to be subjugation of the weak.

That question of the future of the British imperial race is precisely the one
we are left with at the conclusion of *The Whirlpool*. Harvey has taken little
Hughie out for another visit to the Mortons at Greystone, and sits on their
porch reading passages to Basil Morton from Kipling's *Barrack-Room Ballads*
"with no stinted expression of delight, occasionally shouting his appreciation"
(449). Rolfe acknowledges the brutality of the verse:

> "The Empire; that's beginning to mean something. The average En-
> glander has never grasped the fact that there was such a thing as a British
> Empire. He's beginning to learn it, and itches to kick somebody, to
> prove his Imperialism. The bully of the music-hall shouting 'Jingo' had
> his special audience. Now comes a man of genius, and decent folk don't
> feel ashamed to listen this time. We begin to feel our position. We can't
> make money quite so easily as we used to; scoundrels in Germany and
> elsewhere have dared to learn the trick of commerce. We feel sore, and
> it's a great relief to have our advantages pointed out to us. By God! we
> are the British Empire, and we'll just show 'em what *that* means!" (450)

Numerous contemporary reviewers of the novel interpreted this passage, and
others like it, straightforwardly. Foremost was H. G. Wells's review, containing this assessment of Rolfe: "here, in the mouth of a largely sympathetic
character, is a vigorous exposition of the acceptance, the vivid appreciation of
things as they are."[41] Gissing was deeply upset by that remark, and attempted
to clarify his intentions to Wells: "In that last talk with Morton, I never meant
to suggest that Rolfe tended to the "Barrack-room" view of life. In all he says,
he is simply expressing his hopeless recognition of facts which fill him with
disgust. Thus and thus—says he—is the world going; no refusing to see it; it
stares us in the eyes; but what a course for things to take!—He talks . . . in a
voice of quiet sarcasm. . . . I have a conviction that all I love and believe in is
going to the devil; at the same time, I try to watch with interest this process of
destruction, admiring any bit of sapper-work that is well done."[42] To Eduard

Bertz, a German friend and correspondent, Gissing expressed more dismay that critics read the book as an endorsement of Kipling, and again vigorously asserted that Rolfe spoke "*in bitterest irony*. . . . No man living more abhors the influence of Kipling than I do. . . . I thought the meaning was unmistakable to any intelligent person."[43]

The dispute demonstrates a central problem in reading Gissing: are we to understand his books and characters on their own terms, or do we judge his central protagonists as merely voices emitting from an authorial ventriloquist? If the former, Rolfe seems not merely resigned, but even affirmative, of the Social Darwinian law of the jungle. If the latter is our method, then the irony of Rolfe's voice cannot be in dispute, because what Gissing says of Kipling elsewhere is unremittingly harsh. While praising Kipling's early work, for instance, Gissing called *Stalky & Co.* "the most vulgar and bestial production of our times," and repeatedly assailed Kipling's glorification of bloodshed.[44]

The only internal evidence in this novel, however, that Rolfe finds the balladeer of empire repulsive, is Harvey's son Hughie, who has been raised on a steady diet of classics. Little Hugh hardly resembles his namesake Carnaby, a beef-eating, gin-drinking paragon of English might. Instead, Rolfe's son is feeble, "slight, and with little or no colour in his cheeks; a wistful, timid smile on the too intelligent face" (451). This seems none other than Hardy's Little Father Time reincarnate,[45] and like that ill-fated child, he is the offspring of an unfulfilled intellectual. Watching his unhealthy son who prefers to read rather than play, Rolfe says, "It won't do; he must be among boys, and learn to be noisy. Perhaps I have been altogether wrong in teaching him myself. What right has a man to teach, who can't make up his mind on any subject of thought? Of course I don't talk to *him* about my waverings and doubtings, but probably they affect him" (452). Rolfe's waverings are also Gissing's, and they pervade every ironic inflection in the book. Eduard Bertz grasped just how indeterminate such fine-edged irony can be: "Several times I was struck with the likeness of the state of things, as you have reported it, to Nietzsche's ideals. For, though he believes himself, and his disciples believe him, to be a preacher *against* our time, in reality he is a mouthpiece of all that is worst in the *actual* tendencies of our present life."[46]

Culture over Conscience: Late Gissing

"The world frightens me." So writes the narrator at the most confessional moment of *The Private Papers of Henry Ryecroft* (288), resuming where Harvey

Rolfe left off in *The Whirlpool*. Gissing can no longer summon up liberal fury about the rotting slums or the beating imperial drums. Nor can he muster, except occasionally, an ironic edge against the "blood-drenched chaos" (209) which he sees the world becoming. In a pattern that will repeat itself in several of his Edwardian peers, Gissing literally puts his liberal guilt to pasture, through an act of therapeutic self-preservation. Retired writer Ryecroft has withdrawn to a country haven to live out his remaining years. We should note, however, that in the choice of a literary device that makes such retirement possible—the legacy—Gissing resorts to the tired clichés of an earlier literary period. Liberal guilt that has run out of gas tends to look backward for inspiration. Yet the book is not without charm and continues to draw devotees. Ryecroft ranges with eccentric wit over a miscellanea of topics: the unsurpassable pleasure of English beef and gravy; gardening; the English pastoral tradition in literature. This charm has proven more attractive to readers than the moral seriousness invested in the earlier works. Yet it should not obscure the solidly reactionary message at the core. In linking the pastoral tradition with aristocratic values, Ryecroft echoes both the archconservative Hubert Egdon of *Demos* and Morton of *The Whirlpool*.

The form of the book would indicate that Gissing, near his death, wished to step out from behind the mask of author to speak directly to his audience; as he says in the book's preface, the "irregular diary" (xiii) from which he claims to have chosen Ryecroft's "fragmentary pieces" reveals someone "saying exactly what he thought; he spoke of himself, and told the truth as far as mortal can tell it" (xiii–xiv). In passages such as this, employing an explicitly confessional as opposed to ironic voice, Gissing suggests more than a fictional identity is at stake:

> I had stepped into a new life. Between the man I had been and that which I now became there was a very notable difference. In a single day I had matured astonishingly. . . . I suddenly entered into conscious enjoyment of powers and sensibilities which had been developing unknown to me. To instance only one point: till then I had cared very little about plants and flowers, but now I found myself eagerly interested in every blossom. . . . As I walked I gathered a quantity of plants, promising myself to buy a book on the morrow and identify them all. . . . never since have I lost my pleasure in the flowers of the field, and my desire to know them all. My ignorance at the time of which I speak seems to me now very shameful; but I was merely in the case of ordinary people, whether living in town or country. How many could give the familiar name of half a

dozen plants plucked at random from beneath the hedge in springtime? To me the flowers became symbolical of a great release, of a wonderful awakening. My eyes had all at once been opened; till then I had walked in darkness, yet knew it not. (25)

My eyes had all at once been opened; till then I had walked in darkness, yet knew it not. Darkness and light, the error and even shame of youthful waywardness versus the "springtime" of "wonderful awakening": here is the story of a guilty liberal's epiphany, the gospel according to Gissing. Thus the Pauline conversion language overlaid on the final revelatory words of John, who has found in Patmos not his prison but his earthly paradise. Like Morton, Ryecroft has found home. "My house is perfect," he repeats (6, 7).

Still, from this secure vantage point Ryecroft allows himself, briefly, to consider how all this would look to his younger activist self, the self that had not yet abandoned social conscience for the pleasures of botany. Ryecroft does not forget where he has been: "There was a time in my life when, if I had suddenly been set in the position I now enjoy, conscience would have lain in ambush for me. What! An income sufficient to support three or four working-class families—a house all to myself—things beautiful wherever I turn—and absolutely nothing to do for it all! I should have been hard put to it to defend myself. In those days I was feelingly reminded, hour by hour, with what a struggle the obscure multitudes manage to keep alive" (12, 13). The reference to youthful privations periodically surfaces in *Ryecroft*, and when the narrator catalogs those sufferings, it is for the express purpose of justifying his present viewpoint. Mrs. Clennam's moral bookkeeping, perhaps? Suffering becomes the primary apologetic for the present life of aestheticist value.[47] Of course, that reclusive aestheticism has not been actually chosen, but granted by fiat, although the Ryecroftian voice ultimately confuses such privilege with some kind of innate worthiness of character. Defensive about his guilty pleasures, Ryecroft must assert "destiny" as a tag for moral worthiness. His allusion to the "multitudes" and their bitter lot is followed immediately by his assertion that he, all along, was deserving; the multitudes, less so: "Nobody knows better than I do *quam parvo liceat producere vitam.* I have hungered in the streets; I have laid my head in the poorest shelter; I know what it is to feel the heart burn with wrath and envy of 'the privileged classes.' Yes, but all that time I was one of 'the privileged' myself, and now I can accept a recognized standing among them without shadow of self-reproach" (13).

The passage, like Gissing's reminiscence about Hardy, reveals immediately the insecurity of the arriviste, the man who in his boast that he no longer feels

ashamed, wears his inferiority all too visibly. Ryecroft, like Richard Mutimer in *Demos*, demonstrates that any predilections for the poor are rooted
exclusively in personal ressentiment—one has to share their condition, and
such sharing, such advocacy, is never purely motivated. Furthermore, the cure
for such burdensome social activism, based as it is on the false guilt of ressentiment, is instantaneous upon the individual's entry into the ranks of the
privileged. Once removed from the unhappy lot of the "multitude," the "ordinary people," Ryecroft finds the problem of their plight irrelevant. Ryecroft
now also insists that in spite of youthful radicalism—"to think that at one time
I called myself a socialist, communist, anything you like of the revolutionary
kind!" (113)—he could never fully identify with the poor, even had he wanted
to. "I have known revolt against the privilege of wealth (can I not remember
spots in London where I have stood, savage with misery, looking at the prosperous folk who passed?), but I could never feel myself at one with the native
poor among whom I dwelt. And for the simplest reason; I came to know them
too well. . . . I knew the poor, and I knew that their aims were not mine"
(194). Here class consciousness has changed to immutable doctrine, and the
individual moral distinctions between "worthy and aspiring" and "vile" members of the lower and middle classes that Gissing made earlier in his career
have disappeared. From the heights of a newly found, carefully groomed aristocracy of culture, such individual distinctions are lost. From the distance, it
all looks vile. The Sidney Kirkwoods and Clara Hewetts become obscured in
the mass, and likewise any imaginative sympathy for their particular situation
becomes blunted by the dogma of class.

At the same time, entrance into the ranks of the privileged by one who has
been on the outside looking in most of his life leads to the time-honored equation between moral worthiness and aristocratic privilege. The roots of such
sentiment go deep in the English subconscious, as Ryecroft himself observes
in this adulation for the feudal formula:

Profoundly aristocratic in his sympathies, the Englishman has always
seen in the patrician class not merely a social, but a moral, superiority;
the man of blue blood was to him a living representative of those poten-
cies and virtues which made his ideal of the worthy life. Very significant
is the cordial alliance from old time between nobles and people; free,
proud homage on one side answering to gallant championship on the
other; both classes working together in the cause of liberty. However
great the sacrifices of the common folk for the maintenance of aristo-

cratic power and splendour, they were gladly made; this was the Englishman's religion, his inborn *pietas*; in the depths of the dullest soul moved
a perception of the ethic meaning attached to lordship. (135–36)

Notable is the emphatic relationship between religious order and social order,
that affirmed by Mrs. Morton in her view of the relation of the sexes. With
this affirmation of the feudal order, Ryecroft's antiliberalism seems solidly in
place. He glorifies the servants and peasantry of old, who knew their position,
likewise praising his present barely literate, blessedly obedient housekeeper:
"She is fulfilling the offices for which she was born" (49). In this fantasy, Gissing the artist has lost his imaginative desire, and ability, to render any kind
of character with precision, and chooses instead to romanticize a throwback
servant insofar as she contributes to his comfort and convenience. A narrowing of the imaginative range occurs in direct proportion to Ryecroft's fulfilling
his cultural destiny as a connoisseur of the good and beautiful. As Irving
Howe was to observe in his argument with Trilling about James's Hyacinth
Robinson, "Culture, no less than politics, can harden into ideology."[48]

Like many of his contemporaries, Gissing perceived the country house as a
kind of cultural lifeboat in a time of turbulent and unwelcome change. This
inclination was to become a strong feature of Edwardian writing and to continue unabated as late as 1930, with publication of Vita Sackville-West's novel,
The Edwardians. But whereas writers such as Wells, Forster, and Ford all tem-
per their nostalgia with both an apprehension of the capitalist forces propping
up the country order, as well as a cynicism about the inherent nobility of the
gentry itself, Gissing's celebration of landed privilege in *Ryecroft* seems by
comparison naive.

If so naive, then why is it so compelling, and why did it exercise such a
hold on the Edwardian generation? The most revealing aspect of that unqualified praise is the way Gissing insulates his gentry from the very material
basis of capital that makes their cultured leisure possible. If men like Carnaby
and Rolfe find themselves sullied by the effort to maintain a certain standard
of living—by work itself—Gissing's country elite are never subjected to such
degradation.

One of the attractions of Gissing for critics of Marxist persuasion is that he
sometimes sounds like a thoroughgoing materialist, arguing that moral systems ultimately derive from the presence or absence of money. As Ryecroft
observes early in his narrative, "there is no moral good which has not to be
paid for in coin of the realm" (15–16). And we recall that in *The Whirlpool*,

Rolfe admits his moral refinement followed rather than preceded his reception of a legacy.[49] But the consistency of this materialist conception of things breaks down once Gissing begins his chant in praise of country aristocracy. For the fallacy of Gissing's class consciousness becomes most apparent in his division between two kinds of capital: the filthy middle-class kind pursued in the midst of London's commercial darkness, and the invisible good kind that gives the country gentry time to pursue their botanical hobbies. To recall Morton: "He lived by trade, but trade did not affect his life." This wishful thinking dovetails perfectly with Gissing's other notion that it is more blessed to receive than to earn one's keep, because that makes the matter of qualification for genteel status uncomplicated. Gissing, writes Gillian Tindall, "gives the impression of believing that those who do not actually labour directly for money themselves never have to think about it at all. It is as if Gissing himself, despite his consciousness of the suffering of the exploited classes, in general accepted the prevailing middle-class idea that, sitting on your lovely lawn in Surrey, you are not 'tainted' by commerce or industry even if that is the true source of the wealth you are enjoying."[50] Similarly, this leisurely withdrawal seems to enable Ryecroft the luxury of taking a tone of moral superiority to those rabid imperialists who would "paddle in blood and viscera" (97). Ryecroft does not show quite the awareness that Margaret Schlegel will: namely, that standing on "islands of money" does not necessarily remove one from responsibility for the commercial and imperial enterprise that makes those islands possible.

The Private Papers of Henry Ryecroft proves to be a fantasy garden of bliss that not very successfully covers over the garden of pain tilled by Gissing in his earlier work. For most of his career Gissing is caught up, by his own confession, in "the study of things which I yet condemn": the misery of the poor, the brutal will conveyed in imperialist jingoism. That sensibility defines his best work, and it is in the particulars of those phenomena, and not the assurances granted by any of the late nineteenth-century metanarratives—Marxism, positivism, Social Darwinism—that Gissing found his métier. And at the end, the surrender of his liberal guilt for a peaceful bed of tulips perhaps suggests how difficult the pain was to deal with. The memory of his youth, continually surfacing in *Ryecroft*, suggests that the hardening of his heart via Schopenhauer's regime of renunciation was a process never quite completed.

Gissing's role in the history of liberal guilt is one of the most poignant, if most obscure pieces of this story overall, but it deserves attention, and he deserves to be read. Maybe not the least reason is that two of his Edwardian contemporaries, Joseph Conrad, and E. M. Forster, moved by a similar sense of indignity about England's power and the condition of her people, were to create the most articulate voices of liberal guilt yet: an adventurer named Marlow, and a young woman named Margaret. It is not exaggerating to say both voices carry the Gissing imprimatur.

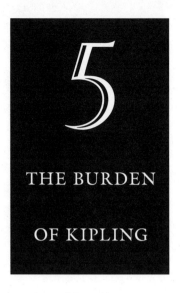

5

THE BURDEN

OF KIPLING

LORD JIM

AND HEART OF DARKNESS

It is wrong, of course, of Mr. Kipling to address a large audience;
but it is a better thing than to address a small one. The only better thing is to
address the one hypothetical Intelligent Man who does not exist and who
is the audience of the Artist.

T.S. ELIOT,
"Kipling Redivivus"

With these words Marlow had ended his narrative, and his audience had
broken up forthwith, under his abstract, pensive gaze. Men drifted off the
verandah in pairs or alone without loss of time, without offering a
remark. . . . Each of them seemed to carry away his own impression, to carry
it away with him like a secret; but there was only one man of all these
listeners who was ever to hear the last word of the story. It came to him at
home, more than two years later, and it came contained in a thick packet
addressed in Marlow's upright and angular handwriting.

JOSEPH CONRAD,
Lord Jim

Liberal guilt is an attitude which cannot be entirely understood apart from a particular reaction to Rudyard Kipling. Gissing's response to Kipling, which overflowed the bounds of personal antipathy onto the pages of *The Whirlpool*, *The Crown of Life*, and *Ryecroft*, anticipates later Edwardian strategies to combat the force of this bespectacled muse from India. Indeed, two of the finest novels of the period, to be taken up in subsequent chapters — *Howards End* and *Tono-Bungay* — can be read as rejoinders to the imperial gospel with which Kipling came to be identified. But they are strange rejoinders. Forster's book attempts to answer the question of how a humanitarian-minded liberal can coexist with the "Imperial type"; the solution proposed is to marry him, and then in true Ryecroft style, to retreat promptly to the spiritual shelter of the country house. Wells's book, equally ambivalent, projects a uniquely twentieth-century intellectual who, while building the ultimate weapons of destruction, wishes to retain the graces of a cultured intellectual, distancing himself from naive jingoist spouters of "turgid degenerate Kiplingese."[1]

"Kiplingese," the "Kiplingesque," or "Kiplingitis" as critic Richard Le Gallienne put it in his scathing book-length attack in 1900, comprise just some of the currency of abusive terms used at the turn of the century to whittle the reigning literary lion down to the sum of his political convictions.[2] The assertion of such terms became a reliable strategy for enforcing the critic's own moral and literary superiority and was anticipated already in 1897 by Henry James. "In his earliest time," James wrote to Grace Norton privately, "I thought he perhaps contained the seeds of an English Balzac; but I have quite given that up in proportion as he has come steadily from the less simple in subject to the more simple — from the Anglo-Indians to the natives, from the natives to the Tommies, from the Tommies to the quadrupeds, from the quadrupeds to the fish, and from the fish to the engines and screws. But he is a prodigious little success and an unqualified little happiness and a dear little chap."[3]

Belittlement on this scale was acknowledgment of a big talent. Martin Green argues that almost every self-consciously literary writer in the English language since Kipling has written in reaction against him, even if they have not read him.[4] To qualify this ambitious claim, Green explains that "Kipling" signifies not a specific "literary influence" but rather a marker for a whole constellation of cultural attitudes. Understood in this way, Green's sprawling thesis makes sense, although I believe it is more persuasive when deployed more specifically. I want to argue that a comprehensive survey of Edwardian literary responses to Kipling can prove a valuable means toward understanding the seminal place of Kipling in the birth of liberal guilt. In a sudden flash at the turn of the century, Kipling became the lightning rod for every spark of liberal fury—and his literary reputation still shows the effects.

Beyond the personal disparagements of the man, what was it about Kipling's idea of empire which liberal critics could not tolerate? And more importantly, why did the fictional responses to Kipling repeatedly mix opposition with acquiescence? Often, it seems, the attacks on Kipling degenerated into name-calling because his liberal antagonists operated on assumptions uncomfortably close to his own. Thus a substantive criticism of him became difficult. Even Robert Buchanan, whose sharply accusatory "The Voice of the Hooligan" in late 1899 helped steer literary opinion decisively against Kipling, displays an ideological predisposition which to our ears sounds remarkably like that usually attributed to the poet of empire. Fulminating as Gissing did against *Stalky & Co.*, Buchanan promulgates a "true Imperialism" meant to contrast Kipling's "mere lust of conquest": "its object is to diffuse light, not to darken the sunshine; to feed the toiling millions, not to immolate them; to free man, not to enslave him. . . . Some of its ways, like the ways of nature herself, must inevitably be destructive; the weaker and baser races must sooner or later dissolve away; but the process of dissolution should be made as gentle and merciful as possible, not savage, pitiless, and cruel."[5]

Buchanan, like Gissing, objects to Kipling's taste for violence, but in fact endorses his opponent's underlying assumptions of an inevitable imperial mandate and white racial superiority. Genocide, couched euphemistically here in terms of "dissolution," is the way of nature and empire, says Buchanan; therefore let us make the destruction kinder and gentler. But Buchanan is not alone in these sentiments. The same kinds of Spencerian assumptions also mark early Conrad, for instance the narration at the outset of *The Rescue*: "Their [the Malays'] country of land and water—for the sea was as much their country as the earth of their islands—has fallen a prey to the Western race—the reward of superior strength if not of superior virtue."[6] Likewise, when James describes Kipling's descending order of subject matter, he reveals similar assumptions on the part of the critic; the hierarchy, meant to induce a smile, is dangerously suggestive: natives are "more simple" than Anglo-Indians, a revealing racial slip that becomes more remarkable when we realize this is exactly the kind of thinking for which Kipling gets damned. (That the Tommies rank even lower on the scale indicates something about James's class snobbery.) The case is rendered more perplexing because some of Kipling's early Indian stories, and even *Kim*, often subvert this sort of hierarchy by showing Indians to be just as complex (sometimes more so) and sympathetic as the British in India. That may well account for Kipling's early "subversive" reputation,[7] as well as the fact that he continues to attract a global readership today.

Kipling's literary stock turned decisively downward only after publication in the *Times* of his two most famous poems, "Recessional" (17 July 1897), and "The White Man's Burden" (4 February 1899). While Gissing, James, and others had praised Kipling's early volumes of short stories as brilliant, the solid consensus that Kipling had turned from literature to jingoism was fixed by Le Gallienne's and Buchanan's articles, both respectively published as book-length works in 1900. Buchanan sealed the indictment: "There is an universal scramble for plunder, for excitement, for amusement, for speculation, and, above it all, the flag of a Hooligan Imperialism is raised, with the proclamation that it is the sole mission of Anglo-Saxon England, forgetful of the task of keeping its own drains in order, to expand and extend its boundaries indefinitely, and, again in the name of the Christianity it has practically abandoned, to conquer and inherit the earth."[8] Tomes have been written about the major features of European and particularly British imperialism at the turn of the century: its reliance on "scientific" racial categories on one hand, its religious invocation of the white man's burden as a high civilizing mission on the other. But there remains one relatively empty space on this map of critical responses to Kipling. By this I mean conscious, direct literary responses such as those found in the novels by Gissing, Forster, and Wells. That empty space is occupied by the other truly global writer of the time, and like Kipling a man with some sense of being an alien among the English: Joseph Conrad.

This is not to say that Conrad and Kipling have not been compared; they have been, and at length.[9] Indeed the literary history of their relationship constitutes a story in itself. At first both regarded as writers of exotic adventure, for roughly half a century they were seldom mentioned in the same breath. Conrad was considered one of the modernist masters while Kipling was relegated to ignominy as a politically incorrect versifier and children's book writer. Then, beginning with Alan Sandison's *Wheel of Empire* (1967), certain critics, whose major interest was the explication of imperial ideology, once again began to juxtapose the two authors' work.[10] Curious revisionist eddies developed in the main critical currents: while novelist Chinua Achebe touched off a huge debate by accusing Conrad of being "a bloody racist"[11] in his depiction of Africans in *Heart of Darkness*, other writers led by Elliot Gilbert were busy rehabilitating Kipling's reputation. They argued that he was a modernist in his own right, an aesthetic innovator in the short story form who was a victim of a curious double standard within the literary academy. His questionable politics, Gilbert suggested, ought not be denied but rather be treated apart from his literary contribution—just as the right-wing, and sometimes fascist, politics of Lawrence, Yeats, Pound, Eliot, and Lewis are generally not considered germane to considerations of their respective literary achievements.[12]

If Conrad had ever expressed a consistent opinion about his more famous—at that time—contemporary, as other Edwardian writers seemed more than willing to do, this matter of the two authors' relative positions on the spectrum of imperial ideology would be greatly clarified. But the exact relationship between the two men remains something of a mystery. One of Kipling's biographers, Charles Carrington, says Conrad "visited Kipling at 'Bateman's' and each was an admirer of the other's work," [13] but he offers no documentary evidence for this claim. Frederick Karl notes that the correspondence between Kipling and Conrad has disappeared; moreover, contradicting Carrington, he asserts that the two were not on social terms whatsoever.[14] We know they did correspond, for in October 1906 Conrad wrote both J. B. Pinker and John Galsworthy that Kipling had praised *The Mirror of the Sea*: "Kipling sent me an enthusiastic little note," Conrad told Galsworthy. "The Age of Miracles is setting in!" [15] And elsewhere Conrad alludes to Kipling. At the beginning of his own writing career, Conrad sent T. Fisher Unwin this cryptic letter, commenting on several reviews of *An Outcast of the Islands*: "I am condemned for not being like Kipling (that was a stupid phrase of the Spectator's (?)) but as I never tried to be, I can't pretend to be much upset by that. I *was* upset by a letter from Mrs Garnett telling me of his serious illness. Through the community and also diversity of ideas I have become much attached [to] the man." [16]

This is suggestive of polite and indirect acquaintance, not friendship, but "much attached" is an interesting choice of words. To R. B. Cunninghame Graham, Conrad expressed an attitude toward Kipling rather like James's: admiration for the craftsman, but with reservations. "Mr Kipling has the wisdom of the passing generations—and holds it in perfect sincerity. Some of his work is of impeccable form and because of that little thing he shall sojourn in Hell only a very short while." [17] Then, attempting to clarify himself to Cunninghame Graham a few days later: "You understand perfectly what I tried to say about Mr Kipling—but I did not succeed in saying *exactly* what I wanted to say. I wanted to say in effect that in the chaos of printed matter Kipling's 'ebauches' [rough drafts] appear by contrast finished and impeccable. I judge the man *in* his time—and space. It is a small space—and as to his time I leave it to your tender mercy. I wouldn't in his defence spoil the small amount of steel that goes to the making of a needle." [18] Cunninghame Graham was contemptuous of Kipling, so Conrad's tone here seems guarded and judicious; the repetition of "small" and "little" anticipates James's words to Grace Norton. But Conrad does indicate that he has seen some of Kipling's work in rough drafts. What are we to make of this? Does it not imply a degree of familiarity more intense, maybe, than Karl would admit? I am not suggesting these two very un-English Englishmen played croquet on each other's lawns, but circumstantial evidence exists for at least some degree of communication, even trust, between them.

Six months later, early in 1898, Conrad wrote an article for *Outlook* magazine, defending Kipling against a hostile reviewer. For reasons unknown the article was never published, although Conrad's apologies for it as a "silly thing," "unredeemed trash," and "a chatter about Kipling provoked by a silly criticism"[19] suggest he had reservations about the piece even as he wrote it. Like the Conrad-Kipling correspondence, the article disappeared, and Zdzislaw Najder notes it is "the only nonepistolary text of Conrad's which certainly existed, but which has remained unknown."[20] One of the final twists in this gnarled yarn came in a letter Conrad wrote to his cousin Aniela Zagórska during Christmas of the same year. In describing the British literary scene, Conrad dispatches quickly with popular authors Grant Allen and Hall Caine, but then makes this bold pronouncement: "Among the writers who deserve attention the first is Rudyard Kipling."[21]

This welter of commentary, rather like the collage of verdicts on Jim's fate in *Lord Jim*, is so diverse as to be self-canceling; it defies interpretation. Conrad vacillates between irony and praise, contempt and admiration. Chronologically there is no discernible pattern of change in Conrad's attitude toward his famous contemporary; if we conclude anything it is that Conrad probably attuned his remarks for different ears.

But I want to suggest that Conrad did feel compelled, like his other Edwardian contemporaries, to go beyond private assessments of Kipling; that he responded within his fiction to Kipling, and indeed more directly than has previously been supposed. Finally, that response takes on directly "the idea" of the imperial mission enshrined in "Recessional" and "The White Man's Burden."

These assertions are made in a spirit of hypothetical and necessarily speculative judgment, gathered largely from a close look at an anonymous figure who appears briefly in chapter 36 of *Lord Jim*. Introduced simply as the "privileged man," he is but one member of Marlow's original audience on a verandah two years prior. Yet he carries a special distinction. Marlow has chosen him to be the only worthy reader for the remainder of Jim's story:

You alone have showed an interest in him that survived the telling of his story, though I remember well you would not admit he had mastered his fate. You prophesied for him the disaster of weariness and of disgust with acquired honour, with the self-appointed task, with the love sprung from pity and youth. You had said you knew so well "that kind of thing," its illusory satisfaction, its unavoidable deception. You said also—I call to mind—that "giving your life up to them" (*them* meaning all of mankind with skins brown, yellow, or black in colour), "was like selling your soul to a brute." You contended that "that kind of thing" was only endurable and enduring when based on a firm conviction in the truth of ideas racially our own, in whose name are established the order, the morality of an ethical progress. "We want its strength at our backs," you had said. "We want a belief in its necessity and its justice, to make a worthy and conscious sacrifice of our lives. Without it the sacrifice is only forgetfulness, the way of offering is no better than the way to perdition." In other words, you maintained that we must fight in the ranks or our lives can't count. Possibly! You ought to know—be it said without malice—you who have rushed into one or two places single-handed and come out cleverly, without singeing your wings.[22]

Surprisingly little has been said about this character, although he occupies, as Albert Guerard was first to point out, a most strategic place in the novel's narrative structure.[23] Not only is he the sole audience for the "last word" of the story; he also receives the invitation to act as final judge, final arbiter, and interpreter of the tale. "I affirm nothing," Marlow characteristically declaims; "Perhaps you may pronounce—after you've read" (206). Here Conrad may well be addressing the "ideal reader," a notion which has preoccupied critics from T. S. Eliot to Stanley Fish, but John Feaster on a very different level speculates that the privileged man is none other than Tom Lingard, the sea captain of Conrad's earlier Malayan trilogy, whose last whereabouts were supposedly Europe where he sought new financial backing.[24] Linda Shires eschews such a literalistic search for his identity and instead considers him simply as one more important voice in the Bakhtinian play of Conrad's story, one perhaps meant to complement Stein's.[25]

The shortcoming of these approaches—literalistic source hunting on one hand, theoretical sophistication on the other—is that both avoid the most evocative and concrete information Marlow provides about the privileged man: his clear articulation of the white man's burden. This individual proclaims, rather unambiguously, both imperialism and racism. And he does so histrionically, with "the firm conviction in the truth of ideas racially our own, in whose name are established the order, the morality of an ethical progress" (206). The few critics who have anything to say about the privileged man repeatedly avoid comment on this most blatant aspect of his character. It is maybe just too embarrassing. Stephen Barza acknowledges in a brief note that Marlow chooses this individual as his final confidant because he "has recognized a kindred spirit, one as mentally perambulatory as himself. Both reconnoiter other men's minds like exploring scouts." [26] But if we take this as true, then we must also wonder how far that kinship extends, for the privileged man's racial, imperial convictions are bound to make some of our commonly held perceptions of Marlow more problematic.

Let us suppose Conrad intended the privileged man as an overtly Kipling-esque figure in his narrative. The term "Kiplingesque" is used advisedly but can be justified given the controversy that swirled around Kipling even as Conrad wrote *Lord Jim*. Not only does this character in Marlow's audience sound uncannily like the composer of "Recessional" and "The White Man's Burden"; he also by the same token seems the most appropriate audience for the final Patusan episode, which contains strong thematic echoes of Kipling's early stories. James Dale observes that "Kipling's Indian stories abound in men of Jim's type," [27] but we might go further in suggesting Marlow's tale of Jim is an inscription or commentary on Kipling's themes themselves. First, there is the question of whether Jim is master or captive of Patusan, a query pertinent to Kipling's understanding of colonial administration as a sacrifice; second, the question of miscegenation and "going native" is raised by Jim's liaison with the Eurasian Jewel and his refusal to live among his own people. The latter might bear only minor importance to contemporary readers—indeed Conrad's handling of the Jewel-Jim relationship seems the weakest aspect of the book—but even to such disparate characters as the privileged man and Gentleman Brown, that relationship and what it says about Jim's self-imposed exile from white society becomes a prime interest.

Conrad had taken up these themes before in such works as *An Outcast of the Islands*, *Almayer's Folly*, and "The End of the Tether." [28] But a couple of evoca-tive letters Conrad wrote in the period 1899–1900 suggest Kipling was very much on his mind during the process of composing *Lord Jim*. In December 1899, when the third installment of the novel had run in *Blackwood's*, Conrad wrote to Cunninghame Graham, alluding playfully to God, the Boer War, and Kipling's "Recessional": "Allah *is* careless. The loss of your MS is a pretty bad instance; but look—here's His very own chosen people (of assorted denomi-nations) getting banged about and not a sign from the sky but a snowfall and a fiendish frost. Perhaps Kipling's Recessional (if He understood it—which I doubt) had offended Him?"[29]

Only a year before, in his letter to Zagórska, Conrad had ranked Kipling at the front of English writers. Was Kipling now being reassessed? Perhaps, but we must also allow for the possibility of a letter merely being tailored to the tastes of a familiar audience. Either way, Kipling had Conrad's attention. Maybe more suggestive is this note about Lord Jim (19 May 1900) to David S. Meldrum, the Blackwood editor: "It has not been planned to stand alone. H of D was meant in my mind as a foil, and Youth was supposed to give the note. All this is foolishness—no doubt, the public does not care—can not possibly care—for foils and notes. But it cares for stories and Jim is as near a story as I will ever get. The title will have to be altered to Lord Jim. A tale—instead of A sketch. And yet it is a sketch! I would like to put it as A simple tale A plain tale—something of the sort—if possible. No matter."[30]

Like Gissing, Conrad was driven to write short stories out of financial need. The public's appetite for magazine fiction and the emergence of well-paid writers working primarily in the short story form—preeminent among them Kipling—insured a happy fulfillment of supply and demand.[31] Conrad's comments here reveal his understanding of this popular market, as well as exasperation with a story intended for four installments having mushroomed out of control.[32] That Conrad still wants to call Lord Jim a "sketch" or "A plain tale" is rather humorous. But it also seriously suggests, by alluding to Kipling's first collection of short stories, Plain Tales from the Hills (1888), a frame for interpreting the book, especially for the Patusan episode. No fewer than five of the original Plain Tales are concerned with actual or potential miscegenation: the often-anthologized "Lispeth" as well as "Yoked with an Unbeliever," "Kidnapped," "Beyond the Pale," and "To Be Filed for Reference." The prime thematic vein running through that collection is the disastrous loss of personal identity while serving the Empire far away from home. In the most spectacular instance of such loss, "Thrown Away," an immature youth unable to function in Indian culture by the norms learned in an English boys' school commits suicide, while his army companions subsequently attempt to cover up the truth about his death.

The pattern of congruence between these stories of Kipling's and Conrad's own "plain tale" of Jim might be coincidental. Nevertheless, if Conrad intended the privileged man as a stand-in for Kipling, then that mysterious figure's title gains additional resonance as an inside joke about Kipling as literary superstar, the most "privileged" writer of the moment.

Reading Conrad through Kipling

To begin with, of what other writer, except maybe John Buchan, does Marlow's address in chapter 36 remind us, except Kipling? The privileged man's outlook tallies with Kipling's too perfectly, especially in the depiction of Europeans acting as servants to colonized populations. Is not Jim both "lord" and captive? As Marlow observes, "all these things that had made him master had made him a captive, too" (152). It is a wonderful rhetorical trick. "Giving your life up to them" is how Marlow quotes the privileged man. When mastery cloaks itself in the mantle of sacrificial servanthood—much like Jim's career in Patusan—we witness the transformation of ideology into a kind of religion, a transformation which had been achieved first by Kipling. But whereas Kipling's refrain in "Recessional" yokes the idea of imperial humility with divine blessing,

> Lord God of Hosts, be with us yet,
> Lest we forget—lest we forget!

his "White Man's Burden" makes even more clear the view that world domination consists not of taking, but of giving, and that real mastery is gained only in relinquishing one's own freedom. Ingenious, indeed devious argument, this— but argument that electrified England when it came into print, addressed to the United States in regard to its recent acquisition of the Philippines. The advice came from an established member to a newcomer in the club of imperial nations:

> Take up the White Man's burden—
> Send forth the best ye breed—
> *Go bind your sons to exile*
> *To serve your captives' need;*
> *To wait in heavy harness*
> *On fluttered folk and wild—*
> Your new-caught, sullen peoples,
> Half devil and half child.
>
> Take up the White Man's burden—
> In patience to abide,
> To veil the threat of terror
> And check the show of pride;
> By open speech and simple,

An hundred times made plain,
To seek another's profit,
And work another's gain.[33]

[my italics]

What obsessed Conrad in *Lord Jim* and its shorter "foil," *Heart of Darkness,*
also completed in 1900—was precisely "the idea" of imperialism proposed by
Kipling. The idea promised to dispel doubts about England's world mission
by its compound of mystical belief and language of servanthood. " 'We want
its strength at our backs,' " says the privileged man. " 'We want a belief in
its necessity and its justice, to make a worthy and conscious sacrifice of our
lives' " (206). Words themselves, Marlow admits, are tenuous means of form-
ing a bulwark against the uncertainties of existence, but they "also belong to
the sheltering conception of light and order which is our refuge" (190). In
this way Marlow suggests the fiction of imperial destiny is nevertheless one
which palliates, even glorifies, the sordid business of carving out an empire.
At the outset of *Heart of Darkness* Marlow meditates on the Romans who conquered Britain, comparing them to their modern-day counterparts, the British
imperialists:

> What saves us is efficiency—the devotion to efficiency. But these chaps
> were not much account, really. They were no colonists; their adminis-
> tration was merely a squeeze, and nothing more, I suspect. They were
> conquerors, and for that you want only brute force—nothing to boast
> of, when you have it, since your strength is just an accident arising from
> the weakness of others. They grabbed what they could get for the sake
> of what was to be got. It was just robbery with violence, aggravated
> murder on a great scale, and men going at it blind—as is very proper for
> those who tackle a darkness. The conquest of the earth, which mostly
> means the taking it away from those who have a different complexion or
> slightly flatter noses than ourselves, is not a pretty thing when you look
> into it too much. What redeems it is the idea only. An idea at the back
> of it; not a sentimental pretence but an idea; and an unselfish belief in
> the idea—something you can set up, and bow down before, and offer a
> sacrifice to.[34]

The end of this oft quoted passage suggests the "idea" is nothing less than an
idol of our own creation, invested with the certainties and dogmas of religion.
Indeed, John Buchan's spokesman for empire in *A Lodge in the Wilderness*
(1906), the "intelligent millionaire" Francis Carey, calls the imperial mission

a "faith" and "a religion."[35] Alan Sandison observes that Buchan viewed the Empire as "the means whereby man in his secular condition could be integrated with his spiritual ideal,"[36] and it would seem Marlow takes a similar view. Even though Marlow sees through the human artifice of the idea, he willingly grants it authority. He acknowledges rather matter-of-factly the human need—and power—to create new gods in place of the old one.

Avrom Fleishman, one of the numerous commentators on the idolatrous "idea" proposed in this passage, suggests it can be understood entirely in terms of a distinction between rapacious conquerors (Kurtz, naturally, among others) and caring colonists such as Jim and Lingard.[37] On inspection, however, Fleishman's argument does not hold up. Just moments earlier, Marlow describes the initiators of Britain's rise to power, pirates including Francis Drake who guaranteed their place in history by preying on another empire's treasure ships: "Hunters for gold or pursuers of fame, they all had gone out on that stream, bearing the sword, and others the torch, messengers of the might within the land, bearers of a spark from the sacred fire" (492). To the English, knights; to the Spanish, just one more species of ruthless marauder, out to steal what had already been stolen. In buccaneers like Drake, parasitic savagery is elevated to heroism and becomes the means to knighthood; and in *Lord Jim* this scenario of one white man preying on another's empire is reenacted, but without the benefit of a sacred fire to light it up. Gentleman Brown, himself a pirate, contemplates "stealing the whole country. Some confounded fellow had apparently accomplished something of the kind—single-handed at that" (223). If there is any single thrust to Conrad's treatment of the idea, it is the power of that idea to transform what are otherwise banal, low, purely mercantile activities. In Stein's case, Marlow suggests such a transformation is chosen to evade the kinds of stark, amoral vocabularies of a guano-hunting Chester, or a Brown, who revels in his dirtiness: "Stein was the man who knew more about Patusan than anybody else. More than was known in the government circles, I suspect. I have no doubt he had been there, either in his butterfly-hunting days or later on, when he tried in his incorrigible way to season with a pinch of romance the fattening dishes of his commercial kitchen. There were very few places in the Archipelago he had not seen in the original dusk of their being, before light (and even electric light) had been carried into them for the sake of better morality and—and—well—the greater profit, too" (133-34).

Stein, like the privileged man, simultaneously shows toward Jim sympathy and patronizing judgment; both men see in Jim the mirror of their younger selves.[38] Stein most immediately diagnoses Jim's case because he was once like him: "romantic" (129). Here the essence of that romantic spirit is explained.

It includes the wish to do good, and in the case of Patusan, to bring a "better morality." But Stein, like Marlow, has grown into an ironist who sees the motive for what it is: profit. If Kurtz's original notions about "humanizing, improving, instructing" Africans (535) are in part subverted by an uncontrollable, raging appetite for ivory, Stein on the other hand has successfully negotiated the opposing crosscurrents of desire and restraint: this is one of the things that swimming in "the destructive element" means. (It also means ditching altogether cumbersome moral vocabularies.) And so Marlow perceives with a divided mind that Jim's work on Patusan means no one single thing. Again the narrative becomes an exploration of, a circling around, critical events, the meanings of which multiply in direct relation to innumerable perspectives. The Patusan episode, then, turns out to be just as difficult to describe as the *Patna* episode, as Marlow's narrative reveals following his letter to the privileged man. Marlow cannot make up his mind which interpretive language to use in describing Jim's activity on the island.

What is that activity to Jim himself? Solely the means to reestablish his heroic, chivalric image of himself as good and brave in the wake of the jump from the *Patna*: "He had the gift of finding a special meaning in everything that happened to him" (185). He takes for granted the goodness of the work itself— his rule over dependent natives, his expression of the white man's burden: "I am responsible for every life in the land" (240). As Marlow observes, "Now and then . . . a word, a sentence, would escape him that showed how deeply, how solemnly, he felt about that work which had given him the certitude of rehabilitation" (152).

Stein, however, willing to indulge Jim's need to salve a tortured conscience—sees the work in a wider frame: it serves the pragmatic purpose of shoring up a troubled part of the trading empire. Whenever we get too enamored of Stein's cultured mystique, Marlow throws in a reminder of Stein's public character—for just as Kurtz achieves godlikeness through firepower, so Jim enforces his short-lived rule in Patusan by the same means, supplied by his powerful Dutch sponsor. "Stein . . . had obtained from the Dutch Government," Marlow observes, "a special authorisation to export five hundred kegs of it [gunpowder] to Patusan" (220).

What does Jim's activity mean to Jewel? Abandoned originally by her father—who in all likelihood seems to have been Stein himself[39]—and left to the dubious care of a stepfather, Cornelius, Jewel is again shattered when Jim's public activity as Patusan chief leads to yet another abandonment.

And to the Patusan inhabitants? Tuan Jim's rule will deteriorate into a bloody massacre far worse than any they suffered in their own tribal warfares prior to his coming: "Some remarked that it was worse than in Sherif Ali's war. Then many people did not care; now everybody had something to lose" (238).

And finally, to Gentleman Brown, the most subversive voice in this chorus, the work of Jim is pure exploitation, something he understands perfectly, nothing less than "stealing a country," a theft made hypocritical by appeals to "responsibility," the defense of "innocent lives," and "duty" (233). In Marlow's story, Brown is not only the final interviewed source but also the unmasker who, like Marlow in *Heart of Darkness*, exposes the inherent rapacity at the heart of the benevolent imperial "idea."

Marlow's continually split consciousness between the noble "idea" of the imperial torch on one hand and the material greed and destruction lighting it on the other recurs throughout both *Lord Jim* and *Heart of Darkness*. The consequence of this vision is an endlessly ruminative bad conscience. Marlow is partly sympathetic to Jim's own case of guilt because he himself suffers from it, but we must discriminate the very different kind from which he suffers. Marlow does not have the excuse of seeing with naively "unconscious eyes," of living still in an atmosphere of "undisturbed rectitude" (208). The final episode of the novel reveals that quite unlike Jim, who is trapped within a narrowly individualistic moral frame, Marlow clearly sees the wider imperial and commercial frame within which Jim has worked out his own private "redemption" and "sacrifice," a frame which throws the very significance of Jim's salvation into doubt. Jim can feel only the particular trespass of his own soul—the breaking of the naval code in abandoning the *Patna*. (Ironically, his obsession with his own guilt about breaking an honor code obscures real recognition of the hundreds of lives that might have been lost; later, when Dain Waris and his men are butchered, Jim seems not so much to grieve as to acknowledge the tragedy as predetermined. When considering Jim we are in the presence of a supercharged Augustinianism.) And Jim is as sanguine in his expectation of redemption as he is narrow in his conception of sin, uncritically seizing on the Patusan opportunity as the means of salvation, never doubting it right down to the final act of suicide martyrdom.

But Marlow sees things whole, which means he cannot deny the various sources for his story. The resulting multiple vocabularies interpret Jim's work in Patusan as alternately destructive, imperial, egotistical—external voices that demand to be heard along with Jim's internal one, the unchanging voice of youth that sees all of history building toward his own particular martyrdom. Jim's voice is that of individual Christian conscience seeking redemption; Marlow's story is that of collective British liberal guilt beginning to identify the spectacular gap between its Victorian ideals of Christian duty and its ineradicable lust for booty. Maybe even more importantly, Marlow begins to recognize through the Patusan story that the imperial mandate, even in its most benign and altruistic form, is an ambiguous one. Jim's crisis of conscience is one-dimensional and relatively simple: how does one make up for breaking a cardinal rule? Marlow's crisis, however, is endlessly complex, and ever more compelling on further rereadings of the novel, because it takes as its starting point not the question of individual conformity to prescriptions, but rather the troublesome matter of how the activities of white adventurers like himself and his audience can possibly serve the goal of human solidarity. Jim asks, how can I be saved? Marlow asks, how can we live together?

Sometimes Marlow tries to pull together by the force of his rhetoric the irreconcilable sides of his vision. On the early history of Patusan, and certainly anticipating the young Stein's arrival there, Marlow reflects in a brilliant passage (matched perhaps only by Nick Carraway's musings on the gangster-visionary Gatsby):

> The seventeenth-century traders went there for pepper. . . . For a bag of pepper they would cut each other's throats without hesitation, and would forswear their souls, of which they were so careful otherwise: the bizarre obstinacy of that desire made them defy death in a thousand shapes—the unknown seas, the loathsome and strange diseases; wounds, captivity, hunger, pestilence, and despair. It made them great! By heavens! it made them heroic; and it made them pathetic, too, in their craving for trade. . . . To us, their less tried successors, they appear magnified, not as agents of trade but as instruments of a recorded destiny, pushing out into the unknown in obedience to an inward voice, to an impulse beating in the blood, to a dream of the future. (138–39)

Nowhere does Marlow better express the pull between his maudlin sentimentalism, and corroded cynicism—and the desire to fuse them. But what is perhaps most striking about the privileged man's response to Marlow's tale is that he refuses the dualistic choices Marlow presents in depicting Jim, the split vocabulary of greed versus romantic honor. The privileged man utterly excludes mention of material or economic motives at the back of Stein's dropping Jim in Patusan; and he views Jim's efforts in Patusan to regain his lost honor as illusory and bound for disappointment. Both extremes in Marlow's description of Jim's case are negated. We could say the privileged man finds the allegory of money-grubbing beetles and romantic butterflies inadequate.

Instead, the privileged man's judgment on Jim falls from another quarter. One would think he would approve of the work Jim accomplishes on Patusan.

After all, listened to with a selective ear, enough of Marlow's account supports a positive and conventional reading of Jim's reign, a point of view maybe suggested in one Edwardian sociologist's plea that "the higher nations . . . regard themselves as possessing a high and important trust for common humanity to protect and guide and inspire the lower races."[40] According to Marlow, Jim "had proved his grasp of the unfamiliar situation" (159), quickly establishing his superiority above warring factions, defeating Sherif Ali and thereby becoming the "virtual ruler of the land" (166). And Marlow blesses this consolidation of the white man's rule: "this power that came to him was the power to make peace. It is in this sense alone that might so often *is* right" (159). Moreover, Jim's triumph is unmistakably linked to his whiteness—"Patusan was recovering its belief in the stability of earthly institutions since the return of the white lord" (236)—and the people readily accede to that man's greatness, even by their tributes to chieftain Doramin's son. Marlow chimes in with these voices: "Of Dain Waris, his own people said with pride that he knew how to fight like a white man. This was true; he had that sort of courage—the courage in the open, I may say—but he had also a European mind. You meet them sometimes like that, and are surprised to discover unexpectedly a familiar turn of thought, an unobscured vision, a tenacity of purpose, a touch of altruism" (160).

This might be Cooper describing Chingachgook. Taken together, these voices seem to confirm nothing less than the privileged man's argument for "a firm conviction in the truth of ideas racially our own, in whose name are established the order, the morality of an ethical progress" (206). And as in Kipling's doctrine in "Recessional" and "The White Man's Burden," the profit motive is neatly excluded from this altruistic strand of imperial ethical progress. Recall Orwell's telling remark "that Kipling does not seem to realise, any more than the average soldier or colonial administrator, that an empire is primarily a money-making concern. Imperialism as he sees it is a sort of forcible evangelising. You turn a Gatling gun on a mob of unarmed 'natives,' and then you establish 'the Law,' which includes roads, railways and a courthouse."[41]

The privileged man's objection to Jim is not that he has refused to shoulder the white man's burden, but rather that in doing so he has made the unforgivable mistake of isolating himself from other white men. We have already noted that both Kipling's and Conrad's colonial fiction is full of characters who either go mad, commit suicide, or go native—or some combination of the above—as a result of such isolation. Jim has incorrectly identified himself *with* the people of Patusan, growing much too enmeshed, even to the degree of taking a lover from among the local population, Jewel. This adds yet another meaning to the privileged man's harsh racism: "'giving your life up to them' (*them* meaning all of mankind with skins brown, yellow, or black in colour), 'was like selling your soul to a brute'" (206). Furthermore, when he states "'that kind of thing' was only endurable and enduring when based on a firm conviction in the truth of ideas racially our own" (206), he suggests that the burden should not be enjoyed, but only tolerated out of an unsentimental and ironclad sense of duty. Jim's notion that he has redeemed himself, argues the privileged man, will sour once he realizes the society that matters, white society, knows nothing of that redemption. And finally, the privileged man seems a little irritated that Jim should be having so much fun. The dutiful and sober paternalism that can be maintained only by keeping oneself apart from the "lower races" has broken down in Jim's case. When the privileged man argues "we must fight in the ranks or our lives can't count" (206), he speaks rather plainly about Jim's refusal to rejoin white society. One can serve the empire in remote and dangerous places, goes the argument, but it is quite another matter to cut oneself off intentionally from the imperial community and get spiritually attached to the locals. That egotism the privileged man finds intolerable, and Marlow seems to rub salt in the wounds by his response in defense of Jim: "of all mankind Jim had no dealings but with himself, and the question is whether at the last he had not confessed to a faith mightier than the laws of order and progress" (206). Call it love; call it taboo love. Jim no longer needs white civilization to guarantee his identity. Imperialism requires the cohesion of the white community, especially white male bonding, and in that imperial credo by which the privileged man lives, Jim has broken the prime directive.

One other strand in Marlow's narrative bears out this reading: the episode where Marlow tries to talk Jim—unsuccessfully—into leaving Patusan. Two years after dropping Jim off the island's coast, Marlow goes back as Stein's emissary, this time with the task of presenting Jim with Stein's payment, "the house and the stock of trading goods" (151), and of asking him whether he would like to return to civilization. Marlow assumes here that Jim will end his isolation, but instead Jim shouts, "Leave! For where? What for? To get what?" (151). Jim's choice in making exile permanent demonstrates his social allegiances. To the privileged man, that choice can only be interpreted as an affront, a demonstration of his refusal to "fight in the ranks." But even more galling to the privileged man is Marlow's suggestion that "Perhaps, indeed, nothing could touch him [Jim], since he had survived the assault of the dark powers" (151). Unlike Kurtz, who did not survive such an assault, but who caved in according to Marlow to the "unspeakable rites" and "unlawful" ways of the local African population,[42] Jim has managed to maintain his identity in Patusan's surroundings through sheer personal willpower and imagination.

The enduring problem raised by Marlow's choice of the privileged man as the final audience and judge is simply this: why a man with such an overtly racial and imperial perspective? In his appeal to him, it would seem Marlow grants him just as much authority as is given to Stein, whose gnomic and dominating presence exactly in the middle of the book has been noted so often. Like Stein, this individual seems at one level to personally identify with Jim, and like Stein, he has retired from the life of adventure, viewing Jim's youth and energy with a kind of wistful nostalgia.

Maybe more importantly, like Marlow, the privileged man seems to be a writer, but one who now lives strictly on his store of memories, whose "wandering days were over. No more horizons as boundless as hope, no more twilights within the forests as solemn as temples, in the hot quest of the Ever-undiscovered Country over the hill, across the stream, beyond the wave. The hour was striking! No more! No more!—but the opened packet under the lamp brought back the sounds, the visions, the very savour of the past—a multitude of fading faces, a tumult of low voices, dying away upon the shores of distant seas under a passionate and unconsoling sunshine. He sighed and sat down to read" (205). Radically unlike Stein—whose words convey a detached twentieth-century ironic sensibility, in demeanor clinical and therapeutic, in language more like a playful swami—the privileged man holds Jim accountable exactly because Jim has violated conventional Victorian codes of behavior inherent to white imperial ideology. In fact, in this respect the privileged man epitomizes Marlow's initial audience. "The listeners," Michael P. Jones writes, ". . . are probably very much like the ones Conrad might imagine reading the story in *Blackwood's*. . . . We may assume this audience's values to be commercial, nationalistic, and perhaps colonialistic."[43] Jones notes further the similarity between this audience and the internal audience in *Heart of Darkness* that is given distinct professional identity: the unnamed frame narrator of Marlow's tale, the Director of Companies, the Lawyer, the Accountant. In both narratives, "Marlow is a part of his audience's world and yet both his sentimentality and his . . . esoteric moral consciousness tend to isolate him in personal reflections which his listeners frequently do not seem to understand."[44]

Orwell remarks that Kipling's "admirers are and were the 'service' middle class, the people who read *Blackwood's*."[45] Thus by choosing a man who seems rather typical rather than untypical of this identical readership, Marlow makes plain his allegiances to this group. These are his people. And yet. That "yet" becomes ubiquitous whenever we attempt to pierce the Marlovian mask for the obscure Conradian face. Even the possibility—which I think a good one— that the privileged man represents Kipling's point of view in the novel does not provide a point of entry into the text that will solve its mysteries. Like efforts to locate in Stein a kabbalistic key to the book's central wisdom, efforts to extract from the privileged man some clue that will definitively interpret the story are bound to fail. If anything, Marlow reveals the "privileged" perspective in chapter 36 to be a limited perspective—like all the others. The parroting of Kipling's popular racial, imperial ideology leaves out too arbitrarily the economic factor of the equation, one of which Marlow is perfectly aware, and denies too completely Jim's personal triumph. This is maybe why Marlow makes the point to him in the cover letter that Jim was "overwhelmed by his own personality" (207); that is a point to which the privileged man has not so far proven amenable. And the fact that Gentleman Brown is Marlow's prime source for the final installment suggests a destabilizing and unmasking perspective to be essential in correcting the "privileged" point of view.

Who has the last word? Marlow's quest for the final say, the last word on Jim's case, denies the possibilities of a last word.[46] Brown is the final source for the story, the privileged man the final judge, Marlow the final storyteller (although who is the ghost who tells us Marlow sent the privileged man the final installment—the privileged man himself?)—but the result is that none have the last word in any final sense.

And yet. The idea that Conrad's best work is endlessly dialogic, or polyphonic, has become a truism applied not only to Conrad but to a host of other novelists, and anyway, the Bakhtinian phrase does not tell us much. It provides a grid for the interpretive task, but does not constitute the actual work of interpretation. In Marlow's case, we apprehend that convictions about imperial conquest evolve to a level differentiated from either solipsism or relativism. Marlow is caught in the wish to bow down to an ideal of the white man's burden with its implicitly imperial and racist components, but strong enough to resist the impulse too completely, wise enough to notice the contradictions inherent in even the most benevolent expressions of the ideal.

Marlow stops short of outright condemnation; he finds expressions of doubt more comfortable than any declarations of certainty. An incident toward the end of *Heart of Darkness* is suggestive. In a scene of indescribable chaos, the boat with Marlow and Kurtz aboard has just pulled away from the riverbank at Kurtz's station. Marlow recollects:

I pulled the string of the whistle, and I did this because I saw the pilgrims on deck getting out their rifles with an air of anticipating a jolly lark. At the sudden screech there was a movement of abject terror through that wedged mass of bodies. "Don't! Don't you frighten them away," cried someone on deck disconsolately. I pulled the string time after time. They broke and ran, they leaped, they crouched, they swerved, they dodged the flying terror of the sound. The three red chaps had fallen flat, face down on the shore, as though they had been shot dead. Only the barbarous and superb woman did not so much as flinch, and stretched tragically her bare arms after us over the somber and glittering river.

And then that imbecile crowd down on the deck started their little fun, and I could see nothing more for smoke. (588)

It is a parable of liberal Edwardian responses to the imperial mandate. Marlow can blow the whistle, but the thought of commanding the pilgrims down below on his vessel to stop shooting never crosses his mind. Liberals find the thud of bullets on "native" flesh distressing—but ultimately no less inevitable than do Kipling and kin.

PRIVATE GARDENS,

PUBLIC SWAMPS

HOWARDS END AND THE REVALUATION
OF LIBERAL GUILT

"I know that personal relations are the real life, for ever and ever."
HELEN SCHLEGEL,
in *Howards End*

"We merely want a small house with large rooms, and plenty of them."
MARGARET SCHLEGEL,
in *Howards End*

"Reality" and "realty" derive from the same root word, so it is not too surprising that the Schlegel sisters' premium on personal relationships, the "real life" named by Helen, reveals itself to be equally preoccupied with the business of real estate. Of what, after all, does the "real life" consist? Friendships or property?

The question is never put quite that baldly, and Forster endows it with equally serious, equally comic proportions. But such a query goes to the heart of what has been variously called the liberal "dilemma," "paradox," or, as pejoratively denoted by Marxist critics, "the liberal confusion." [1] Through Margaret and Helen, Forster succeeded in delineating the most comprehensive picture of liberal guilt in this century. As an Edwardian, however, Forster was by no means alone in this obsessive desire to reconcile liberalism's commitment to the life of the spirit, if you will, with the competing tugs of power and property. Forster's contemporaries—journalists such as Masterman and Hobson, and novelists such as Gissing and Conrad—share with him the view that social, collective guilt coalesces around the two prime issues of imperial power abroad and growing urban poverty at home. George Gissing's fiction repeatedly examines the plight of the domestic underclass and its effect on intellectuals, while Conrad contemplates most thoroughly the effects of imperialism through the mind of his primary thinker, Marlow. Yet of the Edwardians, it was chiefly Forster who perceived how intimately bound up these two concerns actually were. And it was Forster who wove that sense of interdependence into the fabric of a single literary masterpiece.

The plight of this world's Leonard Basts is connected with the activities of the Henry Wilcoxes: the Schlegels cannot help but see that. Even more importantly, Forster noticed how the privileged vantage point of liberal intellectuals, while it enabled them to see "things whole," still compromised and complicated their disinterestedness: for is the privileged vantage point not dependent on and allied with the very power that liberals mistrust? And corollary to this, is that same power not in part responsible for a socially abhorrent and all too visible poverty? The Schlegel sisters are painfully aware of this condition—at least at the novel's outset.

The unresolved tension of *Howards End* has been stated on many occasions—and, one should note, stated rather gleefully—by critics on both left and right. How can liberal intellectuals reconcile the private activities of aesthetic contemplation, friendships, spiritual formation, with a broader concern for the public and social interest? That is the defining problem for Lionel Trilling's understanding of the "liberal imagination," and, in discussing *Howards End*, he illuminates that question's vital historical importance:

The 18th century witnessed such a notable breaking up of religious orthodoxies and such a transference of the religious feelings to secular life that it is surely the true seed-time of the intellectual as we now know him. One observes in the social circles of the first generation of English romantic poets the sense of morality, the large feelings of intellectual energy that had once been given to religion.

This moral and pious aspect of the intellectual's tradition is important. Intellectuals as a class do not live by ideas alone but also by ideals. That is, they must desire the good not only for themselves but for all, and we might say that one of the truly new things in human life in the last two centuries is the politics of conscious altruism.[2]

Thus liberal intellectuals, if perceived within this historical tradition, are defined as individuals who seek to integrate their private and public selves. To a degree, this is exactly what the tension between the pursuit of the "real life" and of realty is about in *Howards End*. As numerous critics have noted, the novel is preoccupied with houses, interiors, and real estate;[3] discussion of values in *Howards End* is never rarefied or pursued apart from a material context of physical living space. It is as if Stein's central query in *Lord Jim*, "How to live?" were converted to that of "Where to live?" and Forster succeeds in treating the question with utter seriousness, without banality. Real estate permeates the novel: personal relations never proceed within a material vacuum. Seen this way, a preoccupation with surfaces, houses, and the substance of material living hardly means *lack* of moral penetration—the famous charge Virginia Woolf brought against the Edwardian writers; instead, that preoccupation, at least in Forster's hands, becomes a *strategy* of moral penetration.

Forster, of course, consciously allied himself with a passing intellectual and literary generation. "I belong," he said, in one of his famous quips, "to the fag-end of Victorian liberalism."[4] By calling himself a dinosaur, Forster perhaps thought he could escape the charge of being one. But from our present vantage point it seems he wrote himself off prematurely. For why should such an "old-fashioned" narrative—one seeking, in Forster's words, the channel whereby "private decencies can be transmitted to public affairs"[5]—still maintain its grip on us?

Quite simply, the novel vitally engages present debates about the future of liberalism itself. My approach to the book emphasizes the specific texture of Edwardian liberalism, but ends with reflections on how the novel addresses our situation. Particularly interesting is the way this novel serves as a gloss on the contemporary framing of pragmatic liberalism by philosopher Richard Rorty. Rorty, himself much preoccupied with this question of private and public value, ascribes to imaginative narrative and the activity of reading it the highest rewards possible; yet *Howards End* can itself be read as a criticism of Rorty's influential brand of neoliberal thought.

What is especially ironic is that Rorty, who holds Trilling in the highest regard, should disavow the very endeavor that shapes Trilling's understanding of the liberal intellectual: the attempt to fuse private and public virtue. Rorty argues in *Contingency, Irony, and Solidarity* that "self-creation" and social justice are incommensurate activities. He speaks about the impossibility of ever uniting self-creation and justice, private perfection and human solidarity, in a single vision.

There is no way in which philosophy, or any other theoretical discipline, will ever let us do that. The closest we will come to joining these two quests is to see the aim of a just and free society as letting its citizens be as privatistic, "irrationalist," and aestheticist as they please so long as they do it on their own time—causing no harm to others and using no resources needed by those less advantaged. There are practical measures to be taken to accomplish this practical goal. But there is no way to bring self-creation together with justice at the level of theory. The vocabulary of self-creation is necessarily private, unshared, unsuited to argument. The vocabulary of justice is necessarily public and shared, a medium for argumentative exchange.

If we could being ourselves to accept the fact that no theory about the nature of Man or Society or Rationality, or anything else, is going to synthesize Nietzsche with Marx or Heidegger with Habermas, we could begin to think of the relation between writers on autonomy and writers on justice as being like the relation between two kinds of tools—as little in need of synthesis as are paintbrushes and crowbars.[6]

If Rorty is right, then what are we to make of the frequently agonized posture of the Schlegel sisters in *Howards End* or the central tension of Forster's authorial voice? If Rorty is right, then all such agonizing is wasted energy. Yet, the activity of reading Rorty through the lens of *Howards End* may prove as informative a task as reading *Howards End* through the lens of Rorty. Especially in his portrayal of Margaret Schlegel, Forster anticipates some of the more privatistic conclusions to which Rorty's theory leads. Margaret, like Rorty, eventually abandons the attempt to articulate a unifying vision for her private and public discourse. And the resulting limitations of her character, I want to argue, have premonitory value in anticipating similar limitations of Rorty's argument.

Forster's novel need not be rescued; it has steadily endured. Yet the tone of much criticism does treat the book, in the spirit of Forster's own wry self-appraisal, as if it were a fossil, an elegiac swan song for an ailing liberal creed. Rorty's pragmatism might be taken to be one more example of this impulse to consign Forster's position to the closet of worn out philosophical postures, for that pragmatism renders any kind of progressivist view of history—crucial for traditional liberalism—naive and any rhetorical articulation of liberalism's philosophical tenets wrongheadedly "foundational." Other, older arguments proposed against the liberalism taking shape in *Howards End* are more familiar. It has become a truism, though one perhaps in need of renewed debate, that World War I effectively shattered for all time liberal humanist conviction. Indeed, the final scene of *Howards End* carries the consciousness of the encroaching "red rust" of suburbia, which also may be read symbolically as the gathering red tide of blood explicitly identified by George Gissing in *The Private Papers of Henry Ryecroft*. Forster himself suggests the tenuousness of his affirmative vision by the novel's end. Other facets of the book, as well, cast doubt on the viability of Forster's liberal affirmation, and we must face these aspects in turn. Liberalism's de facto alliance with imperialism, suggested by Margaret's marriage to Henry Wilcox; liberalism's uncertain response to the plight of the people of the abyss, represented by Leonard and Jackie Bast; and liberalism's less than convincing answer to suburbia, a response couched in nostalgic country-house pastoralism—these features of the Schlegelian outlook do not as a whole impress us with their potency.

So it is that many critics, of practically every ideological persuasion, have perceived the novel as a touching but nonetheless terminal account of flawed liberalism. And yet here it becomes imperative to note: eighty years after the novel's appearance, we find ourselves in a peculiar position relative to a phenomenon usually pictured as enfeebled, ailing, gored by the horns of its own dilemma, or already dead. It seems now that liberalism is not as doddering as either Forster or his critics believed, or at least one can say that liberalism's rivals are all equally bedeviled by disabilities. In fact, the present seems oddly dominated by gloating about liberal democracy's possibilities, although I suspect that this too shall pass.

At any rate, much of the criticism of Forster, in its tacit assumptions about liberalism's decay and death, sounds premature. The time is ripe to take new stock of Forster's novel. The intellectual currents of the moment stand to gain by reconsidering Forster's voice, one which stands implicitly behind Schlegelian liberalism, but often subjects it to scathing interrogation. Maybe this very method suggests Forster's faith in liberalism and its self-correcting potential. Yet part of the problem of reading the book is discovering where Forster's voice separates from Margaret's; the process is much like discerning when Jane Austen's narrator speaks sympathetically through a favorite heroine and when she speaks more critically of her. Certainly it is a game of aesthetic pleasure, but its ethical stakes are never frivolous, for even while giddy in the pleasures of Austen's prose, we feel the bite of her sobriety. Trilling notes,

"For all his long commitment to the doctrines of liberalism, Forster is at war with the liberal imagination."[7]

It was partly this moderation in him which led Trilling to comment even more tellingly: "He is sometimes irritating in his refusal to be great."[8] Forster is a writer of cautionary reflection, not Napoleonic intellectual thrusts, and my treatment of the novel may be accused of the same wavering back and forth. Liberalism, as an attempt to find a middle way, is often characterized by its extreme antagonists as shipwrecking not on the shoals of ambition but rather the sandbar of compromise and mediocrity. But in counterpoint to the common assumption that liberal humanism is but a nostalgic whiff to be experienced in books like this, I assume that the milieu within which *Howards End* takes place is not an endpoint or cul-de-sac. The novel represents not a tombstone of liberal crises, but rather a good place to begin sorting them out. As Bakhtin puts it,

> in the ideological horizon of any epoch and any social group there is not one, but several mutually contradictory truths, not one but several diverging ideological paths. When one chooses one of these paths as self-evident, he then writes a scholarly thesis, joins some movement, registers in some party. But even within the limits of a thesis, party, or belief, one is not able to "rest on his laurels." The course of ideological generation will present him with two new paths, two truths, and so on. The ideological horizon is constantly developing—as long as one does not get bogged down in some swamp.[9]

Situation Comedy or Class Struggle?

Sometimes a text can be grasped anew only if ossified assumptions about it are swept away. In this respect, Trilling's analysis of the novel, still preeminent, needs revision on one crucial point. Most distorting is his insistence that the novel's characters all belong to the middle class. This denial of class differences obscures far more than it illuminates, yet few readers have bothered to question it. The flaccid term, "middle class," made here to encompass at one stroke the poverty-line Basts, the independently wealthy Schlegels, and the rapidly rising Wilcoxes, might be an indisputable label as defined by Trilling: everyone who is neither destitute nor blue-blood royalty. Yet the more we consider the term, the less meaningful it becomes.

There seems to be one reason alone for Trilling's use of that tag: that "the class struggle," as he puts it, "is not between the classes but within a single class." [10] Does the finicky distinction matter? It might—but only if one is attempting to combat some narrow strain of Marxist dogma.

There are good reasons to clear away this misleading nomenclature. First, as already suggested, it is descriptively inadequate. When we ponder the enormous differences in cultural outlook, living space, and habits of the Basts, the Schlegels, and the Wilcoxes, the blanket term "middle class" is rendered empty. Second, Trilling's definition, including as it does people of independently wealthy means, alters beyond recognizable form the term "middle class." Imprecise as the term may be, it has usually had associations with working for your living, as opposed to living off interest. Finally, and most importantly, one hardly needs claim a Marxist pedigree to suggest that Trilling's framing of social relations in this way takes the edge off the actual struggle in the book. There is a struggle—Leonard's—demanding recognition. There is economic oppression; there are possessors, and dispossessed. Although Trilling recognizes the pain underlying the humor—"The situation is sad but comic" [11]—his distinctively reassuring, American propensity to see everybody as middle class projects the novel more as living room situation comedy than as economic war. As a rhetorical tag, the term smooths out disjunctions and erases difference. It declaws the cat, makes Forster too benign.

The claws reappear rather sharply when we give even the most cursory nod in the direction of history. For the Edwardians, the spread of the middle-class label was not what it is today. (Of course for the British, it has never been so.) Far more prevalent was a perception of plutocracy on one hand and a growing abyss on the other. Consciousness of the latter pervades *Howards End* and raises several questions: how does Forster use that term, what is its specific meaning for the Edwardian audience, and, finally, what is Leonard and Jackie Bast's relationship to it?

The existence and characteristics of the "abyss" were impressed on the Edwardian reading public most repeatedly by the Liberal journalist C. F. G. Masterman. In *From the Abyss: Of Its Inhabitants by One of Them* (1902), Masterman conceived the abyss as a general class marker and associated it with slum dwellers' alleged physical characteristics as well as their living space. Today, perhaps, we too easily lose sight of this initial sociological significance, when understanding of the word "abyss," at least since the modernists, more likely conjures generalized notions of spiritual angst, akin to Helen's experience of the "goblins" in Beethoven's Fifth and conveyed by the Forsterian voice as "Panic and emptiness! Panic and emptiness!" [12] The rich, too, experience the abyss, but as Masterman and Forster remind us, theirs is of a different kind.

Masterman had first detailed the features of the abyss in *The Heart of the Empire: Discussions of Problems of Modern City Life in England. With an Essay on Imperialism* (1901). There he delineated the composite for Forster's Leonard Bast, calling him "the New Town type," [13] someone

> physically, mentally, and spiritually different from the type character-
> istic of Englishmen during the past two hundred years. The physical
> change is the result of the city up-bringing in twice-breathed air in the
> crowded quarters of the labouring classes. This as a substitute for the
> spacious places of the old, silent life of England; close to the ground,
> vibrating to the lengthy, unhurried processes of Nature. The result is the
> production of a characteristic *physical* type of town dweller: stunted,
> narrow-chested, easily wearied; yet voluble, excitable, with little ballast,
> stamina, or endurance. . . . Upon these city generations there has oper-
> ated the now widely spread influence of thirty years of elementary school
> teaching. The result is a *mental* change; each individual has been en-
> dowed with the power of reading, and a certain dim and cloudy capacity
> for comprehending what he reads.[14]

The empirical relationship between "stunted" physique and "crowded quar-
ters" is the controlling hypothesis of Masterman's argument. A year later, in
From the Abyss, Masterman describes that tight space more distinctly:

> The three-roomed tenement forms the staple abode of our people, the
> characteristic "home" of the dwellers in the Abyss. In some cases a three-
> storied house cut into layers; in others tenements in a swarming human
> hive of "artisans' buildings;" in the vast bulk four-roomed cottages, of
> which one is let off to a lodger. The number in these must run to mil-
> lions; here is being reared the coming race. Civilization has commenced,
> though in rudimentary form. The oleographs on the wall, the framed
> burial-cards of defunct relatives, the cheap white curtains pathetically
> testify to unconquered human aspiration.[15]

Jack London's *People of the Abyss* (1903), a muckraking, firsthand narrative of
the author's experience living in the East End, asserted Masterman's claims
even more forcefully. After a lengthy and statistic-ridden account of the cubic
feet required to sustain a single human life, London concludes:

> It is incontrovertible that the children grow up into rotten adults, with-
> out virility or stamina, a weak-kneed, narrow-chested, listless breed,

that crumples up and goes down in the brute struggle for life with the invading hordes from the country. . . .

So one is forced to conclude that the Abyss is literally a huge man-killing machine, and when I pass along the little out-of-the-way streets with the full-bellied artisans at the doors, I am aware of a greater sorrow for them than for the 450,000 lost and hopeless wretches dying at the bottom of the pit. They, at least, are dying, that is the point; while these have yet to go through the slow and preliminary pangs extending through two and even three generations.[16]

Together, Masterman and London's accounts of the poor city dweller form the prototype in practically every detail for Forster's own Leonard Bast:

One guessed him as the third generation, grandson to the shepherd or ploughboy whom civilization had sucked into the town; as one of the thousands who have lost the life of the body and failed to reach the life of the spirit. Hints of robustness survived in him, more than a hint of primitive good looks, and Margaret, noting the spine that might have been straight, and the chest that might have been broadened, wondered whether it paid to give up the glory of the animal for a tail coat and a couple of ideas. Culture had worked in her own case, but during the last few weeks she had doubted whether it humanized the majority, so wide and so widening is the gulf that stretches between the natural and the philosophic man, so many the good chaps who are wrecked in trying to cross it. She knew this type very well—the vague aspirations, the mental dishonesty, the familiarity with the outsides of books. She knew the very tones in which he would address her. (90)

Now for his depiction of the Porphyrion Insurance clerk, Forster has been much castigated. Commentators have called Bast "one of the most interesting and least convincing characters in the book," [17] "an inspired guess at an unknown class," [18] and "Forster's one outstanding failure." [19] Peter Widdowson, who accuses Forster of both condescension and ignorance about people like Bast,[20] is especially incensed by Forster's famous disavowal at the beginning of chapter 6: "We are not concerned with the very poor. They are unthinkable, and only to be approached by the statistician or the poet. This story deals with gentlefolk, or with those who are obliged to pretend that they are gentlefolk" (34). Without worrying too much whether Bast has been brought into line with strict standards of literary realism (however those standards may be defined), we can see how carefully Forster relies on contemporary understandings of the abyss to draw his portrait of Bast. Even to the detail of Leonard's death from a weak heart, which we perhaps see too symbolically, Forster's depiction confirms common Edwardian notions about the physical deterioration of the city-dwelling poor. Overlaid on this pattern, there is also much that is reminiscent of Gissing, especially Gissing's proletarian intellectuals who, barely scraping by, manage despite exhaustion to read a little literature in their shortened evenings. Like Gilbert Grail in *Thyrza*, or even Hardy's Jude, Bast has achieved tragic consciousness of his condition. And he is arguably more realistic than many suppose. We might think, in parallel terms, of the university adjunct English instructor. Hopes of finishing the dissertation fade, as he or she signs on to teach one more section of freshman writing. Rent must be paid.

Forster, in his careful description of the Basts' apartment, punctuates both Masterman's and Jack London's observations about the dwellings of the urban poor. The interior of the flat, three rooms railroad style, seems lifted straight out of *From the Abyss* and is fully visualized, down to the kitschy details of "a draped mantelshelf bristling with Cupids" (37). It is "what is known to house agents as a semi-basement, and to other men as a cellar" (36). Forster sums it up as "an amorous and not unpleasant little hole when the curtains were drawn, and the lights were turned on, and the gas-stove unlit" (37).

In the phrase "other men," Forster obviously includes himself. To Widdowson's accusation that Forster is calloused, we can point out that he at least reveals the vantage point from which his observations are made. "Realism" is always an illusion, its effect of objectivity achieved by excluding overt reference to the subjective vantage point and biases of the observer. Therefore, Forster's willingness to reveal his own position vis-à-vis Leonard Bast displays not ignorance of Bast, but in fact necessary recognition that "realism" about Bast is problematic. Forster is undoubtedly guilty of condescension toward Bast; remarks that men of Leonard's "type" show a "familiarity with the outsides of books" seem especially gratuitous and cruel. Yet when Forster comments on Bast's attempts at self-education, he shows not only Leonard's inadequate grasp of Ruskin, but also, and just as pointedly, social critic Ruskin's inability to understand men like Leonard. Forster's implicit criticism of himself seems almost as harsh. In this passage, his identification with Ruskin, verging almost on confession, can be heard:

> Leonard was trying to form his style on Ruskin: he understood him to be the greatest master of English Prose. He read forward steadily, occasionally making a few notes.

"Let us consider a little each of these characters in succession, and first (for of the shafts enough has been said already), what is very peculiar to this church—its luminousness."

Was there anything to be learnt from this fine sentence? . . . Could he introduce it, with modifications, when he next wrote a letter to his brother, the lay reader? For example—

"Let us consider a little each of these characters in succession, and first (for of the absence of ventilation enough has been said already), what is very peculiar to this flat—its obscurity."

Something told him that the modifications would not do; and that something, had he known it, was the Spirit of English Prose. "My flat is dark as well as stuffy." Those were the words for him.

And the voice in the gondola rolled on, piping melodiously of Effort and Self-Sacrifice, full of high purpose, full of beauty, full even of sympathy and the love of men, yet somehow eluding all that was actual and insistent in Leonard's life. For it was the voice of one who had never been dirty or hungry, and had not guessed . . . what dirt and hunger are. (38)

More cruelties ensue, when Forster goes on to describe Leonard's "half-baked mind" (38), his pathetic belief that he could "come to Culture suddenly, much as the Revivalist hopes to come to Jesus" (39). Yet Forster's satire cuts both ways, especially later on in the dinner party (chapter 15), complete with the reading of a paper in typical Bloomsbury style. Forster's criticism savages those who make a pretense of concern about the plight of people like Leonard, all the while deciding how to dispose of family fortunes. That these women imagine themselves having millions to give away makes scant difference; their leisure time to even speculate about such a thing reveals how comfortable they truly are. (Indeed, Margaret and Helen do have enough of a fortune to allow them independent wealth, and Helen attempts to give hers away, in one of the book's most blatant examples of liberal guilt.) The scene reminds us, uncomfortably, that the book is about rich and poor, and that for all their talk, the Schlegel sisters are firmly allied with the former. A middle-class label such as that proposed by Trilling glosses over the fundamental social problem. Just a year before publication of *Howards End*, Masterman had summarized England's distress this way: "Public penury, private ostentation—that, perhaps, is the heart of the complaint." [21]

The Faint Smell of the Abyss: Margaret and Matrimony

The rich get richer, and the poor get poorer. This common cry of Edwardian social critics,[22] who lashed out repeatedly against a swollen plutocracy, is thus implicit as well in *Howards End*. Yet, as Jamie Camplin has observed, the focus on the evils of money became largely an excuse for breast beating and righteous indignation. While the social commentators pointed out that inequity of income distribution had become greater than at any other period of history, "the strange result was that radical politicians and conservative critics of contemporary morality engaged in an obsessive and empty concentration on the evils of modern society."[23] In short, indignation does not necessarily spell thoughtfulness or reform. But even more disturbing in *Howards End* is that these very expressions of remorse seem to vitiate, or to substitute, the possibility of meaningful thought or reform. Here Schlegelian liberalism, of both the Helen and Margaret varieties, deserves the sharpest criticism. If Forster satirizes Ruskin's ability to respond to the urban poor, he is just as damning of the Schlegel sisters themselves.

Helen's shortcomings have been frequently noted, usually in counterpoint to the supposed wisdom and perspicacity of Margaret. The novel begins by exposing this younger sister's foolishness; we see her progressive mind-set co-opted instantly by the Wilcox élan. Hormones triumph over political convictions with ridiculous ease. Later, Helen repeats an even more destructive cycle of infatuation with Bast. "Leonard seemed," Forster wryly observes, "not a man, but a cause" (246). Here we are reminded of the earlier dinner party, where Leonard's case had been pondered in scholastic and comprehensive fashion. It is after Leonard learns he has been ruined by Wilcox's financial advice—advice conveyed by the Schlegels—that Helen offers both herself and her money to Leonard in a dramatic gesture, "not in the spirit of instinctive joy," John Colmer observes, "but 'heroically,' as a sacrificial victim from the class responsible for his ruin."[24] The offer of 5,000 pounds further demonstrates the destructive nature of Helen's pity. She confesses: "I wanted to give him money, and feel finished" (247). A few pages later, Forster abandons his usual humorous lilt for this dagger: "She and the victim seemed alone in a world of unreality, and she loved him absolutely, perhaps for half an hour" (250).

If Forster makes Helen an easy target, Margaret's case is more subtle, both because Forster identifies her with the healing earth mother spirituality of the first Mrs. Wilcox, and also because he so often blends his voice with Margaret's own. Yet disturbing conclusions are in store when we consider the eldest Schlegel at length. Chief among the discoveries is this: for all her talk about connection, Margaret seems rather ill equipped, and not at all predisposed, to connect with people. Early on she observes, "The more people one knows, the easier it becomes to replace them. It's one of the curses of London. I quite expect to end my life caring most for a place" (102). This proves to be accurate foretelling. And Forster is explicit about the principal factor related to this distancing process: the marriage to Wilcox, and the subsequent necessity of acting the proper housewife to a man of Henry's position:

> So Ducie Street was her first fate—a pleasant enough fate. The house, being only a little larger than Wickham Place, trained her for the immense establishment that was promised in the spring. They were frequently away, but at home life ran fairly regularly. In the morning Henry went to the business, and his sandwich—a relic this of some prehistoric craving—was always cut by her own hand. . . . When he had gone, there was the house to look after, and the servants to humanize, and several kettles of Helen's to keep on the boil. Her conscience pricked her a little about the Basts; she was not sorry to have lost sight of them. No doubt Leonard was worth helping, but being Henry's wife, she preferred to help someone else. As for theatres and discussion societies, they attracted her less and less. She began to "miss" new movements, and to spend her spare time re-reading or thinking, rather to the concern of her Chelsea friends. They attributed the change to her marriage, and perhaps some deep instinct did warn her not to travel further from her husband than was inevitable. Yet the main cause lay deeper still; she had outgrown stimulants, and was passing from words to things. (206)

Most particularly, these "things" for Margaret are houses, real houses, and the sense of permanence they impart. Margaret wants a home; from the start she worries incessantly because the flat at Wickham Place is about to be pulled down by a developer in order to make way for smaller, cheaper apartments. The neighborhood is in decline.

Critics have paid too much attention to Margaret's rhetoric about connection and not enough to this primary obsession with realty—the matter largely responsible for her marriage to a man so incompatible as Wilcox. Yet, unless we are clear about her drive for a proper, spacious home, we will be as puzzled as Leavis was about the marriage she chooses. His complaint continues to resound in much of the criticism:

The Wilcoxes have built the Empire; they represent the "short-haired executive type"—obtuse, egotistic, unscrupulous, cowards spiritually, self-deceiving, successful. They are shown . . . as having hardly a re-deeming characteristic, except that they are successful. Yet Margaret, the elder of the Schlegel sisters and the more mature intelligence, marries Mr. Wilcox, the head of the clan; does it coolly, with open eyes, and we are meant to sympathize and approve. . . . Nothing in the exhibition of Margaret's or Henry Wilcox's character makes the marriage credible or acceptable. . . . We are driven to protest.[25]

As Leavis rightly points out, Margaret marries Wilcox with "open eyes." But Leavis, unwilling to follow his own observation to its logical conclusion, finds this marriage inexplicable because he refuses to situate Schlegelian moral values within their threatened urban context.

Forster indicates in the passage above that Margaret knows the distanc-ing between herself and Henry to be "inevitable." Forget the argument about Margaret reforming Henry's views; she knows perfectly well that marrying an imperialist to change him is like marrying an alcoholic to save him. Why, then, does Margaret seek this matrimonial "connection" that she understands will never fulfill the terms of personal connection in any significant sense? Though it may seem harsh to accuse Margaret of making fiscally opportunistic mar-riage vows, it is just as dangerous to ignore altogether, as Leavis does, the economic shrewdness of her decision to wed. Leavis radically underestimates the allure of Wilcox's "success" for Forster's heroine.

The desire to find a safe, permanent home exists, as well, in direct propor-tion to Margaret's need to escape contact with the abyss. This is evident long before her marriage to Wilcox. When Jackie initially comes to Wickham Place, under the alias of Mrs. Lanoline, to inquire about Leonard's missing umbrella, Margaret reflects gloomily after her departure: "The flats, their only outlook, hung like an ornate curtain between Margaret and the welter of London. Her thoughts turned sadly to house hunting. Wickham Place had been so safe. She feared, fantastically, that her own little flock might be moving into turmoil and squalor, into nearer contact with such episodes as these" (89). Margaret is de-pressed, "her thoughts . . . poisoned. Mrs. Lanoline had risen out of the abyss, like a faint smell, a goblin footfall, telling of a life where love and hatred had both decayed" (90). The urban blight of London has begun to invade the pri-vacy of the Schlegel home; Forster dramatizes Masterman's trenchant analysis: "The Abyss has budded."[26] Masterman and London both document the process by which old buildings are knocked down to build suburban houses or cheap apartments, and the subsequent deterioration in which these slapdash dwellings are further subdivided for a landlord's economic gain—until a slum has been created.[27] Fully conscious of this progressing blight, Margaret does all within her power to escape it. Aware that her income is ample, she also knows it is fixed. Even the "islands" of money (47) upon which she and her siblings stand are finite, and, given the skyrocketing values of London real estate (64), she recognizes the slim likelihood of finding living comparable to Wickham Place. How convenient, then, for a Mr. Wilcox to appear.

Fear that one's neighborhood is decaying, and the desire to escape it, dominates Forster's Londoners. For all their differences, in this respect Margaret and Henry are identical. Shortly after proposing to her, Wilcox comments on the house at Ducie Street—where they plan to reside temporarily while a lavish, new country house is under construction. The awareness of a neighborhood change for the worse resembles the descriptions of deterioration made by Masterman and London, although here there is added irony: the so-called bad element comes from that very artistic class with which Margaret and Helen had previously rubbed shoulders. Henry says, "The house opposite has been taken by operatic people. Ducie Street's going down, it's my private opinion" (143). One can practically imagine the consequences about to ensue: badly sung arias disturbing the tranquillity of the neighborhood, suspicious-looking bohemians trailing fumes of tobacco and red wine. Most interesting about the exchange between Henry and Margaret, within which we find this observation, is Margaret's playing to Henry's business sense, her denigration of Helen's lack of such a sense, and the merging of common pragmatic interests: "she was penetrating to the depths of his soul," Forster observes, "and approving of what she found there" (144). And then follows immediately this most cryptic Forsterism, just preceding their first kiss: "And if insight were sufficient, if the inner life were the whole of life, their happiness has been assured" (144).

Such is the synopsis of a conversation dominated almost entirely by observations about real estate. But this is not contradictory, for the "real" life as Forster shows us, and as Margaret would certainly agree, is in fact grounded in realty. As she tells Helen shortly before this scene with Henry: "He has all those public qualities which you so despise and enable all this—" She waved her hand at the landscape, which confirmed anything. "If Wilcoxes hadn't worked and died in England for thousands of years, you and I couldn't sit here without having our throats cut. There would be no trains, no ships to carry us literary people about in, no fields even. Just savagery. No—perhaps not even that. Without their spirit, life might never have moved out of proto-plasm. More and more do I refuse to draw my income and sneer at those who guarantee it" (137–38).

Margaret's thinking is part of what makes Forster's book one of the most insightful and disquieting fictional treatments of the relationship between culture and capital. Moreover, her wish for a grand house providing permanence outside the flux of London's unceasing development unmistakably indicates where the forces of culture and capital can be wed most felicitously. Once inside the house that has been made into a home, all so-called distinctions of inner and outer life fade. "Buildings, and the design of them, the architectural character of a civilization," John Hardy observes, "would seem to be in Forster's mind fundamentally related to its character of manners and morals." [28] Just as the loving description of Howards End is meant to reveal what Schlegel character is about, so a tiny basement apartment conveys the Bast state of mind: dark and cramped. Likewise, the Ducie Street house, when initially let by Wilcox to the Schlegel sisters, is imbued with the imperialist character of its inhabitants on account of the furnishings. Seen through Margaret's eyes, a room can tell us everything we need to know about its owners: "The room suggested men, and Margaret, keen to derive the modern capitalist from the warriors . . . of the past, saw it as an ancient guest-hall, where the lord sat at meat among his thanes. Even the Bible—the Dutch Bible that Charles had brought back from the Boer War—fell into position. Such a room admitted loot" (128). In Margaret's case, the consciousness of rooms of her own means a great deal, means practically everything. Here Woolf's attack on Forster because he dwelt overly much on physical detail ("He has recorded too much and too literally." [29]) can and should be deflected. Take the houses out of *Howards End* and you take the heart out of the novel, for it is this very impulse toward home that puts the liberal conscience to its ultimate test.

This impulse, I would argue, lands Margaret squarely in the arms of Henry Wilcox, whose plenitude of apartments, if not soul, has the potential of re-furbishing. Moreover, this same impulse of Margaret's rather neatly coincides with a distancing from the unsavory odors of the abyss. But the joys of establishing one's private garden are not adequate to dispel awareness of the seething, advancing public swamp, and, as so many critics have pointed out, the novel's concluding hymn to pastoral calm does not drown the more disturbing urban sights and sounds.

The Schlegel response to those sounds is far from reassuring. Helen wants to rescue Bast, discovers her own revulsion, and then attempts to assuage the guilt with an offering of money. By contrast, Margaret, very early on, mainly wants to forget he exists; toward him, disengagement and not connection is her actual if unspoken motto. Forster can have him conveniently killed, but it is very hard to make him quiet. Even the pastoral retreat to the green world of the first Mrs. Wilcox's wych-elms cannot quite do the trick.

The Lure of the Private Refuge

Must the liberal response to Bast be all heart and no head, or all head and no heart, as Forster suggests in this novel? Perhaps Forster only shows us the wrong roads taken. Perhaps a depiction of other, more successful responses is indeed, as Woolf said, better left to legislators than to novelists. Maybe Richard Rorty is right: attempting to integrate private and public value is an abortive enterprise.

Yet a central observation needs to be made about Forster's final resort to the escape-retreat green world of the Howards End estate. Principally, it must be seen as the typical Edwardian gesture to the urban crises of the time: the pastoral escape hatch has exact parallels in Gissing and Masterman. The cry is sounded for the rural virtues. The ideal of the ancient English yeoman is invoked as antidote to modernity, imperialism, and all the attendant crises that made liberals nervous. It almost seems as if these writers, longing for the return of Gabriel Oak, go about composing belated versions of *Far from the Madding Crowd*.[30] Forster's glorification of an organic society is embarrassing stuff: "The feudal ownership of land did bring dignity" (118). And this nostalgic tribute strikingly resembles those of T. S. Eliot and Yeats, who never apologized for linking their ideas of spiritual and aesthetic wholeness with a conservative, authoritarian political order located in a golden past.[31]

What, then, remains at all of Forster's liberal imagination? Commenting on Masterman, from whom Forster seems to derive much of this rosy-hued country gestalt, Samuel Hynes observes:

> The most striking thing about this Liberal's description of the condition of England is its close resemblance to the Tory version. Masterman's account of the loss of national altruism would have pleased Baden-Powell, and his description of suburban idleness and vacuity could have come from any pamphlet of the National Service League. . . . His predictions of increasing lawlessness, his fears of government by violence, and his mood of irresolution and discouragement are all echoed in Tory writings of the time. And so is the note of nostalgia that he struck again

and again—nostalgia for a simpler and better past, when life was decent because men were decent, and men were decent because they were in touch with the English earth. This note one expects from Conservatives, but in a Liberal it suggests a facing in the wrong direction. Masterman could write movingly about the things that moved him, and his deep sympathies for the poor sometimes made him sound like a radical reformer; but his emotions were not directed toward action; they were, apparently, sufficient in themselves. If he wrote feelingly about the urban poor, he wrote in the same mood about the decline of the rural peasantry, and in each case the burden of his argument was not reform but decent feelings.[32]

The last phrase is especially telling in the case of Margaret Schlegel. When she towers in righteous fury over Wilcox for his sexual double standard, her intent is that he gain awareness, consciousness of self (perhaps to see, as the Forsterian-Schlegelian voice puts it later in chapter 43, "the inner darkness in high places that comes with a commercial age" [262]); but she hardly proposes any concrete means of reparation to the disenfranchised Basts, whose lives have been sexually and financially destroyed by Henry. On the same note, Jackie Bast's absolute disappearance after Leonard's death is suggestive. She does not come around to spoil the idyll in the hay field; while the child of Leonard and Helen's union seems to trail clouds of glory, the odors of the abyss clinging to her are not allowed to taint this meadow. The feudal past is glorified, the unified culture signified by Helen's son gets deferred to the future, and the ignominies of the present hour are avoided. Margaret fully intends to block the chance of any more of that unpleasantness. As she tells Helen,

> "Then I can't have you worrying about Leonard. Don't drag in the personal when it will not come. Forget him."
> "Yes, yes, but what has Leonard got out of life?"
> "Perhaps an adventure."
> "Is that enough?"
> "Not for us. But for him." (267)

Is Forster aware of the frequent chill he puts into Margaret's voice? I think so. In spite of all his identification with her, Forster depicts her in such a way that our disquiet is bound to increase upon every rereading of the novel. How, we ask, can her rhetoric of connection be reconciled with such coldness?

I would suggest that true connection, to borrow Margaret's term, means at the very least a willingness to ponder, and not forget, the discontinuities between one's private garden and the public swamp, or as the Edwardians named it, the abyss. The connection can be painful, the process of reconciling private pleasures and the public good difficult. Both Schlegel sisters seem perfectly aware of that tension at the outset of this novel, when a man named Leonard Bast walks into their lives. And this tension results in guilt, the painful awareness of the gap, in Trilling's words, between one's "ideas" and one's "ideals." The guilt necessarily forces an examination of personal circumstances, as well as some kind of personal gesture or response to the discontinuity.

The dangers of hasty response become all too clear in Helen's behavior, and conservative critics of liberalism are fond of pointing to the often destructive action generated by liberal pity.[33] For Margaret, though, a movement beyond liberal guilt seems to be the goal early on, and she accomplishes it by removing herself from the place where class disjunction is most obvious: the city. The quality of this detachment finds uncanny expression in Rorty: "My 'poeticized' culture is one which has given up the attempt to unite one's private ways of dealing with one's finitude and one's sense of obligation to other human beings."[34] This is a long way from Arthur Clennam. Elsewhere, Rorty, like Margaret, acknowledges the financial order upon which the life of the mind and culture rests: "We should be more willing than we are to celebrate bourgeois capitalist society as the best polity actualized so far, while regretting that it is irrelevant to most of the problems of most of the population of the planet."[35] Rorty's argument severs all connection between the private pleasures made possible by bourgeois capitalism—including the luxury to contemplate it from within the academy, as Rorty does—and the public crises engendered by it. Yet Rorty does not want to admit that the sources of one's private pleasures are quite conceivably the sources of other people's pain. Rorty's choice of the word "irrelevant" in the above passage may be most liable to question, as Jeffrey Stout suggests:

If the concession tagged onto the end of this sentence were intended only to say that bourgeois capitalist society is unlikely to solve most of the problems of most of the population of the planet, Rorty is certainly right. But it is hard to see how bourgeois capitalist society could be deemed irrelevant to most of those problems, at least as a source of dramatically important unintended consequences, many of them bad enough to make celebration seem the wrong tack to take. With no more than asides like this to go on, we are left with what seems a dangerously myopic moral vision, apparently blind to relations of interdependence and dominance within the economic world-system from which we derive our wealth, a vision compatible with gross insensitivity to that system's sorrows, injustices, and corrupting influences.[36]

Rorty's position, like Margaret's, finally is meant to relieve us of the burden of guilt—a guilt engendered by seeing systemic connections. And given the supposedly irreconcilable nature of private pleasures and public crises, it should not take us long to realize which distinct order of being, in Rorty's schema, is more likely to be slighted. For once liberalism abandons its traditional concern to integrate private and public modes of discourse, once liberalism becomes exclusively privatistic, it becomes an intellectual game of diminished energy, and then finally altogether unnecessary. Rorty wants to affirm both private ironists and public ethicists as ongoing, necessary, albeit separate, forms of life. But given the pattern of his thinking, it is almost inevitable that the private ironists—the Tibby Schlegels, perhaps?—will prevail.

That Forster interrupts his final scene with awareness of the encroaching London mass suggests he is not entirely happy with this one-sided vision of serene, private, poeticized culture. The conclusion of the book, which remains stubbornly unsettling, indicates crucial truths about Forster's conception of the liberal imagination: that it cannot relax if it is to remain functional; that any attempt to waft away the odors of the abyss is not only intellectually dishonest, but also damaging to one's liberal ideals; and that the spirit of Bast competes with Mrs. Wilcox for the privilege of hovering over the final scene in the meadow. The suggestion of this novel is a simple one. For Forster, the liberal imagination retains its vitality only so long as we are able to revalue, and not dispense with, liberal guilt.

AFTER

LIBERAL

GUILT?

TONO-BUNGAY AND THE TOXIC IMAGINATION

> But there is also another kind of life that is not so much living as a
> miscellaneous tasting of life. One gets hit by some unusual transverse force,
> one is jerked out of one's stratum and lives crosswise for the rest of the time,
> and as it were, in a succession of samples. That has been my lot, and that
> is what has set me at last writing something in the nature of a novel. I have
> got an unusual series of impressions, that I want very urgently to tell.
>
> GEORGE PONDEREVO,
> in *Tono-Bungay*

> The work calls attention to its arbitrariness, constructedness;
> it interrupts itself. Instead of a single center, there is pastiche, cultural
> recombination. Anything can be juxtaposed to anything else. Everything
> takes place in the present, "here," that is, nowhere in particular. Not only
> has the master's voice dissolved, but any sense of loss is rendered deadpan.
> The work labors under no illusions: we are all deliberately playing,
> pretending here—get the point? There is a premium on copies; everything
> has been done. Shock, now routine, is greeted with the glazed stare of the
> total ironist. The implied subject is fragmented, unstable, even decomposed;
> it is finally nothing more than a crosshatch of discourses.
>
> TODD GITLIN,
> "Postmodernism: Roots and Politics"

In H. G. Wells's *Tono-Bungay* various formations of liberal guilt as we have previously described them are summarized, parodied, cut, pasted, and enlarged; in short, they mutate into something quite new while at the same time maintaining recognizable features. The figure of the commercial titan—Merdle, if you will, of *Little Dorrit*—reappears as Teddy Ponderevo, "the symbol of this age . . . the man of luck and advertisement, the current master of the world."[1] Such an assessment comes from his nephew and narrator George in this beautiful wreck of a novel, the young partner and accomplice whose boyhood repeats with uncanny similarity that of Pip in *Great Expectations*. Like Clennam, who abhors the Merdle empire and yet invests the public's capital in it, George helps engineer the fantastically successful Tono-Bungay enterprise while continually assuring us that he finds the enterprise morally and intellectually repugnant. The major difference is that George applies himself with romping abandon to the patent medicine corporation, the radioactive quap expedition, and the building of superdreadnoughts, in that order, and if he has any reservations about what he is doing, those show no sapping effect on his perkiness. The monstrosity of his projects seems to energize and not paralyze him. George Ponderevo pushes to even greater extremities than Eliot's Grandcourt the question of how—or whether—the will is linked to moral knowledge; and as in Eliot's book, the disquieting impression persists that no such link remains anymore. Ponderevo is a highly intelligent eruption of transgressive behaviors.

The novel exhumes and exposes the passion of Gissing and Forster for the alleged organicism of the country house tradition. The country house emerges in *Tono-Bungay* more as museum than living presence; rather than conclude with a mirage redolent of rural bliss, Wells scatters the bones of the decayed country house order at the narrative's beginning.

Finally, Wells takes the matter of collective guilt about imperial conquest most comprehensively developed by his friend Conrad, and reiterates it in the quap episode of his own novel by rather simple means: stealing outright from both *Lord Jim* and *Heart of Darkness*. Wells's parody of the Conradian voyage of discovery and depredation evolves into a slapstick cartoon of random individual murder superimposed upon the portent of mass radioactive apocalypse. The jarring effect of his morbidly comic tone, which permeates most of the book, seems very far from Conrad's solemnity, and well on the way to something more akin to various artifacts in our own museum of pop culture iconography: *Catch-22*, Stanley Kubrick's *Dr. Strangelove*, or a David Lynch film. The characteristic signature of postmodern art is exactly this unsettling disjunction: the more inappropriate the mood to the subject treated, the more effectively postmodern the piece. The work preferably should unsettle, often by treating the horrific not in a tone of dismay but instead high comedy. However, unlike the satire of Swift, which in certain ways anticipates this movement, postmodern expression is not confident, but unsure, continually making us ask as art consumers or readers whether we ought to be laughing.

Although many critics agree that *Tono-Bungay* rates among Wells's best novels, it hardly occupies a distinguished place in the pantheon of English fiction. The history of its critical reception explains why. To begin with, *Tono-Bungay* has often been held hostage to the Wells-James debate about the nature and form of the novel, and has been read merely as an appendage to that debate, which largely bolstered modernist claims to literary ascendancy. This, taken together with various perceptions of Wells as scientist manqué, frustrated visionary social planner, science fiction hack, eccentric Fabian and socialist, and (too) prolific journalist, impedes our ability to see Wells as an important writer, let alone artist.

I would argue that *Tono-Bungay* can be considered the first postmodern novel in the English language, anticipating much of the discussion in the last twenty-five years about postmodern art.[2] One of the particular effects of this sensibility is nothing less than the disappearance of the liberal guilt whose features I have delineated previously. If, for the Victorians, guilt persisted in spite of the death of God, Wells's *Tono-Bungay* manufactures a new intellectual terrain where not only God but also guilt as a subjective mode of moral awareness has approached the vanishing point. For Gitlin, one major feature of the postmodern mind is "a knowingness that dissolves commitment into irony."[3] Utilized in this way, irony arouses major questions, chief among them whether it can serve in an adversarial or oppositional capacity to the larger culture, or rather signals a weak gesture of defeat or accommodation to it. This question engages most of the commentators on postmodernism, from Habermas to Jameson to Graff,[4] and is one especially appropriate to the case of narrator George Ponderevo, whose career calls for a response that is larger than the terms of accommodation or opposition that the novel itself continually wants to outflank.

What are the major implications of this reading of the novel? There is the utterly disjointed narrative ("a succession of samples") as well as the problematic nature of Ponderevo's self, and a consistent disjunction between the book's theme of commodified destruction and the tone Ponderevo takes toward it. Finally, I want to reflect on what the narrator's freedom from the grasp of liberal guilt might signify for us, and will seek the answer to that question in the internal evidence provided by Ponderevo's own commentary.

One aside seems necessary before proceeding. The traditional understanding of voice or character within fictional discourse is viewed as an archaic activity by not a few poststructuralist critics, so even to inquire into the character of Ponderevo might seem odd in light of my argument that this book is best explicated in postmodern terms. Does it make sense anymore at all to speak of selves or unified consciousnesses? The consensus among poststructuralists is that it does not make sense, and for them, terms such as the self should come prepackaged in quotation marks. The "individual," goes the argument, is merely a bourgeois myth masking the way institutional and mass cultural languages shape, control, and circulate through the alleged subject, whether the subject in question be the reader, the author, or a character within the work at hand. In this sense liberal faith in the individual is itself evaporated.

Now it is quite another task than the one outlined here to go into all the implications of this perspective. Such an argument seems to me indispensable for grasping the social nature of language, yet less useful when turned into totalized and rigid dogma. The particular problem for poststructuralist critics is this: how can we claim to rise above the determinist nature of language in order to expose its hidden politics (the "political unconscious") if the subject is, at worst, a misleading category, or at best, radically "decentered"? More telling is that even while the death of "the self" and "the author" have rapidly passed to the status of clichés within the marketplace of poststructuralist theory, heavy reliance on personal assertion, as well as a general resurgence of both the personal essay and autobiography distinguish much poststructuralist practice.[5] If the autonomous self must indeed be put under absolute question in the poststructural dispensation, then on what personal terms can a critic claim to unmask the hidden power networks of language, let alone claim, on any occasion, exemption from the blind spots such networks imply? This dilemma has not been adequately addressed by the poststructuralists—whose confident rhetoric exceeds in its oracular gravity even that of their predecessors, the New Critics. Where the poststructural reading of the self has gone wrong is in its heavy-handed literalizing of a useful caricature of emptied, fragmented selfhood—Tyrone Slothrop of *Gravity's Rainbow* might serve as the prime example of this caricature—and turning the insights of the cartoon into an article of faith. Overused, the intriguing and useful insight becomes trivialized, and after a while, the novelty wears off of categorical claims for the hegemony of untethered discourse, accompanied by repeated proclamations of the death of the author, the subject, and the self.

These reservations need not turn into another form of reaction, though. It should be acknowledged how far such a poststructuralist view of the self goes toward explaining Ponderevo, who as a character is very difficult to describe, who impresses us finally as a continuous eruption of transgressive behaviors. Ponderevo's narrative does find a mappable order of sorts despite the apparent chaos, because this transgressiveness defines both his aesthetic and ethical being: whether he is trying to violate our sense of what to expect in a novel, deceive the consumer public, escape the bond of gravity through flight, or steam down the Thames toward the open sea, Ponderevo exemplifies a life devoted to the breaking of barriers, the seeking of new space. However, it is unclear whether Ponderevo ultimately achieves his desired freedom or rather confirms the domination of instrumental forces of knowledge and power to which he himself is subjected. In spite of his high degree of self-consciousness, at times it appears he is a conduit for the greater social forces which he cognitively disavows or despises. "I still clung to the idea that the world . . . was or should be a sane and just organisation" (113), he says, while noting with dismay his role as operations manager in Uncle Teddy's huge bottling plant. And perhaps his confession on another level can be read as Wells the novelist spoofing Wells the hyperrational social planner.

We will begin with the way he tells his story. He ignores, or claims ignorance of, standard aesthetic prescriptions, and alters narrative form without fully understanding where his own story is going. This book, he announces at the outset, is "something in the nature of a novel." In other words, he tells us, throw out all prescriptive aesthetic formulae before you proceed any further. The words might have come from Lyotard, writing seventy years later: "A postmodern artist or writer is in the position of a philosopher: the text he writes, the work he produces are not in principle governed by preestablished rules, and they cannot be judged according to a determining judgment, by applying familiar categories to the text or to the work. Those rules and categories are what the work of art itself is looking for. The artist and the writer, then, are working without rules in order to formulate the rules of what *will have been done.*"[6]

Formalist Preoccupations and Critical Appraisals of Tono-Bungay

Scholarly treatments of *Tono-Bungay*, usually preoccupied with its structure, reveal more about the evanescence of successive schools of critical thought than about the form of Wells's novel. The dispute about *Tono-Bungay* begins with Henry James, who worked hard to define what the novel, or at least the literary novel, was supposed to be: a work of seamless unity, both on formal and psychological levels. To better understand the feud that divided James and Wells, we can usefully consider Gitlin's summary of the premodernist definition of artistic work. It

> aspires to a unity of vision. It cherishes continuity, speaking with a single narrative voice or addressing a single visual center. It honors sequence and causality in time or space. Through the consecutive, the linear, it claims to represent a reality which is something else, though to render it more acutely than happens in ordinary experience. It may contain a critique of the established order, in the name of the obstructed ambitions of individuals; or it may uphold individuals as the embodiments of society at its best. In either event, individuals matter. The work observes, highlights, renders judgments and exudes passions in their names. Standing apart from reality, the work aspires to an order of beauty which, in a sense, judges reality; lyrical forms, heightened speech, rhythm and rhyme, Renaissance perspective and compositional "laws" are deployed in the interest of beauty. Finally, the work may borrow stories or tunes from popular materials, but it holds itself (and is held, by its audience) above its origins; high culture holds the line against the popular.[7]

Wells's novelistic method in *Tono-Bungay* throws sand in the face of Jamesian assertion. Though there is a single narrator, narrative unity has become a joke, with a continual jerking back and forth between the author-inventor's current activities—writing a novel, building warships, inventing aircraft, etc.—and past history. Of course, a unified consciousness can engage a variety of pursuits, but whether Ponderevo conforms to any standard of psychological realism is an open question; as Wells commented in *Experiment in Autobiography*, "Only one or two of my novels deal primarily with personality, and then rather in the spirit of what David Low calls the caricature-portrait, than for the purpose of such exhaustive rendering as Henry James had in mind."[8] Ponderevo puts in question the whole implicit assumption of the self's coherence or unity. "I must sprawl and flounder" (12) he announces early on. As to the form of the book, and the drawing on disciplines such as science or borrowing from popular media, *Tono-Bungay* violates entirely James's canon of taste. Ponderevo leaps jaggedly between different topics: advertising, class difference, English nobility, house design, technology, science, flight, capitalism, love affairs. This eclecticism bears out Wells's rejection of the Jamesian sensibility, a rejection summarily expressed in *An Englishman Looks at the World* (1914): "We are going to write about it all." Wells went on to scoff: "The novel has been treated as though its form was as well-defined as the sonnet."[9]

Finally, on the matter of high and low culture—or even the distinction between culture and commerce, those problematic antitheses within James's own work—*Tono-Bungay* collapses the distinction entirely, conveying by its very title the dominance of name brands, mass culture, and advertising. The intersection of advertising copy with cultural commentary finds most comic expression when the table of contents of a learned journal, "The Sacred Grove"—containing pretentiously erudite titles about Pater and Brontë (188)—is reproduced as actually appearing sandwiched between ad copy for a liver pill.[10] Wells would keep showing disrespect in the sacred grove of art to the end of his career, holding out against every form of aesthetic prescription and proscription.[11] During World War II, when Shaw circulated a letter requesting that warring nations "respect art objects," Wells refused to sign, saying, "I'd like to keep them but not if they lead to idolatry."[12] The attitude, in key with the formative years spent in a Nonconformist evangelical milieu, also finds affinity with poststructuralist theory that openly challenges efforts to grant literature a special status above "non-literary" discourse.[13] Wells disdains art worship.

From the outset of their mutual acquaintance, James qualified his admiration for Wells's work, reserving judgment, quite often by silence, on the question of his actual skill. Writing to Wells in 1905 about *Kipps*, James said, "the book has, throughout, such extraordinary life; everyone in it, without exception, and every piece and part of it, is so vivid and sharp and *raw*."[14] The razor edge of condescension slips through the compliment. By 1914 James was less subtle and had dismissed Wells in the manner of Woolf; that year, in "The New Novel," James formulated the criticism that still holds for many of Wells's books: too many of them, he suggests, "are so very much more attestations of the presence of material than attestations of an interest in the use of it."[15] From here it was only a short distance to the indignities of ad hominem attack. Wells's *Boon*, published a year later in response, contained the famously nasty portrait of James as "a magnificent but painful hippopotamus resolved at any cost, even at the cost of its dignity, upon picking up a pea which has got into a corner of its den."[16]

Modernism and its critical handmaiden within the academy, New Criticism, amplified and refined much of the Jamesian verdict on Wells's novel. In Walter Allen's words, it amounts to "excellent interludes in an embarrassing muddle"; what it "conspicuously lacks, is, of course, a Commanding Center, the principle making for unity."[17] Premodern and modernist standards merge for Allen; the benchmarks of achievement are James's novels, *Nostromo*, and *Ulysses*, all of which are praised as "highly organized."[18] This assessment consolidated many of the pronouncements made by Mark Schorer, who had employed *Tono-Bungay* as an exhibit for everything a novel ought not to be.[19]

Yet Schorer's essay sets the stage for a number of the most critical inquiries about *Tono-Bungay*: in light of the novel's chaotic structure, exactly what is the relationship between Ponderevo's consciousness and Wells's own? And are we to read the ending of the book straightforwardly or ironically, with Ponderevo steaming full speed out to sea in his latest destroyer? If Schorer's essay belies the New Critical premium put on coherence, craftsmanship, and Jamesian attitude, it also suggests the central features of the novel's structure that in retrospect seem remarkably compatible with the "Junk Heap" school of postmodern pastiche coming into vogue during the sixties.[20] As Ponderevo apologizes in one of his numerous asides, "I've given, I see, an impression that I want to make simply a hotch-potch of anecdotes and experiences with my uncle swimming in the middle as the largest lump of victual" (11). Call it junk heap, call it stewpot, such antimethod turns the Jamesian formula on its head. Schorer sums up the complaints about *Tono-Bungay* to which all subsequent critics have had to respond:

> The novelist flounders through a series of literary imitations—from an early Dickensian episode, through a kind of Shavian interlude, through a Conradian episode, to a Jules Verne vision at the end. The significant failure is in that end, and in the way that it defeats not only the entire social analysis of the bulk of the novel, but Wells's own ends as a thinker. For at last George finds a purpose in science. . . .
>
> But science, power and knowledge, are summed up at last in a destroyer. As far as one can tell Wells intends no irony, although he may here have come upon the essence of the major irony in modern history. The novel ends in a kind of meditative rhapsody which denies every value that the book had been aiming toward. For of all the kinds of social waste which Wells had been describing, this is the most inclusive, the final waste. Thus he gives us in the end not a novel, but a hypothesis; not an individual destiny, but a theory of the future; and not his theory of the future, but a nihilistic vision quite opposite to everything that he meant to represent.[21]

David Lodge began both the dismantling of this formalist reading as well as the novel's literary rehabilitation with an essay in 1966, arguing that the book was a mess, but a purposeful one. It "sins," he said, "deliberately, against most of the Jamesian commandments: it is picaresque, full of apparent digressions in the form both of episodes, and of expository comment."[22] The departure from Jamesian codes now got recast as nerve rather than incompetence. Following Lodge's lead, other critics also suggested the mess did have a certain kind of order, at least thematically, insofar as the Tono-Bungay quack remedy, the quap episode, the trajectory of flight, and the steady advance of bad urban housing creeping like cancer all signify a pattern of rise and fall, decay, or entropy.[23] As Ponderevo himself makes obvious in his discussion of the title, "I have called it Tono-Bungay, but I had far better have called it Waste" (311).

Other aspects of Schorer's formalist reading also came under fire. At bottom there lay his naive confusion of Ponderevo's voice with Wells's own, a presumption based on Wells's presumed inability to create narrators very different from himself.[24] And this confusion led to others, most notably, the error of the intentional fallacy, something rather surprising in a formalist reading. Schorer's assertion that "Wells intends no irony" in the final symbol of the destroyer, that it is "a nihilistic vision quite opposite to everything that he meant to represent," suggests that Schorer wanted to find Wells the melioristic social planner in the place of Ponderevo, and was disconcerted to discover an uneven, even impossible, fit. As numerous critics since have suggested, throughout his career Wells presented alternating methods of the optimistic social planner on one hand and the apocalyptic dystopian on the other. Against Schorer, Lodge asserts, "Wells is fully aware of the irony of making this achievement a destroyer," and furthermore, the novel "is not the only one of his imaginative works which disturbingly questions the meliorism of his public self."[25] So that even if we wish to identify Ponderevo with Wells, we have to decide which Wells we're talking about. We must acknowledge that his popular reputation—as opposed to the academic one—rests primarily on his most pessimistic works: The Time Machine, The War of the Worlds, The Island of Dr. Moreau.

There is one other twist to the evolving literary reputation of Tono-Bungay. Most recently, because of certain stylistic features that are granted special favor in the moment's dominant aesthetic theories, Tono-Bungay has been elevated to increasingly higher status. Not that the novel hasn't always had some defenders. Beginning with a review by Masterman, and picked up later by Bergonzi and Lodge, the novel has been praised as a Condition of England book, in Bergonzi's words, for "the breadth of its panoramic vision, where the sociological imagination works through metaphor and symbol to achieve a memorable analysis—and indictment—of a whole social order."[26] In this frame, aesthetic criteria have always been rendered secondary to the book's importance as a social document. But of late the book has been granted special dispensation because it (1) shows a sophisticated self reflexivity (much writing by Ponderevo about the process of writing itself—shades of metafiction?);

(2) defies conventional realism and modes of representation, however that realism is to be understood; and (3) continually "draws attention to its fictionality."[27] By way of these arguments, J. R. Hammond wishes to turn the novel into a modernist one.

Now focusing on self-referentiality, or granting a novel some cachet by its passing connections with *Tristram Shandy*,[28] are not in themselves sufficient strategies or evidence for treating a work as modern, or even for justifying its evaluation as a work of literature. More crucially, Hammond's effort to save the work by designating it "modern" comes up short because it simply ignores Wells's overtly antiaesthetic, antimodernist posture about novel writing.

Such cautionary skepticism needs equally stringent application to my reading of the novel as a postmodernist one. What follows is an effort to substantiate this claim, by drawing attention to some parallels between *Tono-Bungay* and contemporary postmodern works that begin to emerge during the 1960s. I do not want to belabor the structural similarities; some of those have been already duly pointed out. Rather, by showing how the consciousness of George Ponderevo has moved beyond the grasp of liberal guilt into a new, uncharted realm, I will elaborate the most prominent thematic aspect of postmodernism, one which has been relatively ignored in studies that treat postmodernism almost entirely in terms of formal techniques.

Postmodernity and Comic Violence

The most bizarre effect of reading *Tono-Bungay*, one critic observes, is that "although George . . . says that his theme is 'waste' the tone throughout has been that of buoyancy and achievement."[29] This point becomes all the more noticeable in the context of the novelists I have discussed previously. There is none of Gissing's defeatism, Forster's wistful organicism, the obsessive rumination of Conrad, or even the muted victories attempted earlier by Dickens and Eliot. Social change is focused in the lens of all these writers, but not without profound disquiet and reservation.

Then along comes Wells's Ponderevo, who jumps into the twentieth century with furious gusto, projecting a radically new voice in fiction. It is not that a spirit of indomitable jauntiness had not been seen before; that quality is endemic to the picaresque. But never before had that spirit been coupled with the magnitude of destructive capability and equally powerful reflection embodied in a character such as Ponderevo. It is as if Wells, in the manner of Pip ripping down the heavy draperies of Miss Havisham's chambers, decided to start all over again, by going one step further and blowing the whole house down. For at the outset of *Tono-Bungay* he puts away forever the kind of house so central to the fictional strategy and cultural goal of his contemporaries' work. That house, longingly asserted as the aim in Forster's and Gissing's novels, marks by contrast the beginning point of *Tono-Bungay*, its legitimacy promptly demolished. Ponderevo sweeps the stage clear at the outset, making plain that his novel belongs to the future, not the past. He does this by presenting the estate and its residents as dying grotesques:

> In that English country-side of my boyhood every human being had a "place." It belonged to you from your birth like the colour of your eyes, it was inextricably your destiny. Above you were your betters, below you were your inferiors. . . . Head and centre of our system was Lady Drew, her "leddyship," shrivelled, garrulous, with a wonderful memory for genealogies and very, very old, and beside her and nearly as old, Miss Somerville, her cousin and companion. These two old souls lived like dried-up kernels in the great shell of Bladesover House, the shell that had once been gaily full of fops, of fine ladies in powder and patches and courtly gentlemen with swords. . . . When I was a boy I used always to think of these two poor old creatures as superior beings living, like God, somewhere through the ceiling. . . . I remember her "leddyship" then as a thing of black silks and a golden chain, a quavering injunction to me to be a good boy, a very shrunken loose-skinned face and neck, and a ropy hand that trembled a halfcrown into mine. Miss Somerville hovered behind, a paler thing of broken lavender and white and black, with screwed up, sandy-colored eyes. (15)

This is strongly permeated by Dickens's picture of Chesney Wold, the Dedlock residence in *Bleak House*. Like Dickens, Wells displays his fundamentally anticonservative cast of mind by disavowing any hopes that England's future lies in a revitalized country aristocracy. But Wells's voice, loaded with class resentment expressed in a hardened, strident key, contains less shame and more rage. It makes us imagine Leonard Bast finally given a powerful enough voice to be heard. George describes his intellectual maturation percolating from this adolescent pain; class consciousness, if ending in theory, must certainly begin with hard experience:

> Now the unavoidable suggestion of that wide park and that fair large house, dominating church, village and the country-side, was that they represented the thing that mattered supremely in all the world, and that

all other things had significance only in relation to them. They represented the Gentry, the Quality, by and through and for whom the rest of
the world, the farming folk and the labouring folk . . . the upper servants
and the lower servants and the servants of the estate, breathed and lived
and were permitted. And the Quality did it so quietly and thoroughly . . .
that it was only when I was a boy of thirteen or fourteen and some queer
inherited strain of skepticism had set me doubting whether Mr. Bartlett,
the vicar, did really know with certainty all about God, that as a further
and deeper step in doubting I began to question the final rightness of
the gentlefolk, their primary necessity in the scheme of things. But once
that skepticism had awakened it took me fast and far. By fourteen I had
achieved terrible blasphemies and sacrilege; I had resolved to marry a
viscount's daughter. (13)

The voice—leveling, brash, outrageous—carries the declaration of war against
the monolithic partnership of religious and social oppressors. The very "rightness of things" that Gissing's and Forster's protagonists assume as the bulwark
against disorder is the barrier George wants to break down. Toward the old
England Ponderevo expresses an attitude of good riddance rather than longing. This itself makes him a new kind of Englishman, and it is altogether fitting
to find him at the novel's outset standing in a shipyard "amidst the fine realities
of steel" (10), building destroyers. If he observes "how extensively this ostensible order" of old things "has even now passed away" (14), his own embrace
of the most powerful destructive technology known to Wells's readers at the
time suggests he is no mere bystander to the process of change, but one of
its accelerators: dreadnought construction in the period 1908–9, as the reading audience was well aware, obsessed most of Europe, principally England
and Germany. George has admittedly few moments of doubt about the social
transformations taking place. He recalls with some fondness his youthful exposure at Bladesover to the library's books as well as the beauty of the parks:
the place "had not altogether," he grudgingly concedes, "missed greatness"
(22). And he also confesses that "in a sense Bladesover has never left me. . . . It
is my social datum" (54). Yet in what seems a final thrust at belated Edwardian
romanticism about rural value, Ponderevo delivers this edict. He has chosen
the city, and he has chosen modernity: "No, I didn't like those young country-
men, and I'm no believer in the English country-side under the Bladesover
system as a breeding ground for honourable men. One hears a frightful lot of
nonsense about the Rural Exodus and the degeneration wrought by town life
upon our population" (60).

Ponderevo's tone alters once he moves from the relatively easy assertions about what must be swept away, to the more difficult question of what will replace it. Just as he confesses he "must sprawl and flounder" in finding a new shape for a new kind of book, likewise he suggests:

> The new order may have gone far towards shaping itself, but just as in that sort of lantern show that used to be known in the village as the "Dissolving Views," the scene that is going remains upon the mind, traceable and evident, and the newer picture is yet enigmatical long after the lines that are to replace those former ones have grown bright and strong, so that the new England of our children's children is still a riddle to me. The ideas of democracy, of equality, and above all of promiscuous fraternity have certainly never really entered into the English mind. But what *is* coming into it? All this book, I hope, will bear a little on that. (14)

But the prospects which subsequently unfold are unnerving, not only on account of the utter disparity between the narrator's rhetoric and action, but more so because it is never apparent to what extent Ponderevo recognizes the split. We can say he shows awareness of the split but has lost all signs of what clinical psychologists call "affect" about it; somewhere along the way personality has been altered, the moral and the intellectual capacities severed. Building the destroyers and offhandedly murdering an islander near the quap deposit seem to be complementary tasks of the same impulse, but George nonetheless implicitly affirms "fraternity"; manipulating the public to buy "slightly injurious rubbish" (120), he can still claim allegiance to notions of socialism and "equality." Although he decries the advance of London's tumor-like suburbs and the "dingy lives" of their inhabitants (77), he repeatedly undertakes enterprises which hasten the advance of disease, decay, and death. Near the end of the book he reflects fully on his title:

> I have called it *Tono-Bungay*, but I had far better have called it *Waste*. I have told of childless Marion, of my childless aunt, of Beatrice wasted and wasteful and futile. What hope is there for a people whose women have become fruitless? I think of all the energy I have given to vain things. I think of my industrious scheming with my uncle, of Crest Hill's vast cessation, of his resonant strenuous career. Ten thousand men have envied him and wished to live as he lived. It is all one spectacle of forces running to waste, of people who use and do not replace, the story of a country hectic with a wasting aimless fever of trade and money-making and pleasure-seeking. And now I build destroyers! (311)

This combination of jeremiad and confession, denunciation and Augustinian soul searching, is Ponderevo's primary means of camouflaging moral monstrosity. In the second paragraph of his narrative, he announces with unabashed candor: "And once (though it is the most incidental thing in my life) I murdered a man" (9).

The effect of this utterance, however, is opposite to what we might expect. In spite of its inappropriate abruptness within the text, it works to draw us into the narrator's confidence; we believe that he will tell all. He is humanized; we trust him. And thus rather than fully appraise Ponderevo as the serial killer he turns out to be—destruction and killing are hardly "incidental" but in fact the very design of his existence—numerous critics ignore his pathology and concentrate instead on the formal aspect of his narrative and how it does or does not conform to someone's idea of the "novel."

Ponderevo's alleged confessions draw attention away from his activity and produce by their repetition a numbing effect. On the murder: "It is remarkable how little it troubles my conscience and how much it stirs my imagination, that particular memory of the life I took" (182). On the quap expedition: "an enterprise that was after all, to put it plainly, stealing" (186). On the Tono-Bungay conglomerate: "For now it was open and manifest that I and my uncle were no more than specimens of a modern species of brigand, wasting the savings of the public out of the sheer wantonness of enterprise" (301).

Alfred Borrello argues that George Ponderevo discovers "damnation is not as horrible as it first appears";[30] John Batchelor sums up the narrator as "the inner-directed, self-seeking and somewhat cold-blooded nephew"[31] of Teddy. Relying on traditional moral vocabularies, however, both of these descriptions fall somewhat shy of explaining the absolutely contemporary feel of George's personality. Batchelor's stress on the psychological jargon of "inner-directed" and "self-seeking" may begin to point us in a fruitful direction. Consider, for instance, Philip Rieff's explanation of the historic emergence of Freud's "ethic of honesty." Only within this therapeutic vocabulary, and not an earlier religious or moral one, do Ponderevo's frequent confessions become more intelligible. Such an intellectual framework also suggests the extent to which the notion of confession itself has altered: "In place of reticence, Freud prescribes talk—thorough, ruthless talk. Honest talk fills the gap in ideals, creates the condition of a new personal integrity. This painful intellectual working-through of illusions contrasts sharply with the romantic conception of honesty as a leap beyond the paralyzing dialectic of illusion and disillusion—into decision."[32] Yet while this "honest talk" presumably accomplishes or accompanies the process leading to individual mental health, in social terms it does not answer the question of where or to what end such a society of individuals might take us. Bearing in mind Ponderevo's almost obscenely prolific self-revelations, Rieff's commentary gains even more resonance:

> As a purely explanatory and scientific ideal, honesty has no content. Though the Freudian training involves intellectual judgment . . . based on a calm and neutral appraisal of all the demanding elements of a life-situation, still, the freedom to choose must end in choice. Here, at the critical moment, the Freudian ethic of honesty ceases to be helpful.
>
> Being honest, admitting one's nature, does not resolve specific issues of choice. The Freudian ethic emphasizes freedom at the expense of choice. To achieve greater balance within the psyche, to shift the relative weights of instinct and repression, installs no new substantive rules of decision.
>
> In this final suspension, Freud's ethic resembles Sartre's existentialism, which offers a related criterion, authenticity, as a way of judging what is good in human action. André Gide offers lucid disillusionment as the distinguishing mark of humane conduct. But what guarantees that an authentic action, or one conceived in perfect lucidity, will be good or in conformity with human nature? Similarly, after a long process of self-recuperation through lucidity, the Freudian choice may be not more humane but rather more arbitrary. One need not be self-deceived to act maliciously. Freud gives no reason why unblinking honesty with oneself should inhibit unblinking evil. Lucidity may render us exquisitely articulate and unapologetic about our aggressions. . . . Openness of character may well elicit more, not less, brutality. Unaided by the old transcendental ethics of guilt, or by the rationalist ethics of a future harmony through knowledge, the Freudian lucidity may pierce the deepest shadows of the self without dispelling one degree of gloom.[33]

This spells out Ponderevo's case: utter clarity about his toxic activities, even, as he puts it, possession of "what the old theologians call a 'conviction of sin' " (164), without any attendant desire to reverse course. Confession in this mode signifies not the start of genuine ethical decision, but rather an endlessly repeating purgative. Ponderevo achieves his tone of buoyant sincerity precisely by such complete and repeated divulging of misdeeds. By burying us with details—the strategy of all convincing first-person narrators—George renders himself forthcoming, the cooperative couch client, or in a less professional mode, the good buddy who pours out his soul.

The most fully developed example of this strategy is his account of murder committed on Mordet Island. The quap expedition within which this event occurs is read generally as a parody of Conrad, or as a "structural tumor" within the novel that enhances the pervasive carcinogenic themes and imagery found throughout the book.[34] From a strictly formal standpoint, both these observations about the episode are illuminating. It does indeed echo Conrad, although in a more exact way, I think, than in merely replaying the narrative of journey into the wilderness. The episode is not merely a structural excrescence, but operates as the explicit reminder that all Ponderevo's vocations lead in the same direction. The murder at first seems gratuitous, out of place, given Ponderevo's continued self-representation as an educated, rational, and affable being. He wants to bracket it off as "apart from all the rest of my life. . . . so far as this novel of mine goes . . . merely an episode, a contributory experience, and I mean to keep it at that" (260). But the episode actually provides the glue at the bottom of all Ponderevo's enterprises. He never brings himself to articulate openly how the Tono-Bungay, the quap, and the destroyers are all carriers of mass death. About the quack remedy he continually employs offhanded euphemism, calling it "mischievous trash" (112) and "rubbish" (113), while admitting it contains strychnine (125) and is "insidiously dangerous to people with defective kidneys" (112). The radioactive quap, a heavy-handed portent of the nuclear age discovered in the midst of a blighted wasteland,[35] and the stealing of which Teddy warns could provoke an "international outrage" (253) causes fever, blisters, sores in the crew, and ultimately destroys the ship *Maud Mary*. Finally, Ponderevo symbolically links the high-technology destroyers culminating in the X2 with his desire for open space, unencumbered either by England's decaying urban landscape or its suffocating social history. But not once does he articulate the destroyer's literal function. Only in his encounter with the Mordet Islander does Ponderevo meet one of his victims face to face. And only there is Ponderevo's action named for what it is: murder.

As Orwell and others have observed, the most grim achievement of the twentieth century has not been simply the infliction of mass death on entire populations, but also the facility with which such action finds articulation in rational, abstract discourse, making more of it possible down the line. Killing on a big scale deploys a vocabulary that dispenses with talk of killing altogether. This urge to detach one's own action from murder is most common in the midst of the bureaucratic systems through which the century's enormous genocides have been implemented.[36] What becomes immediately plain by Ponderevo's account of his individual act of murder is that for him, this mental disengagement now filters into even a face-to-face engagement. Confessing to the act, Ponderevo indicates that he feels nothing whatsoever:

"It was the most unmeaning and purposeless murder imaginable. Even as I write down its well-remembered particulars there comes again the sense of its strangeness, its pointlessness, its incompatibility with any of the neat and definite theories people hold about life and the meaning of the world. I did this thing and I want to tell of my doing it, but why I did it and particularly why I should be held responsible for it I cannot explain" (271). This is the logic of Dickens's Circumlocution, though when we get to the description of the man about to become victim, we are deep in Conrad territory:

> He was very black and naked except for a dirty loin-cloth, his legs were ill-shaped and his toes spread wide, and the upper edge of his cloth and a girdle of string cut his clumsy abdomen into folds. His forehead was low, his nose very flat, and his lower lip swollen and purplish red. His hair was short and fuzzy, and about his neck was a string and a little purse of skin. He carried a musket, and a powder flask was stuck in his girdle. It was a curious confrontation. There opposed to him stood I, a little soiled perhaps, but still a rather elaborately civilised human being born, bred and trained in a vague tradition. In my hand was an unaccustomed gun. And each of us was essentially a teeming vivid brain, tensely excited by the encounter, quite unaware of the other's mental content or what to do with him. (271)

As the black man turns to run, Ponderevo has the "preposterous idea" (271) that he will reveal the theft of the quap. Then follows the murder, Ponderevo "coolly" drawing the bead on the retreating figure and shooting him "neatly in the back" (272). To this choice of fastidious adverbs he adds the euphoric announcement: "I saw, and saw with a leap of pure exultation, the smash of my bullet between his shoulder blades. . . . I went to him not as one goes to something one has made or done, but as one approaches something found" (272).

Ponderevo's subsequent mood shifts from horror, to one of a boy who had been caught "poaching" (272). Still later "the business only began to assume proper proportions . . . as I got near the ship, to seem any other kind of thing than the killing of a bird or rabbit" (272). The corpse enters his dreams as "a horrible obsession," confused with a vision of Uncle Teddy found with a slashed throat. Drawn to the corpse as if by a fetish, George goes back into the wilderness to find it. When he does, he comments: "Some evil and detestable beast had been at him, and he lay disinterred" (273). It is beyond George to make the connection between beast and himself, just as it is beyond him to see how the quap expedition parabolically sums up the significance of his numerous careers. Flooded with a wealth of detail, the "well-remembered particulars," Ponderevo cannot fit them to any structure of meaning. Details register but do not cohere.

Ponderevo's murder of the islander, then, reveals all at once the discovery and denial of his own Marlovian heart of darkness. Yet it is in this episode's rather close resemblance to one of Stein's tales in *Lord Jim* that we begin to perceive a dramatically new sensibility toward human suffering and death, toward violence per se. This attitude involves both a different kind of representation of violence than is previously employed by writers, as well as a different set of human emotions connected with violent acts. But before we consider how those peculiar features work themselves out in some postmodern texts, I want to look at the Stein passage to which Wells seems indebted.

Marlow has just arrived at Stein's house to discuss Jim's "case," and the two men sit amidst Stein's vast butterfly collection. Stein recalls, as a kind of prolegomenon to his own assessment of different specimens of man and insect, an incident in his youth. Unlike Ponderevo's act of murder, committed without provocation, Stein's happened ostensibly in the cause of self-defense during an ambush:

> After all, there were only seven of these rascals. They get up from the grass and start running with their sarongs tucked up, waving spears above their heads, and yelling to each other to look out and catch the horse, because I was dead. I let them come as close as the door here, and then bang, bang, bang—take aim each time, too. One more shot I fire at a man's back, but I miss. Too far already. And then I sit alone on my horse with the clean earth smiling at me, and there are the bodies of three men lying on the ground. One was curled up like a dog, another on his back had an arm over his eyes as if to keep off the sun, and the third man he draws up his leg very slowly and makes it with one kick straight again. . . . And as I looked at his face for some sign of life I observed something like a faint shadow pass over his forehead. It was the shadow of this butterfly. Look at the form of the wing. This species fly high with a strong flight. I raised my eyes and I saw him fluttering away. . . . At last I saw him sitting on a small heap of dirt ten feet away. At once my heart began to beat quick. I let go my horse, keep my revolver in one hand, and with the other snatch my soft felt hat off my head. One step. Steady. Another step. Flop! I got him! When I got up I shook like a leaf with excitement, and when I opened these beautiful wings and made

sure what a rare and so extraordinary perfect specimen I had, my head
went round and my legs became so weak with emotion that I had to sit
on the ground. (127–28)

Butterflies, not dead men, make Stein "weak with emotion"; killing without
feeling is one of his gifts, joined with a clinical and cinematic ability to recall
every image of his victims' dying moments. Like Ponderevo's comparison of
murder with the act of shooting a "bird" or "rabbit," Stein remembers one
man curled up like a "dog"; another's death spasm is recorded in the kicking
and straightening of a leg, as if in close-up.

Similarly, Ponderevo goes about the business of killing without registering
strong emotion. Or, when he does express emotion related to such acts, it is
of a jarring, comedic sort. "I saw . . . with a leap of pure exultation, the smash
of my bullet between his shoulder blades" (272). Were this Greek epic battle,
or even a Kipling rendition of a native-white skirmish in the bush, that leap
would be expected. But Ponderevo can find no intelligible explanation for this
kind of behavior. He can only record; the novel has become reportage.

While critics agree that postmodernism should be understood to involve
more than aesthetic techniques or properties,[37] most discussions of it nevertheless focus precisely on formal devices: total fragmentation and discontinuity,
pastiche, collage, nonlinearity, parody, and so forth. To be sure, this phenomenon has been put into broader contexts. Historically, postmodernism
is generally conceived as a sharp reaction to a modernism that had moved
from avant-garde to mainstream status. And the deep connection between
postmodernism, capitalist commodification, and mass culture has been vividly
described, first by Irving Howe, and more recently by Fredric Jameson.[38]

Yet there is another element—a thematic one—in this postmodern stew that
has not received quite so much attention. It is this: a radical obsession with
violence, murder treated both at the individual or mass level; and moreover,
violence rendered not in the traditional generic modes of epic, tragedy, horror,
or melodrama,[39] but rather in a spirit or mood of low comedy or something
approaching the sublime.

Of course the moderns often flirted with a sublime understanding of violence. Yeats's "Easter 1916" with its paean to the "terrible beauty" of political violence is the most noteworthy example; a more extended treatment is
Hemingway's *Death in the Afternoon* (1932) which invests the death of animals
and men with the attributes of ballet-like beauty, employing verbal flourishes
which parallel film's adoption of slow-motion technique. But generally, the
overt and obsessive descriptions within art of violent acts, as well as the treat-

ment of terrible violence as comic material, pertain more fully to postmodern kinds of expression. Reading *Tono-Bungay* and its narrator in this context, I would suggest, yields insights not grasped through the usual discussions that pair Wells and James, or Wells and the moderns.

What are these resonances and parallels I am talking about? Ponderevo's registered emotion upon the killing of the islander—"exultation"—seems as odd as Stein's blasé affect after killing men and watching them twitch in the dirt. This gap between murderous action and attendant emotion grows ever more extreme in twentieth-century art. And in postmodern expressions, particularly in mass entertainment vehicles such as film, the occasion of the kill becomes for the first time the comic climax. Such a moment occurs in Stanley Kubrick's film adaptation of Stephen King's *The Shining* when the crazed father and writer played by Jack Nicholson breaks through the bathroom door with an axe, looking to murder his wife. She cowers in the corner as he, grinning, pokes his demented face through the splintered wood and announces in perfect parody of television's most famous late-night talk show: "He-e-e-e-e-ere's Johnny!" In the same way, the films of David Lynch or the Coen brothers inscribe together disparate elements of horror and kitsch, camp humor and dismemberment. While Ponderevo's murder of the islander does not quite add up to quite the same comic effect, it does underscore, rather than deaden, the "buoyancy" which Batchelor describes. And when Ponderevo keeps returning over a period of time to check the status of the corpse, horror by its very repetition turns into something quite different, although we are not exactly sure what to call it.

The novel delivers its buoyant effect most effectively through the character of Uncle Teddy, whose infectious qualities of the small-time, fast-talking swindler practically camouflage his ominous status as the plutocracy's most corrupt financier. If we look ahead to Joseph Heller's *Catch-22* (1961), Teddy's unique role can be seen in even darker outline. Milo Minderbinder, the lowly air-base cook in Heller's novel, goes about building an international cartel that deals in every kind of merchandise, all sorts of business propositions. He ultimately negotiates with the Germans to bomb his own base and argues later that since it was done for a profit, and since "everyone owns shares" in the worldwide syndicate, everyone benefits. The "apocalyptic" scene of fire and death is rapidly forgotten in the huckster's effervescent rhetoric.[40] Milo incarnates Uncle Teddy all over again, the likeable rogue on the grand scale. Like Teddy, who mints "Faith" (181) and embodies the "Romance of Commerce" (58), Milo visualizes his corporate empire marching across the globe in a way that patronizes nationalist conflicts while utilizing such conflict to maximum capitalist advantage.[41] Milo is nothing less than the fulfillment of Teddy's dream: "I wish to Heaven, George, I'd been born American—where things hum" (57). All the while, as George reminds us, not "a single one of the great businesses we organised added any real value to human life at all" (180). They are about "Waste," putting them in a line with earlier equations of excrement, capitalism, and death: Dickens's dust heaps in *Our Mutual Friend*, the workings of Merdle in *Little Dorrit*, or the equally unsubtle guano expedition headed by Chester in Conrad's *Lord Jim*.

Other instances abound of the characteristic postmodern fracture between theme and tone. In works as different as John Gardner's *Grendel* (1971) and Anthony Burgess's *Clockwork Orange* (1962), violent action comes packaged in cathartic joy and philosophical bemusement. Kubrick's film version of Burgess's novel slows down the rape and murder scenes to allow a complete savoring of the moment, and its techniques anticipate what have become virtually formal clichés in genres such as the slasher film. There once again the sheer repetition of perversity and horror have nowhere to slide but comic parody.[42]

If sex was the great taboo broken down and yet oddly resacralized by the moderns, most notably Joyce and Lawrence, then violence may well be the corresponding totem of postmodern expression. The last remaining possibility for shocking an audience becomes graphic representation of some form of violent sex. Debates in the art community over such kinds of graphic portrayal may seem far afield from George Ponderevo, until we remember certain odd, twisted associations he makes between the female body and his most recent toy, the X_2 destroyer: "There is something links things for me, a sunset or so, a mood or so, the high air, something there was in Marion's form and colour, something I find and lose in Mantegna's pictures, something in the lines of these boats I make. (You should see X_2, my last and best!)" (165).

Tono-Bungay's ending, with Ponderevo at the bridge of his destroyer, steaming out to sea, can be spiritualized—as metaphorical of his ongoing quest for value in the detritus of the Victorian era. In this sense, as one critic argues, the ending is an open and "optimistic"[43] one, as open as the sea on which Ponderevo travels. For other readers, the ending conveys Wells's own bellicosity, of accord with much European sentiment in the years before the Great War, that military destruction would ultimately have a positive and purgative effect on Europe's decadence. In this view, world war was not to be feared but rather embraced as anticipatory of a more rational world to follow.[44]

The problem with the first reading is that it arbitrarily severs the significance of the X_2 from the novel's immediate historical context: the dreadnought arms race between England and Germany, the century's first two superpowers, was rapidly escalating even as Wells composed the novel in the period 1908–9.[45] The second reading, while it appropriately takes the X2 to be more than just metaphor, fails to draw any distinction between Wells the author and George the narrator, and glosses over Ponderevo's own self-assessment that his life-work has been less than salutary. Recalling his uncle's half-finished house, Crest Hill, he reflects: "It struck me suddenly as the compactest image and sample of all that passes for Progress, of all the advertisement-inflated spending, the aimless building up and pulling down, the enterprise and promise of my age. This was our fruit, this was what we had done, I and my uncle, in the fashion of our time. We were its leaders and exponents, we were the thing it most flourishingly produced. For this futility in its end, for an epoch of such futility, the solemn scroll of history had unfolded" (284).

Consciously embracing the knowledge of this "futility," Ponderevo leaves himself free of any obligations save his own pursuit of "power and knowledge" (165). While we can make the argument that this is a nihilistic choice, it does have the beauty of simplifying the ethical life. For such an existential choice, once made, frees the individual from having to make any others. Much like the Schlegelian drive for privacy in one's own garden, it pretends to render questions of social accountability and consequences irrelevant to the interests of a purely personal quest. Yet to define this personal quest in such a way amounts, paradoxically, to a form of self-deception. Note that earlier in his career Ponderevo is troubled to observe how England's ruling elite is busy "calculating . . . how they might use him [Teddy] and assimilate him to their system, the most unpremeditated, subtle, successful and aimless plutocracy that ever encumbered the destinies of mankind" (210–11). However, by the time of his seeming fulfillment in the high-technology armaments business, George no longer asks to whose system *he* is being assimilated: the perfection of destructive capability is the goal, and in the shaping of his personal individualist myth, more searching questions—about the ways political institutions utilize individuals—have become entirely truncated. "I have long since ceased to trouble about such questions" (317) George says. As Linda Anderson astutely observes, Ponderevo's belief that his own individual quest can transcend questions of social interconnectedness ends in an ironic twist whereby he becomes not the maker but the tool of his own science, "which has no other justification than its own inner necessity."[46] His parting remarks in which he attempts to distance himself from "turgid degenerate Kiplingese" (317) become highly significant in this regard. The business of armament, he argues, cannot be tethered by any one particular political program, nor is his activity ultimately controlled by the English. Ponderevo conveys a distinctly postnationalist sensibility but is dangerously unaware that even users such as himself can be used, and his assertion that his weapon "isn't intended for the empire, or indeed for the hands of any European power" (317) does not convince. As with the Edwardian naval arms race of which his shipbuilding is highly suggestive, control by any one party or government is not maintained but finally lost. At the end Ponderevo simply wishes to maintain his own illusion of control.

The parting image of Ponderevo piloting his X2 out to sea finds more recent expression in Kubrick's most brilliant treatment of Cold War paranoia, *Dr. Strangelove, or How I Stopped Worrying and Learned to Love the Bomb* (1963). Updating the X2 is a similar runaway vessel, a nuclear-equipped B-52, another era's culminating technological achievement. And "buoyancy" also describes the B-52's pilot played by Slim Pickens, who ultimately rides an H-bomb bronco-style to its Soviet destination. Does the postmodern sensibility, with its continual effort to shock the audience, arouse resistance to our condition, or does it in fact make us more accepting of what so many thinkers perceive as a drift towards mayhem? [47] Overexposure to the unthinkable, as the postmodern mode expresses it, might provoke increased sensitivity, but can just as well wear that sensitivity down, as yesterday's outrageousness evolves ever more quickly into today's boredom. These feelings, like the term "postmodernism" itself, seem obsolescent almost as soon as they get uttered. Images of apocalypse, which Wells did so much to popularize, become increasingly robbed of their power to amaze or shock us.

There is another troubling aspect to Wells's book that puts it in a line with contemporary postmodern expression. It can be argued that Wells's portrait of Ponderevo definitively unmasks the face and aspirations of "late capitalism," of the direction such unbounded freedom and energy might take. Or, in the words of Judith Shklar, "The liberalism of fear . . . does not, to be sure, offer a *summum bonum* toward which all political agents should strive, but it certainly does begin with a *summum malum*, which all of us know and would avoid if only we could." [48] By showing us the enormity of someone who exorcizes his liberal guilt, Wells bolsters the case for us to maintain our own.

That argument compels up to a point. Perhaps Wells recognized that exposure of the enemy comes only to the degree that his thinking can be imagined from the inside. This reading serves another purpose as well: to demonstrate that the Wells of Fabian sympathies and Wells the artistic creator were in fundamental accord. Yet this interpretation does not adequately account for the tremendous energy of *Tono-Bungay*, however much I want it to. Wells's book hardly distills to some kind of hortatory negative portrait but generates its power equally from a perverse celebration of George and Teddy's unbounded genius. This undertow of currents in *Tono-Bungay* makes it elude singular political or ideological formulation. As with Gissing's portrayal of Sibyl Carnaby, it is difficult to guess where Wells's ostensible purpose in writing the book—exposure of the condition of England—leaves off, and a more uncanny, undiluted fascination with evil takes over. A similar problem of interpretation attends Kubrick's *Dr. Strangelove*, particularly the figure of his bomber pilot. Henry Kariel attempts to argue the value of this ambiguous postmodern strategy by placing the film in the context of the Warhol era:

> Postmodernists . . . engage in the kind of praxis which is so close to the process of reality that it is barely distinguishable from it. During the 1970s the bleached out, deadpan muteness of Andy Warhol showed how it might be done: "If you want to know all about Andy Warhol," he remarked, "just look at the surface of my paintings and films and me—and there I am. There's nothing behind it." . . . Alive to the irreversibility of the prevailing course, such performers follow the resourceful pilot who in Stanley Kubrick's *Dr. Strangelove* obeys instructions to the letter, keeps his plane on course, and like the rest of his crew takes pains to deliver the bomb. Not mechanized, he decides not to let the world end of its own accord but to *make* it end. Not changing the outcome, he but amplifies it.[49]

Critics agree that postmodern art almost always carries with it the dual effect of "critique and complicity."[50] Thus our unease in the presence of, say, Lynch's ever more grotesque portraits of evil—which provoke horror but also a strange kind of attraction. To put it crudely, does Lynch actually make any kind of "statement" about American culture, or are these figures merely the inevitable aesthetic moves in the game to shock an increasingly jaded, knowingly ironic audience? And how quickly do the returns on such a method begin to diminish? The character of Ponderevo anticipates both these strategies and the questions that accompany them, thus making *Tono-Bungay* a novel holding singularly contemporary resonance. And though the analysis that both critique and complicity are at work in this novel may strike us as unsatisfactory to sizing up Wells's book—or any other work of postmodern art, for that matter—such a judgment in spite of its commonness does provide certain reassurances. Namely: the very use of terms such as critique and complicity implicitly acknowledges that moral, ethical judgments can still be made, and that those judgments—and not nihilism as some critics charge—remain central to postmodern discourse. The terms "critique" and "complicity" have little meaning or function unless we attach extraliterary values to them; the terms refute the charge of relativism. Just as well, reliance on such terms has important implications for the way contemporary criticism operates. Most basically, we can recognize that deconstruction's undoing of binary pairs, while useful, is not always useful. Binaries can reify the interests of existing hierarchies and powers. But other oppositional pairings often serve indispensably the process of questioning the powers. For the late Victorian and Edwardian writers considered here, there can be no understanding of the empire without a parallel awareness of those "others" being colonized. Likewise, to understand sympathetically the misery of the poor, to render that pain effectively in the novel as Gissing does, presupposes the contrast provided by the lives of the privileged.

Moved by this basic sense of human contrasts, the products of inequity and injustice, these novelists write their best novels in large measure because of their heightened sense of liberal guilt. Disbelieving, or at least uneasy with the old Christian category of sin, they have not yet defined conscience in terms of strictly personal neurosis. They still attach their guilt to the visible social crises of their age and write with compelling force about them. Although they are unwilling to reduce evil to the level of personal depravity, they harbor no illusions about any fundamental human "goodness"; for them, evil, though detached now from any kind of metaphysic, is not yet explained away as the result of unconscious repression or the effects of environment. It is overwhelmingly social, systemic, and visible.

Tono-Bungay brings these concerns to a head; in the character of Ponderevo we see the disquieting tendencies registered by earlier novelists come to culmination. Ponderevo shows us a series of choices in which he willfully violates the very ethical limits that he can so well articulate. Wells gives us the solution not of how "to connect," that enviable goal of the Schlegel sisters, but instead provides us with the most lasting image of disconnection in all of Edwardian literature. Just as profoundly as Conrad's creation of Kurtz, that favorite and melodramatic specter of evil haunting the liberal imagination, George Ponderevo serves as a startling premonition of our age—closer, I think, to the *summum malum* of all our fears precisely because he has become more commonplace.

CONCLUSION

I am a Liberal, yet I am a Liberal tempered by experience, reflection, and renouncement, and I am, above all, a believer in culture.

MATTHEW ARNOLD,

Culture and Anarchy

That educated liberals lack vitality has been a repeated theme in many novels of the last hundred years. Either instinctively or deliberately, writers have often associated this tradition with sickness.

C. B. COX,

The Free Spirit

Liberal guilt, though a malady, has proven a productive one—acting to stimulate and not block the creative impulse. The body of work coming from these writers attests to that. And the literature of liberal guilt invites, as well, not only standard literary assessments of its value, but also that we assess ourselves in light of the work. Stein's query "How to be?" resonates urgently through all these novels. Giles Gunn argues that "the ethical issue in criticism cannot be confined to the question of what to make of texts in the light of what they presumably say . . . about us. It must be widened to encompass the question of what to make of ourselves in the light of what texts say . . . about others."[1] Reading understood and taught this way affirms the connection between contemplative and active will. As Dennis Donoghue argues,

> It is mischievous to degrade the character of reading by presenting it as merely yet another bout of subjectivity, the consolation prize of bourgeois liberalism. The best way of countering this attitude is by showing that introspection is not the puny, self-regarding act as it is commonly said to be but an act of ethical and moral bearing. When Baudelaire spoke of populating one's solitude, he meant the act by which the mind, in privacy, imagines lives other than its own. Conscience is the capacity by which we reflect upon our actions in the light of our sense of justice. There is no reason why we should allow ourselves to be put out of countenance by attacks upon this sort of subjectivity.[2]

From Dickens's Arthur Clennam, on through to Wells's George Ponderevo —a remarkable mutation of the guilty liberal hero—we encounter the various strands of ethical sensibility that define our subject. Guilt has been severed from its theistic origins, but has not been reduced to a merely emotive feature of subjectivity, of individual personality. These novels entertain the possibility that guilt is a legitimate response to observed social crises in the material world: the persistence of urban poverty, the growth of imperial might. We can say these writers are bothered by history in a way that distinguishes them as a group. Unlike the moderns, whose masterpieces are often read as either transcending history—or else being about the creation of sustaining personal myths that allow one to cope with history—the late Victorians and Edwardians are visibly burdened by their historical milieu; that is why its features are etched so explicitly in their work. Donoghue suggests that "the writers we think of as modern are those who contemplated the possibility of seceding from society and disavowing the social understanding of human life. Not because they wanted more congenial social relationships but because they wanted to escape from all social arrangements."[3] The late Victorian and Edwardian novelists, by contrast, take existing social arrangements to be the material for their art rather than detritus meant to be transcended. The characters in these novels alternately embody the forces that contribute to wretchedness (notably Grandcourt and Ponderevo), articulate concern about the wretched conditions (many of Gissing's alter egos), or most emphatically, as in the case of Clennam and his successors Marlow and Margaret Schlegel, do both.

Conscience is hardly the exclusive purview of liberal, literary intellectuals. Nor can we claim that liberal writers have been the only party to take up the consequences of God's death, the spectacle of urban poverty, the struggle of the colonizers and the colonized, or even the relations between culture and capital as embodied in the English country house. But the guilt mapped and dissected in these novels is unique because it is sustained within a matrix of liberal as opposed to Christian, or conservative, or Marxist ideological values. And liberal guilt carries distinctiveness chiefly on account of its inability to find for the problem of guilt a consolatory response—which the major nineteenth-century metanarratives do. Liberal guilt persists as especially heavy and inescapable. Retaining a belief in personal agency and responsibility, a legacy of the Christian worldview, liberals must confront instances of coercion and suffering without the theists' ability to relax in the belief of a just eternity hereafter. As Clennam reflects in *Little Dorrit*: "Duty on earth, restitution on earth, action on earth" (368). And just as critically, this stress on "earth" must be understood in the present tense, in the here and now, thereby depriving the Victorian liberal of both the future-oriented revolutionary hope of Marxism, and the backward-looking invocation of old "Merrie England"[4] which empowered, among others, Carlyle and the Young Tories. Palliatives, whether sought in glances heavenward, forward, or backward, are hard to come by for writers in the liberal tradition. Hence, the endurance of the "malady."

Other accusations against the liberal tradition, however, deserve emphatic rebuttal in light of a comprehensive and historical understanding of liberal guilt. Most specious of the claims is the enduring polemic that liberalism comes imbued with naive optimism, both about human progress and human nature. (Never mind that this caricature of liberalism as buoyantly optimistic totally contradicts the other straw man of liberal impasse, indecision, weakness, and self-doubt. Antiliberals want it both ways.) The modernist legacy can be held partly to account for this caricature of liberal ideology. If Woolf despised the materially oriented workings of the Edwardian liberal imagination, asserting it to be concerned with "unimportant things,"[5] other modernists including Hulme, Eliot, and Pound, writing for A. R. Orage's *New Age*, asserted their literary and political agenda in reaction to what they depicted as a liberal-romantic cultural hegemony grown soft. "Romanticism" and "liberalism," according to this line of argument, became interchangeable. The charge was made—and stuck—that liberals had a distinct inability to recognize evil, and as antidote to this flawed liberal vision, T. E. Hulme called for dusting off an older doctrine called Original Sin. For many intellectuals, World War I affirmed the rightness of the modernist interpretation: liberalism, so to speak, died in the trenches.

The problem with this caricature of liberalism is that it is false. For practically everywhere in these novels of the guilty liberal imagination there is awareness of radical evil, obsession with it, the bitter flavor of social relations gone awry. Beginning with Circumlocution and Grandcourt, climaxing in the repeatedly toxic activity of master builder George Ponderevo, the reservoirs of the liberal imagination brim to overflowing with imaginative renderings of perversity, evil inhabiting not simply human individual souls as Victorian theists understood it, but evil permeating every level of human social institutions and relations. Liberals did not reject the Christian doctrine of sin. They transmuted and enlarged it.

We need not consider only the novels to make this case. Recent historians, most notably E. P. Thompson, insist that the historic link between Dissenting Nonconformity and nineteenth-century liberalism is of major and not minor importance[6] for understanding the specific texture of the liberal worldview. Following Thompson's lead, E. F. Biagini distinguishes "the anthropological pessimism peculiar to the tradition of British popular liber-

alism, in contrast . . . to the French Jacobin-Republican tradition. Victorian
plebeian radicals believed that the moral nature of man was sinful and—despite
Darwin, Comte and the ideology of progress—basically non-evolutionary."[7]
Nineteenth-century English liberalism, in this framework, sounds more like
Hobbes and less like Rousseau. And the secularized philosophical tradition
of liberalism, particularly that found in Locke and J. S. Mill, confirms these
pessimistic strains that can be glimpsed in spite of the zeal and energy of
nineteenth-century liberal reformers. Locke's constitutionalism, we can argue,
is founded upon a spirit of suspicion, not of optimistic faith;[8] its guiding prem-
ise is that uneven distribution of power, power without counterweights, holds
the potential for great harm. The same attitude pervades J. S. Mill's argument
in On Liberty, which focuses primarily on the need to guard liberty against
the coercive, conformist pressures of social opinion and statist tyranny. This
suspicion of the abuses of concentrated power that work to destroy individual
lives is the strongest inheritance for major twentieth-century exponents of liberal values including George Orwell, Isaiah Berlin, John Rawls, and Judith
Shklar.

Not surprisingly then, Stein's prime question of "How to be?"—which
resonates throughout these works—tends more often than not to get worked
out by negative rather than positive affirmation, turning in practice into a form
of "How not to be." This novelistic practice corresponds closely to the negative
philosophical turn described above, toward what Shklar has aptly described
as a "liberalism of fear."[9] And this brings us to a third and perhaps most
recurrent charge against liberalism today: that it is an ideology of, and for,
atomistic individuals, displaying a sometimes paranoid defensiveness about
individual human rights without a concomitant stress on civic obligations or
virtues. Liberals, it is argued by communitarian theorists, can only argue re-
actively to protect the selfish interests of separate human beings, and fail to
offer any proactive, affirmative vision of the common good, of the community.[10] The communitarian argument also frequently faults liberals for lacking
any kind of spirituality, which echoes strongly of Woolf's insistence for a literature concerned with "the spirit," as opposed to the narrow "materialism"
of the premodern writers.[11]

The attack contains, as well, echoes of Carlyle's angry assault on the liberal
laissez-faire policies of the Manchester thinkers. Granted, if liberalism as an
ideology had remained statically locked in the tenets of its early nineteenth-
century classical framework, the communitarian charge today would carry
more weight. It may be fair to castigate some strains of liberalism this way. But
it will not do to claim that the liberal novelists of the Victorian and Edwardian

periods, at least, in documenting the sickness of existing social bonds, therefore want to explode them. The case of George Ponderevo in *Tono-Bungay* pointedly indicates how pathological and delusional extreme forms of individualism can become. In fact, a unifying thread between all these novels is the pressure on guilty liberal protagonists *not* to withdraw from their communal obligations. Clennam and Amy will go "down into the roaring streets" (895). The temptation to retreat to one's private garden, most strongly conveyed in Gissing and Forster, carries with it the suggestion that such withdrawal carries a high price: the surrender of one's desire and even intellectual ability to "see things whole."

An understanding of liberal guilt allows us, I believe, to reappraise liberalism proper. Arguing for a kind of guilt that has salutary effect, Martin Buber suggests it must take on an "ontic character whose place is not the soul but being." [12] Those are interesting words coming from a mystic, words worth repeating, I think, because they can be grasped by mystic and materialist alike. Buber's assertion cogently explicates the dimensions of the ethical sensibility at work in these novels. Guilt of this kind does not necessitate some essentialist notion of spiritual depravity; in fact, it does not necessitate any kind of spirituality at all. However, Buber at the same time denies that the thinking and feeling capacity for guilt is merely symptomatic of a damaged or maladjusted psyche. Finally, Buber's solid placement of this sensibility at the center of "being," or life in this world, rather than a strictly subjective state of inwardness, allows for a mode of thinking about guilt that propels us away from the dichotomous conception of individual versus community.

What can Buber's assertion possibly mean about guilt having "ontic character" and "being"? By lifting it out of the exclusive domain of the individual inward psyche or, if you will, soul, Buber suggests the character of guilt has more to do with the quality of social relations between people, rather than with states of mind liable to get psychologized, individualized, or theologized. Looking to Bakhtin, another mystic whose commitments are to this world rather than to any to come, we find further clues about the way a new ethical epistemology works:

Separation, dissociation, and enclosure within the self as the main reason for the loss of one's self. Not that which takes place within, but that which takes place on the *boundary* between one's own and someone else's consciousness, on the *threshhold*. . . . Thus does Dostoevsky confront all decadent and idealistic (individualistic) culture, the culture of essential and inescapable solitude. He asserts the impossibility of solitude, the illusory nature of solitude. The very being of man (both external and internal) is the *deepest communion. To be* means *to communicate. . . .* To be means to be for another, and through the other, for oneself.[13]

For the Victorian and Edwardian writers considered in this study, God is dead, but the theological concepts of guilt and evil are secularized instead of eliminated. The secularization of guilt is accompanied by a parallel secularization of evil. And this latter transformation, ironically, results not in a weakening of the liberal concept of evil—the tiresome charge that liberals most consistently have to rebut—but instead in a radically more complicated vision of it. Evil can no longer be restricted to the boundaries of the soul. Theological ideas of individual depravity or villainy no longer adequately explain lived social experience. Dickens's Circumlocution Office and Eliot's Grandcourt uniquely figure in their respective authors' range of aesthetic experimentation because they convey the new apprehension of evil in all its social and institutional complexity. Moreover, as such manifestations of evil make all too plain, complicity with evil has become more troublesome than previously understood, because distinctions between doer and victim blur. No character in English fiction renders this more palpably than Arthur Clennam, stymied by his consciousness that he embodies roles of both victim and perpetrator. Once he recognizes he has willingly entered, and been caught in, the labyrinthine coils of the Merdle financial scheme—the equivalent of Circumlocution—he goes to Marshalsea to die. And the means of redemption through Little Dorrit, paralleled in *Daniel Deronda* by a Zionist national vision of hope, is a miracle unavailable to the subsequent generation of Edwardian novelists.

It cannot be said often enough that strategies to contain or resolve liberal guilt frequently go awry. These novelists not only document the social and political formations pressing in on the guilty liberal conscience; they also explore their protagonists' responses to the weight of that conscience.

One typical strategy, that of Gissing's central protagonists or Forster's Margaret Schlegel, is retreat to a pastoral country estate. To remain sane, one consciously circumscribes the boundaries of vision. The desire grows to turn history back to a good, green world. Seeing things whole for too long can cause unsustainable stress, and so narrowing perspective, in the way Margaret does, at least preserves one's mental health. Other characters, like Conrad's globe-trotting Marlow, display a tenacious ability to forestall decision whether the white man's burden is one of allegiance to the imperial mission's ostensibly noble intent, or one of guilt about imperialism's actual coercive grip of colonialized people. Conrad's ambiguous and shadowy reply to Kipling in the pages of *Lord Jim* seems to indicate willingness, in the end, to march in the ranks of some idealistic intent, and yet Conrad never lets us forget that it is indeed a fiction, an "idol" as he calls it, that we "bow down to." The character of Marlow catches the dominant tone of Edwardian liberalism's attitudes about the colonial enterprise. But if we grant Conrad's liberal complicity with the imperialist gospel, which has been pointed out before, then we should also recognize that prior to any overturning of idols must come their recognition.

Finally, there looms the monstrosity of George Ponderevo, the most uninhibited creature in this gallery of human characters. He defines his personality, if he can be said to have one, in the casting off of all social limits. Yet he also demonstrates how those who make a rule of defying social limits may well become tools of the most entrenched social—in this case military and nationalist—interests, because weapons like the X2 can hardly serve any other. George Ponderevo masks the enormity of his enterprise in exuberant energy: saying yes to life, for him, translates into the service of death: the mass marketing of radioactive and chemical poisons, the development of ever more lethal forms of technology. In spite of these genocidal and carcinogenic qualities, however, George floods us with congenial warmth, in the mode of a homegrown politician. Like his Uncle Teddy, who prefers to clown rather than pontificate, Ponderevo, and not the onerous Kurtz, aptly suggests how modern evil is most likely to infect us.

What Ponderevo shares with this generally more restrained chorus of characters is the propensity to dissect his own motives and actions. And in his case, such a brand of self-critical intelligence ripens into indulgent frivolity—a problem for postmodern art, generally, aspiring to ethical seriousness. Guilt gets practiced as a game of verbal massage. This variety of liberal guilt, one without consequences, is a recurrent temptation that Wells explores brilliantly. But more often than not, I would argue, in most of the novels considered here, self-reflection of a sober and serious kind proves to be one of liberalism's most valuable assets. Persistent interrogation of oneself, often berated by critics on left and right as a sign of bad faith, is in fact the primary trait which makes the liberal sensibility worth saving. These novelists' willingness to confront the temptations of their protagonists provides us with a working model of Trilling's call for a liberalism that will not repress but rather encourage criticism from within. This, too, is a kind of courage.

Our own lived history comes under the gaze of these books, whose impact continues to increase rather than lessen. This is true because these writers were profoundly gifted, but also because the historical crises they confronted are still too much with us. The dimensions of the social abyss grow and show few signs of shrinking even as world capitalism consolidates itself and pushes into the furthest recesses of the globe. Similarly, the ongoing story of bellicose national and imperial interests, after the Cold War's end, shows few signs of hastening to happy conclusion. These writers still speak to our times. These writers are valuable precisely because by articulating the voice of liberal guilt within their novels, they provide us with a means of evaluating our own lives and liberal commitments. They begin to accomplish, indirectly, what one contemporary critic describes as the task of "generating the history we want." [14] They do it by documenting the pain within their own social order, by envisioning precisely the kind of history we do *not* want.

Buber says, "Man is the being who is capable of becoming guilty and is capable of illuminating his guilt." [15] To some, that statement may sound inadequately affirmative. Modest hopes, I would contend, are most appropriate to the present moment. If we are guilty liberals, or have ever been tagged by such an epithet, then we owe something to the light provided by this generation of Victorian and Edwardian novelists. Aware of the guilt's leaden cast, they were able to transform it with their creative gift into a thing called art. The art they made, the culture they proclaimed, is one of the interrogative mode, and only when our unrest congeals into frozen certainties will we find it unnecessary to read their books.

NOTES

INTRODUCTION

1. The books and articles are too numerous to mention; the most comprehensive of the dirges to our growing illiteracy and the death of the book itself amidst the bristle of technological postmodernity is Alvin Kernan's *The Death of Literature* (New Haven: Yale University Press, 1990).

2. Karl Marx, "Theses on Feuerbach," in *Writings of the Young Marx on Philosophy and Society*, trans. Loyd D. Easton and Kurt H. Guddat (Garden City: Doubleday, 1967), 402.

3. Stephen Jay Gould, "Literary Bias on the Slippery Slope," in *Bully for Brontosaurus: Reflections in Natural History* (New York: Norton, 1991), 251.

4. Laurence S. Lockridge, *The Ethics of Romanticism* (Cambridge: Cambridge University Press, 1989), 33–34.

5. J. Hillis Miller, *The Ethics of Reading* (New York: Columbia University Press, 1987), 58. It could be argued that speaking here is the voice of a momentarily forgetful son of a Baptist minister. But I don't think so. More to the point, deconstructionist theory typically presumes a connection between logocentric theories of language and social authoritarianism and oppression. The campaign of deconstructionist critics to hear again marginalized voices and decenter established ones is very much about ethical criteria of justice, fairness, and access to power—criteria which I would insist are not ultimately very different from those espoused within classic liberal, democratic values.

6. Gertrude Himmelfarb, *Poverty and Compassion: The Moral Imagination of the Late Victorians* (New York, Knopf, 1991), 4.

7. Such is the argument in Jonathan Rose's "Secular Religion," chap. 1 in *The Edwardian Temperament, 1895–1919* (Athens: Ohio University Press, 1986). Beatrice Webb remarked in 1884, "Social questions are the vital questions of today: they take the place of religion" (Himmelfarb, *Poverty and Compassion*, 4).

8. Charles Dickens, *Bleak House* (1853; Harmondsworth: Penguin, 1971), 268.

9. Henry Mayhew, *London Labour and the London Poor* (1851); Charles Booth, *Life and Labour of the People of London*, 17 vols. (1892–1903).

10. On the degeneration motif, which was interpreted at biological, racial, economic—indeed every level—of the nation's life, see especially Samuel Hynes's *The Edwardian Turn of Mind* (Princeton: Princeton University Press, 1968), 15–53, and Michael Rosenthal's *The Character Factory: Baden-Powell and the Origins of the Boy Scout Movement* (New York: Pantheon, 1984).

11. Martin Green, *The English Novel in the Twentieth Century: [The Doom of Empire]* (London: Routledge & Kegan Paul, 1984), xii.

12. L. T. Hobhouse, *Liberalism* (1911; New York: Oxford University Press, 1964), 122.

13. Ian Watt, *Conrad in the Nineteenth Century* (Berkeley: University of California Press, 1979), 159.

14. Alan Bullock and Maurice Shock, eds. *The Liberal Tradition from Fox to Keynes* (Oxford: Clarendon Press, 1956), xl.

15. J. A. Hobson, *The Crisis of Liberalism: New Issues of Democracy* (London: P. S. King & Sons, 1909), 259.

16. George L. Bernstein, *Liberalism and Liberal Politics in Edwardian England* (Winchester, Mass.: Allen & Unwin, 1986), 34.

17. Asa Briggs, "The Political Scene," in *Edwardian England 1901–1914*, ed. Simon Nowell-Smith (London: Oxford University Press, 1964), 56.

18. Jefferson Hunter, *Edwardian Fiction* (Cambridge: Harvard University Press, 1982), 108.

19. Lionel Trilling, preface to *The Liberal Imagination: Essays on Literature and Society* (New York: Harcourt, 1949).

20. D. A. Hamer, *Liberal Politics in the Age of Gladstone and Rosebery: A Study in Leadership and Policy* (Oxford: Clarendon Press, 1972), xii, 1–3.

21. D. A. Cook, *A Short History of the Liberal Party 1900–1988*, 3d ed. (London: Macmillan, 1989), 2.

22. Ian Bradley, *The Strange Rebirth of Liberal Britain* (London: Chatto & Windus, 1985), makes a strong case for beginning the genealogy of liberalism with Milton, noting, among other things, that "a copy of the pamphlet" containing the argument of *Areopagitica* "was placed on the high altar of Westminster Abbey at the special service to mark the centenary of the British Liberal Party in May 1977." Furthermore, that work "also serves as the symbol of office of the party president. Every new incumbent receives a bound copy from his predecessor at the annual assembly" (12). See also Bullock and Shock, eds., *Liberal Tradition*, xx–xxi.

23. John Stuart Mill, *"On Liberty" with "The Subjection of Women"; and "Chapters on Socialism"* (1859; reprint, Cambridge: Cambridge University Press, 1989), 15.

24. Ibid.

25. Brian Harrison, *Peaceable Kingdom: Stability and Change in Modern Britain* (Oxford: Clarendon Press, 1982), 390.

26. Eugenio F. Biagini and Alastair J. Reid, *Currents of Radicalism: Popular Radicalism, Organised Labour and Party Politics in Britain, 1850–1914* (Cambridge: Cambridge University Press, 1991), 5.

27. See, for instance, John Gray, *Liberalism* (Minneapolis: University of Minnesota Press, 1986), 27–29; Eugenio F. Biagini, *Liberty, Retrenchment and Reform: Popular Liberalism in the Age of Gladstone, 1860–1880* (Cambridge: Cambridge

University Press, 1992), 107; J. L. Hammond and M. R. D. Foot, *Gladstone and Liberalism* (New York: Macmillan, 1953), 31–32; Bullock and Shock, *Liberal Tradition*, xxxiv, liv.

28. Isaiah Berlin, *Four Essays on Liberty* (New York: Oxford University Press, 1969), 176–77.

29. Lord Acton summarized the liberal understanding of freedom yoked to conscience when he said, "Liberty is not the power of doing what we like, but the right of doing what we ought. . . . [It] is ultimately founded on the idea of conscience." Quoted in Bradley, *Strange Rebirth*, 15.

30. Bradley, *Strange Rebirth*, 26.

31. A. V. Dicey, *Lectures on the Relation between Law and Public Opinion in England during the Nineteenth Century* (1914; reprint, New York: AMS Press, 1978), 254.

32. Bullock and Shock, *Liberal Tradition*, xlv.

33. Ibid.

34. Gray, *Liberalism*, 27; Dicey, *Law and Public Opinion*, 220–24; Bradley, *Strange Rebirth*, 20.

35. Harrison, *Peaceable Kingdom*, 392.

36. Ibid., 390.

37. Bullock and Shock, *Liberal Tradition*, liv, lv.

38. Quoted in Harrison, *Peaceable Kingdom*, 238.

39. Karl Mannheim, "The Utopian Mentality," in *Ideology and Utopia* (London: Routledge & Kegan Paul, 1952), 173–236.

40. Raymond Williams, *Culture and Society 1780–1950* (London: Chatto & Windus, 1958), 100. For a complete genealogy of the phrase "Two Nations," see Gertrude Himmelfarb, *The Idea of Poverty: England in the Early Industrial Age* (New York: Knopf, 1984), 492.

41. *Webster's Ninth New Collegiate Dictionary* (Springfield, Mass.: Merriam-Webster, 1983), 542.

42. Philip Rieff, *The Triumph of the Therapeutic: Uses of Faith after Freud* (New York: Harper, 1966), 14.

43. Ibid., 15.

44. Virginia Woolf, "Modern Fiction," in *The Common Reader* (1925; San Diego: Harcourt, 1984), 146–54.

My separation of Edwardian and modernist writers may seem too conventional in light of recent attempts to minimize the distinctions. While I am in partial sympathy to this effort to uncover modernist indebtedness to Edwardian writers, the break announced by Woolf was more than mere rhetoric, as is implied by Louis Menand in *Sewanee Review* (98 [1990]: 267–74). Menand notes that Arnold Bennett's column in the *New Age* regarding the London neo-impressionist exhibit was "prescient" of aesthetic revolution long before Woolf made her hyperbolic announcement in 1924 that "on or about December 1910, human character changed."

Like Menand, I find the pages of the *New Age* to be one of the most significant sources for understanding literary currents in the period. But by that token, it must be pointed out that Bennett (alias Jacob Tonson) ceased writing his "Readers and Writers" column in September 1911, a couple of months after Wells's views on the novel were roundly attacked by J. M. Kennedy in the same magazine ("The Last Straw," 6 July 1911). Perusing the pages of the *New Age* from 1909 to 1913, it becomes plain that the magazine's broadsides by the end of 1911 against the Victorian and Edwardian writers have grown almost uninterrupted and are also inseparable from an increasingly shrill attack on liberalism, socialism, and democracy—those social doctrines with which many Edwardian writers were associated. Joining A. R. Orage in this vitriol were J. M. Kennedy, T. E. Hulme, and Oscar Levy, who introduced England to the writings of Nietzsche. The break between Edwardian and modernist affinities is unmistakable, with the latter showing themselves to be of the most antiliberal kind.

45. Hunter, *Edwardian Fiction*, 112.

46. Trilling, *Liberal Imagination*, 94.

47. Irving Howe, *The Decline of the New* (New York: Harcourt, 1970), 10. See also John R. Harrison's *The Reactionaries: Yeats, Lewis, Pound, Eliot, Lawrence; A Study of the Anti-Democratic Intelligentsia* (New York: Schocken, 1967).

CHAPTER ONE

1. John Stuart Mill, *Nature and Utility of Religion* (Indianapolis: Bobbs-Merrill, 1958), 68–69.

2. Ibid., 64–65.

3. See, for instance, Eugenio F. Biagini, *Liberty, Retrenchment and Reform: Popular Liberalism in the Age of Gladstone, 1860–1880* (Cambridge: Cambridge University Press, 1992), 218; Edward Royle and James Walvin, *English Radicals and Reformers 1760–1848* (Lexington: University Press of Kentucky, 1982), 184; and Brian Harrison, *Peaceable Kingdom: Stability and Change in Modern Britain* (Oxford: Clarendon Press, 1982), 401.

4. Friedrich Nietzsche, *On the Genealogy of Morals*, in *"On the Genealogy of Morals" and "Ecce Homo,"* trans. Walter Kaufmann and R. J. Hollingdale (New York: Vintage, 1967), 90–91.

5. Friedrich Nietzsche, *Twilight of the Idols*, in *"Twilight of the Idols" and "The Anti-Christ,"* trans. R. J. Hollingdale (Harmondsworth: Penguin, 1968), 53.

6. In his *Autobiography* (1850; London: Cresset Press, 1949), Leigh Hunt retrospectively assessed Shelley: "His want of faith, indeed, in the letter, and his exceeding faith in the spirit, of Christianity, formed a comment the one on the other, very formidable to those who chose to forget what Scripture itself observes on that point."* (*"For the letter killeth, but the spirit giveth life.")

7. The word "flirtation" carries too pejorative a connotation. Critics and biographers are unsure how to assess Shelley's position on nonviolence; perhaps the most exhaustive treatment to date of it is in David Sprunger's "Shelley and His Doctrine of Nonviolence" (unpublished paper, University of Kansas, 1990). Kenneth Neill Cameron, *Shelley: The Golden Years* (Cambridge: Harvard University Press, 1974), argues that "the pacifist element in the poem has been exaggerated and sometimes misunderstood"; that what is being asserted "is not . . . the pacifism of the individual conscience, but a pacifism of massive nonviolent resistance" (349–50). Yet I am uncomfortable with the way Shelley's thinking about pacifism typically gets relegated to minor importance. That move seems typical of liberalism's relationship to pacifism generally. Thus Michael Henry Scrivener can argue in *Radical Shelley: The Philosophical Anarchism and Utopian Thought of Percy Bysshe Shelley* (Princeton: Princeton University Press, 1982) that what matters in the poem *Hellas* "is not whether *Hellas* endorses violence or nonviolence; the important problem is maintaining an *ethical idealism*" (293). However, recent critics on the question of violence and writing, Elaine Scarry and Lynne Hanley, to name just two, take to task this vocabulary of abstract idealism when aesthetic representations of harm to the body are at issue. See Scarry's *The Body in Pain* (New York: Oxford University Press, 1985) and Hanley's *Writing War: Gender, Fiction, Memory* (Amherst: University of Massachusetts Press, 1991).

8. For complete explications of the poem and its publication history, see Cameron, *Shelley*, 343–50, and Richard Holmes, *Shelley: The Pursuit* (London: Weidenfeld & Nicolson, 1974), 529–40.

9. Peter J. Thorslev, Jr., discusses the transformation of the label "Jacobin" to "liberal" in "Post-Waterloo Liberalism: The Second Generation," *Studies in Romanticism* 28 (1989): 444–45.

10. Leigh Hunt, *A Saunter through the West End* (London: Hurst and Blackett, 1861), 235.

11. Thorslev, "Post-Waterloo Liberalism," 437–61.

12. Richard Holmes, citing W. H. Wickwar's *The Struggle for the Freedom of the Press 1819–1822* (1928), notes that in 1819 there were "no less than seventy-five prosecutions for seditious or blasphemous libel" (540).

13. Thorslev, "Post-Waterloo Liberalism," 457.

14. The most complete account of the *Liberal* is W. H. Marshall's *Byron, Shelley, Hunt and "The Liberal"* (Philadelphia, 1960). For contemporary reviews of the magazine's four issues, see James Hogg, "Contemporary Reception of 'The Liberal,'" *Byron Journal* 7 (1979): 61–75.

15. Quoted by Michael Foot in *The Politics of Paradise: A Vindication of Byron* (London: Collins, 1988), 335.

16. Quoted in ibid., 335.

17. Judith Shklar, "The Liberalism of Fear," in *Liberalism and the Moral Life*, ed. Nancy L. Rosenblum (Cambridge: Harvard University Press, 1989), 23.

18. Ann Blainey, *Immortal Boy: A Portrait of Leigh Hunt* (New York: St. Martin's, 1985), 43.

19. J. R. Dinwiddy, "The Early Nineteenth-Century Campaign against Flogging in the Army," in *Radicalism and Reform in Britain, 1780-1850* (London: Hambledon Press, 1992), 125-48. Dinwiddy notes that while the practice did not entirely cease until 1881, it had become relatively rare already in the 1830s (125).

20. John Scott, "One Thousand Lashes!!," *Stanford News*, 24 August 1810; reprint, *Examiner*, 2 September 1810.

21. Rosemary Ashton, *G. H. Lewes: A Life* (Oxford: Clarendon Press, 1991), 88.

22. Leigh Hunt, "Containing Some Remarks on War and Military Statesmen," postscript to *Captain Sword and Captain Pen* (1835; reprint, Iowa City: Friends of the University of Iowa Libraries, 1984), 63.

23. Donald Reiman asks this in his fine summation of Hunt's career, "Leigh Hunt in Literary History: A Response," in *The Life and Times of Leigh Hunt: Papers Delivered at a Symposium*, ed. Robert McCown (Iowa City: Friends of the University of Iowa Libraries, 1985), 81.

24. Reform rhetoric throughout the nineteenth century makes habitual use of the trope linking the plight of African slaves to that of industrial workers, the condition of Africa to the character of city slums. See, for instance, Harrison, *Peaceable Kingdom*, 379-80, 421; Kathleen Tillotson, *Novels of the Eighteen-Forties* (Oxford: Clarendon Press, 1954), 79, 81; Royle and Walvin, *English Radicals and Reformers*, 135; A. V. Dicey, *Lectures on the Relation between Law and Public Opinion in England during the Nineteenth Century* (1914; reprint, New York: AMS Press, 1978), 220; and William Booth, *In Darkest England, and the Way Out* (New York: Funk & Wagnalls, 1891), 11-12, 23. The flavor of this connection is wonderfully captured in a letter written by Unitarian Mary Carpenter to an American abolitionist in 1849: "My mind is now almost as much engrossed by our Ragged School as yours is by the Abolition question. Indeed they are very kindred subjects; you are trying to free the god-like spirit which has been enthralled by the wickedness of man, by external force; we are trying to free that divine nature from the still more than heathenish darkness in which it is growing to become a fiend, a worse than American slave." From *The Life and Work of Mary Carpenter* (London, 1879), quoted in Gertrude Himmelfarb, *The Idea of Poverty* (New York: Knopf, 1984), 381.

25. Thorslev, "Post-Waterloo Liberalism," 450.

26. Benjamin Constant, *On the Spirit of Conquest and Usurpation in Political Writings*, trans. Biancamaria Fontana (Cambridge: Cambridge University Press, 1988).

27. Michael Howard, *War and the Liberal Conscience* (New Brunswick: Rutgers University Press, 1978), 32-33, 40-47. See also F. H. Hinsley, *Power and the Pursuit of Peace in the History of Relations between States* (Cambridge: Cambridge University Press, 1963).

28. Foot, *Politics of Paradise*, 376–81.

29. William St. Clair, *That Greece Might Still Be Free: The Philhellenes in the War of Independence* (London: Oxford University Press, 1972), 184.

30. Carl Woodring, *Politics and English Romantic Poetry* (Cambridge: Harvard University Press, 1970), 329. See also Edward E. Bostetter, *The Romantic Ventriloquists* (Seattle: University of Washington Press, 1963), who contends that Byron's "most concrete idea was of nationalism" (298).

31. Howard, *War and the Liberal Conscience*, 32.

32. St. Clair, *That Greece Might Still Be Free*, 195–204. For a more general discussion of the intersection of evangelical and utilitarian ideals in the Victorian period, see G. M. Young, *Victorian England: Portrait of an Age* (1936; London: Oxford University Press, 1974), 10–12.

33. St. Clair, *That Greece Might Still Be Free*, 198, 202–3.

34. T. A. Jackson, *Charles Dickens: The Progress of a Radical* (1937; New York: International Publishers, 1987), 158.

CHAPTER TWO

1. Alison Adburgham, *Silver Fork Society: Fashionable Life and Literature from 1814 to 1840* (London: Constable, 1983), 2.

2. Kathryn Chittick, *Dickens and the 1830s* (Cambridge: Cambridge University Press, 1990), 22.

3. Kathleen Tillotson, *Novels of the Eighteen-Forties* (Oxford: Clarendon Press, 1954), 73–75.

4. Chittick, *Dickens and the 1830s*, 24.

5. Tillotson, *Novels of the Eighteen-Forties*, 88.

6. Edward Royle and James Walvin, *English Radicals and Reformers 1760-1848* (Lexington: University Press of Kentucky, 1982), 144–45.

7. Derek Beales, *From Castlereagh to Gladstone 1815-1885* (New York: Norton, 1969), 110.

8. Chittick, *Dickens and the 1830s*, 22.

9. For general discussions of the relationship between the British press and politics of the period, see A. Aspinell, *Politics and the Press 1780-1850* (London: Home & Van Thal, 1949). Aspinell takes up specifically the rising social status of journalists in "The Social Status of Journalists at the Beginning of the Nineteenth Century," *Review of English Studies* 21 (July 1945): 216–32.

10. Gaye Tuchman, *Edging Women Out: Victorian Novelists, Publishers, and Social Change* (New Haven: Yale University Press, 1989), describes how this process also meant that women were gradually excluded over the course of the nineteenth century from the ranks of "literary" novelists.

11. Pam Morris, *Dickens's Class Consciousness: A Marginal View* (Houndmills, Basingstoke: Macmillan, 1991), 6.

12. Quoted in ibid., 85.

13. Anita Levy, *Other Women: The Writing of Class, Race, and Gender, 1832–1898* (Princeton: Princeton University Press, 1991), 37.

14. Quoted in ibid., 33–34.

15. Tillotson, *Novels of the Eighteen-Forties*, 79.

16. According to the *Oxford English Dictionary*, the word "entropy" did not enter the English language until 1865; however, Clausius wrote his first full discussion of "entropie" in the German language in 1854 (Paul Edwards, ed., *Encyclopedia of Philosophy* [New York: Macmillan, 1967], 1:526). J. Hillis Miller's essay on *Bleak House* in *Charles Dickens: The World of His Novels* (Bloomington: Indiana University Press, 1958) most fully explores the concept of entropy as key to explicating the novel.

17. *Little Dorrit* (1857; Harmondsworth: Penguin, 1967), 67–68. Subsequent quotations from the novel are cited parenthetically in the text and are from this edition.

18. J. Hillis Miller, writing in *The Disappearance of God: Five Nineteenth-Century Writers* (Cambridge: Belknap, 1963), draws the connection between the experience of the city and post-theist consciousness: "The city is the literal representation of the progressive humanization of the world. And where is there room for God in the city? Though it is impossible to tell whether man has excluded God by building the great cities, or whether the cities have been built because God has disappeared, in any case the two go together. Life in the city is the way in which many men have experienced most directly what it means to live without God in the world" (5). Miller simply confirms that Tillotson is correct in arguing that the two dominant themes emerging in novels of the 1840s are urban crisis and the religious crisis of faith (73–75, 126–30). *Little Dorrit* brings this twin awareness to a head.

19. Owen Chadwick distills it best: "In Comte's mind is a close link between evolution of knowledge and moral progress. As we know more we see relations of things better, we become more benevolent. As we become more intelligent we become more moral" (*The Secularization of the European Mind in the Nineteenth Century* [Cambridge: Cambridge University Press, 1975], 236).

20. Irving Howe, "George Eliot and the Jews," *Partisan Review* 46 (1979): 361, 370. See also Sally Shuttlesworth, "The Language of Science and Psychology in George Eliot's *Daniel Deronda*," in *Victorian Science and Victorian Values: Literary Perspectives*, ed. James Paradis (New York: New York Academy of Sciences, 1981), 272.

21. Alexander Welsh, *The City of Dickens* (Oxford: Clarendon Press, 1971), 134, 135.

22. Howe, "Three Notes on Dickens" (lecture given at the Graduate Center of

the City University of New York, 20 November 1987). Howe argues Little Dorrit's vocation is "for life—not for death, which is the vocation of most saints."

23. Ibid.

24. Lionel Trilling, *The Opposing Self* (1955; New York: Harcourt, 1979), 57.

25. Elaine Showalter, "Guilt, Authority, and the Shadows of *Little Dorrit*," *Nineteenth-Century Fiction* 34 (1979): 35.

26. George Eliot, "Leaves from a Note-Book," in *Essays of George Eliot*, ed. Thomas Pinney (New York: Columbia University Press, 1963), 440.

27. Robert M. Adams, "Religion of Man, Religion of Woman," in *Art, Politics, and Will: Essays in Honor of Lionel Trilling*, ed. Quentin Anderson et al. (New York: Basic, 1977), 177.

28. William Myers, *The Teaching of George Eliot* (Totowa, N.J.: Barnes, 1984), 182.

29. Friedrich Nietzsche, *The Genealogy of Morals*, in *"The Birth of Tragedy" and "The Genealogy of Morals*," trans. Francis Golffing (Garden City, N.Y.: Doubleday, 1956), 194. The *Oxford English Dictionary*'s etymological entry on "guilt" does not explain the connections between "guilt" and "debt," although it is posited that the Old English "scyld" and German "schuld" "have developed the sense of 'guilt' from that of 'debt.'"

30. Ibid., 195.

31. Donald David Stone, *Novelists in a Changing World: Meredith, James, and the Transformation of English Fiction in the 1880's* (Cambridge: Harvard University Press, 1972), 305.

32. Janet Larson, *Dickens and the Broken Scripture* (Athens: University of Georgia Press, 1985), 234.

33. George Holoch, "Consciousness and Society in *Little Dorrit*," *Victorian Studies* 21 (1978): 350.

34. Ibid., 338.

35. Larson, *Dickens and the Broken Scripture*, 235-36.

36. Miller, *Charles Dickens*, 233.

37. Michel Foucault, *Power/Knowledge: Selected Interviews and Other Writings 1972-1977*, ed. Colin Gordon, trans. Colin Gordon et al. (New York: Pantheon, 1980), 98.

38. Charles Taylor, "Foucault on Freedom and Truth," in *Foucault: A Critical Reader*, ed. David Couzens Hoy (New York: Basil Blackwell, 1986), 90-91.

39. Ross Dabney, *Love and Property in the Novels of Dickens* (London: Chatto & Windus, 1967), 123-24.

40. Dennis Walder, *Dickens and Religion* (London: Allen & Unwin, 1981), 124.

41. George Orwell, *A Collection of Essays* (New York: Harcourt, 1946), 52.

42. Barbara Weiss, *The Hell of the English: Bankruptcy and the Victorian Novel* (Lewisburg: Bucknell University Press, 1986), 151.

43. Jeff Nunokawa, "Getting and Having: Some Versions of Possession in

Little Dorrit," in *Charles Dickens*, ed. Harold Bloom (New York: Chelsea House, 1987), 319.

44. Badri Raina, *Dickens and the Dialectic of Growth* (Madison: University of Wisconsin Press, 1986), 18, 19.

CHAPTER THREE

1. Katherine Bailey Linehan, "Mixed Politics: The Critique of Imperialism in *Daniel Deronda*," *Texas Studies in Language and Literature* 34 (Fall 1992): 324-25.

2. Percy Shelley, preface to *Hellas*, in *Shelley's Poetry and Prose*, ed. Donald Reiman and Sharon B. Powers (New York: Norton, 1977), 409.

3. "State of Modern Greece," reprinted from the *Times* in the *Examiner*, 7 October 1821, 627.

4. Leigh Hunt, "The Greeks," *Examiner*, 7 October 1821, 626.

5. Bernard Semmel, *George Eliot and the Politics of National Inheritance* (New York: Oxford University Press, 1994), 141.

6. Henry James, "*Daniel Deronda*: A Conversation," *Atlantic Monthly*, December 1876, reprinted in *Henry James, the Critical Muse: Selected Literary Criticism*, ed. Roger Gard (Harmondsworth: Penguin, 1987), 104-21.

7. F. R. Leavis, *The Great Tradition: George Eliot, Henry James, Joseph Conrad* (New York: New York University Press, 1964), 80.

8. Gordon S. Haight, *George Eliot: A Biography* (New York: Oxford University Press, 1968), 488-90.

9. Ruby V. Redinger, *George Eliot: The Emergent Self* (New York: Knopf, 1975), 473.

10. Mary Ellen Doyle, *The Sympathetic Response: George Eliot's Fictional Rhetoric* (East Brunswick: Associated University Presses, 1981), 168.

11. Calvin Bedient, *Architects of the Self: George Eliot, D. H. Lawrence, and E. M. Forster* (Berkeley: University of California Press, 1972), 44.

12. U. C. Knoepflmacher, *Religious Humanism and the Victorian Novel: George Eliot, Walter Pater, and Samuel Butler* (Princeton: Princeton University Press, 1965), 60 (n. 61).

13. Irving Howe, "George Eliot and the Jews," *Partisan Review* 46 (1979): 365.

14. Badri Raina, "*Daniel Deronda*: A View of Grandcourt," *Studies in the Novel* 17 (1985): 371-72.

15. George Eliot, review of *The Progress of the Intellect, as Exemplified in the Religious Development of the Greeks and the Hebrews*, by Robert William Mackay (Chapman, 1850), in *Westminster Review* 54 (January 1851), reprinted in *Essays of George Eliot*, ed. Thomas Pinney (New York: Columbia University Press, 1963), 29.

16. Robert McCarron, "Evil and Eliot's Religion of Humanity: Grandcourt in *Daniel Deronda*," *Ariel* 11 (1980): 72, 73.

17. *Daniel Deronda* (1876; Harmondsworth: Penguin, 1967), 54. Subsequent quotations from the novel are cited parenthetically in the text and are from this edition.

18. McCarron, "Evil and Eliot's Religion of Humanity," 78.

19. Sally Shuttlesworth, *George Eliot and Nineteenth-Century Science: The Make Believe of a Beginning* (Cambridge: Cambridge University Press, 1984), 190, 191.

20. Sally Shuttlesworth, "The Language of Science and Psychology in George Eliot's *Daniel Deronda*," in *Victorian Science and Victorian Values: Literary Perspectives*, ed. James Paradis (New York: New York Academy of Sciences, 1981), 281.

21. McCarron, "Evil and Eliot's Religion of Humanity," 82.

22. Ibid., 83.

23. William Myers, *The Teaching of George Eliot* (Totowa, N.J.: Barnes, 1984), 182.

24. Raina, "*Daniel Deronda*," 372.

25. Bedient, *Architects of the Self*, 34.

26. Bernard Paris comments in *Experiments in Life: George Eliot's Quest for Values* (Detroit: Wayne State University Press, 1965): "As she has dramatized again and again in her fiction, not all communities provide moral sustenance; many are stultifying" (194). This insight seems to be lost sight of in some more recent criticism—see, for instance, Pam Morris's *Dickens's Class Consciousness: A Marginal View* (Houndmills, Basingstoke: Macmillan, 1991), which would make Eliot out to be simply a reifying force of Victorian moral values (6, 7).

27. T. R. Wright, "George Eliot and Positivism: A Reassessment," *Modern Language Review* 76 (1981): 257. See also Semmel, *George Eliot*, 55-77.

28. Wright, "George Eliot and Positivism," 270. For the pervasiveness of Comte's theories in Eliot's writing, see also William Baker, "The Other George Eliot Notebook at the Folger Shakespeare Library—A Survey," *George Eliot George Henry Lewes Newsletter* (September 1988): 3; also T. R. Wright's *The Religion of Humanity: The Impact of Comtean Positivism on Victorian Britain* (Cambridge: Cambridge University Press, 1986), 173-201.

29. The epigraphs at this chapter's beginning are indicative of the kind of optimism which leading British intellectuals maintained in the 1870s about the possibility of grounding ethics in Darwin's evolutionary theory. Eliot's last novel reveals the beginnings of this disintegrating optimism.

30. Thomas H. Huxley's announcement that ethics would have to be grounded *against* Darwinian principles of nature, rather than *in* them, came in the Romanes Lecture, reprinted in *Evolution and Ethics and Other Essays* (New York: D. Appleton, 1929), 83.

31. Raina, "*Daniel Deronda*," 374.

32. Arthur Schopenhauer, *The World as Will and Representation*, trans. E. F. J. Payne (1958; New York: Dover, 1966), 2:198-99.

33. Ibid., 1:363-64, quoted in E. A. McCobb, "*Daniel Deronda* as Will and

Representation: George Eliot and Schopenhauer," *Modern Language Review* 80 (1985): 548.

34. Myers, *Teaching of George Eliot*, 214.

35. Alasdair MacIntyre, *After Virtue: A Study in Moral Theory* (Notre Dame: University of Notre Dame Press, 1981), 24.

36. Ibid., 24.

37. Terry Eagleton, *Criticism and Ideology: A Study of Marxist Literary Theory* (London: NLB, 1976), 116.

38. Ibid.

39. For a full account of the Jamaica massacre and the Eyre case, see Bernard Semmel, *Jamaica Blood and Victorian Conscience: The Governor Eyre Controversy* (Boston: Houghton Mifflin, 1963), esp. 29-55.

40. Ibid., 115.

41. Ibid., 177-79.

42. Ibid., 51-52.

43. J. A. Hobson, *The Psychology of Jingoism* (London: Grant Richards, 1901), 107. A year later, Hobson denounced imperialism as "motivated, not by the interests of the nation as a whole, but by those of certain classes, who impose the policy upon the nation for their own advantage" (*Imperialism: A Study* [1902; Ann Arbor: University of Michigan Press, 1965], 356). It should be mentioned that Hobson's conspiracy-theory views contained no small part of anti-Semitism; see Bernard Semmel, *The Liberal Ideal and the Demons of Empire: Theories of Imperialism from Adam Smith to Lenin* (Baltimore: Johns Hopkins University Press, 1993), 111-12. Ironically, it would fall to a pro-imperialist writer, Kipling, to illustrate most graphically how the working classes became the cannon fodder of imperial policy even as they cheered the Empire on.

44. Eugenio F. Biagini, *Liberty, Retrenchment and Reform: Popular Liberalism in the Age of Gladstone, 1860-1880* (Cambridge: Cambridge University Press, 1992), 186.

45. Ibid., 51.

46. Semmel, *George Eliot.* "Rather than regarding Eliot as a Victorian liberal," argues Semmel, "and as has been the convention, a liberal whose views were somewhat qualified by a Comtian positivism, one can gain a better understanding of her politics, and of her writings, if we see her as a conservative, enlarged and modified by a heterodox positivism. Not that Eliot did not share many of the interests of Victorian liberals and Positivists. But these interests did not constitute the principal thrust of her outlook. One may better comprehend her position if we take into account her deep sense of dependence on the past, her commitment to the English political tradition, and her vision of the English nationality" (54). Semmel's attempt to remake Eliot in the image of Burke and Disraeli ultimately does not hold up to inspection, especially given her rendering of where English country tradition and inheritance have led: Grandcourt. I concur with Semmel that Eliot wants to

affirm the recovery of a Romantic nationalist tradition. But I prefer to read her embrace of Zionism, with Raymond Williams, as a "deeply felt, deeply desired transcendence" standing in opposition to the English national tradition, not to be conflated with it. See Raymond Williams, *The English Novel from Dickens to Lawrence* (New York: Oxford University Press, 1970), 86–89. For further elucidation of Eliot's position within English liberalism, see Ian Bradley, *The Strange Rebirth of Liberal Britain* (London: Chatto & Windus, 1985), 66–67.

47. Michel Foucault, *Power/Knowledge: Selected Interviews and Other Writings 1972-1977*, ed. Colin Gordon, trans. Colin Gordon et al. (New York: Pantheon, 1980), 97–98.

48. Patrick Reilly, *The Literature of Guilt: From Gulliver to Golding* (Basingstoke, Hampshire: Macmillan, 1988), 4.

49. Samuel Hynes, introduction to *Further Speculations*, by T. E. Hulme (Minneapolis: University of Minnesota Press, 1955), xix, xxx, xxxi.

50. Wallace Martin, *"The New Age" under Orage: Chapters in English Cultural History* (Manchester: Manchester University Press, 1967), 14–16.

51. Ibid., 214, 216.

52. T. S. Eliot, "A Commentary," *Criterion* 2 (April 1924): 231.

CHAPTER FOUR

1. The best biographies of Gissing, Jacob Korg's *George Gissing: A Critical Biography* (Seattle: University of Washington Press, 1963) and John Halperin's *Gissing: A Life in Books* (New York: Oxford University Press, 1982), in the essentials follow Morley Roberts's account of this incident in *The Private Life of Henry Maitland* (New York: George Doran, 1912). By most critical estimates, this crisis is the central shaping event of Gissing's life.

2. Mabel Collins Donnelly, *George Gissing: Grave Comedian* (Cambridge: Harvard University Press, 1954), 29.

3. Austin Harrison, "George Gissing," *Nineteenth Century* 60 (1906): 453–63, reprinted in *George Gissing: Critical Essays*, ed. Jean-Pierre Michaux (Totowa, N.J.: Barnes, 1981), 29. The character Ryecroft expresses the identical sentiment in *The Private Papers of Henry Ryecroft* (1903; Brighton: Harvester Press, 1982): "I had in me the making of a scholar" (51). Subsequent quotations from the novel are cited parenthetically in the text and are from this edition.

4. Gissing to Morley Roberts, 10 February 1895, in *Gissing: The Critical Heritage*, ed. Pierre Coustillas and Colin Partridge (London: Routledge & Kegan Paul, 1972), 244.

5. *London and the Life of Literature in Late Victorian England: The Diary of George Gissing, Novelist*, ed. Pierre Coustillas (Lewisburg: Bucknell University Press, 1978), 210.

6. Ibid., 387-88.

7. Ibid., 413.

8. Roberts, *Private Life of Henry Maitland*, 49.

9. Halperin, *Gissing*, vii.

10. Frederic Harrison to Gissing, 22 July 1880, in Coustillas and Partridge, *Gissing: The Critical Heritage*, 55.

11. Jacob Korg, "Division of Purpose in George Gissing," *PMLA* 70 (1955): 323-36, reprinted in *Collected Articles on George Gissing*, ed. Pierre Coustillas (New York: Barnes, 1968), 71. In his biography of Gissing, Korg notes, "The conflict between esthetic and moral intentions that is so clear in *The Unclassed* continued to embarrass Gissing. He had to make the choice anew with every novel, and yet the choice was never made" (*George Gissing*, 69).

12. Gissing to Algernon, 8 June 1880, in *Letters of George Gissing to Members of His Family*, ed. Algernon and Ellen Gissing (London: Constable, 1927), 73.

13. Korg, "Division of Purpose," 71. The review appeared in *Athenaeum*, 12 June 1880; Gissing's letter to Algernon (15 June 1880) is quoted from *Letters of George Gissing to Members of His Family*, 74.

14. George Gissing, *Workers in the Dawn* (London: Remington, 1880; reprint, New York: Garland, 1976), 1:247. Subsequent quotations from the novel are cited parenthetically in the text and are from this edition.

15. *Letters of George Gissing to Eduard Bertz, 1887-1903*, ed. Arthur C. Young (New Brunswick: Rutgers University Press, 1961), 15 January 1892, 145.

16. Gillian Tindall, *The Born Exile: George Gissing* (London: Temple Smith, 1974), 111.

17. George Gissing, *Pall Mall Gazette*, 14 September 1880, reprinted in *Notes on Social Democracy*, ed. Jacob Korg (London: Enitharmon Press, 1968), 13.

18. George Gissing, "The Hope of Pessimism," in *George Gissing: Essays and Fiction*, ed. Pierre Coustillas (Baltimore: Johns Hopkins University Press, 1970), 96. Coustillas dates the writing of this essay, which Gissing kept from publication, at around October 1882.

19. Korg, *George Gissing*, 33, 34, 259-60.

20. Ibid., 44.

21. The clash of Gissing's classical instincts with naturalistic depiction was always strong. Take, for example, his description and commentary on one artist's rendering of Prometheus: "A thought on realism. In the Corsini Gallery is Salvator Rosa's picture of Prometheus Bound. On a rock lies a naked wretch, whose bowels are being visibly torn out by a huge bird of prey. Blood pours down from the ghastly wounds, and the sufferer's mouth is stretched wide in a yell of agony. The background is black with horror. Well now, *why not* all this? It is a perfectly truthful representation of such an event. Yes, but it happens to be supremely loathsome, and to convey merely the impression of a galley-slave under torture. We know very well that this is *not Prometheus at all*, and there is the answer to all such

nonsense" (*Letters of George Gissing to Eduard Bertz*, 7 December 1888, 27–28).

22. Terry Eagleton, *Marxism and Literary Criticism* (Berkeley: University of California Press, 1976), 47. In *Gissing*, Halperin reiterates this when he says, "One senses his [Gissing's] 'passion of sympathy for the suffering poor' without his writing it down in his Commonplace Book and despite his intellectual antipathy to the lower classes" (10).

23. Gissing, *The Unclassed* (1884; reprint, London: Lawrence & Bullen, 1895; reprint of 1895 ed., Brighton: Harvester Press, 1976), 211. Subsequent references to the novel are cited parenthetically in the text and are from this edition.

24. *London and the Life of Literature*, 1 March 1888, 23.

25. Korg, *George Gissing*, 116.

26. Gissing, *The Nether World* (1889; London: J. M. Dent, 1973), 251–52. Subsequent references to the novel are cited parenthetically in the text and are from this edition.

27. Gissing is partly indebted to Dickens for choosing to depict the poor, but unlike Dickens, he never allows himself to sentimentalize them in any way. He makes this difference between himself and Dickens very clear in *Charles Dickens: A Critical Study* (London: Blackie & Sons, 1903). See also John Halperin, "How Gissing Read Dickens," *South Atlantic Quarterly* 83 (1984): 312–22, and Pierre Coustillas, *Gissing's Writings on Dickens* (London: Enitharmon Press, 1969).

28. C. F. G. Masterman, *From the Abyss: Of Its Inhabitants by One of Them* (London: R. B. Johnson, 1902; reprint, New York: Garland, 1980), 2.

29. Asa Briggs, *Victorian Cities* (London: Odhams Press, 1963), 326. See above, Chap. 1, n. 24.

30. Ibid., 326.

31. Fredric Jameson, *The Political Unconscious: Narrative as a Socially Symbolic Act* (Ithaca: Cornell University Press, 1981), 189.

32. Halperin, "How Gissing Read Dickens," 313. Barbara Hardy's remark about Dickens's technique seems much more in keeping with the notion of "the people" than Jameson's attempt to center Gissing in that tradition. Writing in *The Moral Art of Dickens* (London: Athlone Press, 1967), she observes: "Dickens is interested in the conditioned character, but includes in his fiction a continuing fantasy about the ideal, the unconditional virtue. And in Dickens virtue is often the survivor. His novels show a division between the society he rejects and the humanity he believes in, and that humanity, in different ways, is somehow preserved, frozen, shut off, and saved from the social pressure" (4).

33. John Goode, "George Gissing's *The Nether World*," in *Tradition and Tolerance in Nineteenth-Century Fiction*, ed. David Howard, John Lucas, and John Goode (New York: Barnes, 1967), 235.

34. Korg, *George Gissing*, 68.

35. P. J. Keating, *The Working Classes in Victorian Fiction* (London: Routledge & Kegan Paul, 1971), 134.

36. David Grylls, *The Paradox of Gissing* (London: Allen & Unwin, 1986), 39.

37. Goode, "George Gissing's *The Nether World*," 236.

38. Samuel Hynes, *The Edwardian Turn of Mind* (Princeton: Princeton University Press, 1968), 82, 83.

39. George Gissing, *The Whirlpool* (1897; Brighton: Harvester Press, 1977), 13. Subsequent references to the novel are cited parenthetically in the text and are from this edition.

40. Robert L. Selig sums up in *George Gissing* (Boston: Twayne, 1983) the class bias of *Demos* that seems the equivalent of the antifeminist bias in *The Whirlpool*: "Removed from his proper sphere, this exemplary workingman [Mutimer] becomes an incompetent capitalist, a fiancée deserter, and an insensitive husband" (33). The best discussion of *Demos* is John Goode's "Gissing, Morris, and English Socialism," *Victorian Studies* 12 (1968): 201-26.

41. H. G. Wells, "The Novels of Mr George Gissing," *Contemporary Review* (August 1897), reprinted in *George Gissing and H. G. Wells: Their Friendship and Correspondence*, ed. Royal A. Gettman (Urbana: University of Illinois Press, 1961), 258.

42. Gissing to Wells, 7 August 1897, in *George Gissing and H. G. Wells*, 48.

43. *Letters of George Gissing to Eduard Bertz*, 11 December 1899, 268.

44. Ibid., 269. Gissing affirms Robert Buchanan's attack on Kipling, "The Voice of the Hooligan," which appeared in the *Contemporary Review* in December 1899. See also Gissing's anti-imperialist article "Tyrtaeus" (*Review of the Week*, 4 November 1899, reprinted in the *Gissing Newsletter* 10 [July 1974]: 2-3).

45. Gissing wrote in his diary of his son Walter, "What a terrible lesson is the existence of this child, born of a loveless and utterly unsuitable marriage" (*London and the Life of Literature*, 418). These words recall those uttered by Little Father Time: "I ought not to be born, ought I?" (*Jude the Obscure*, pt. 6, chap. 1).

46. Bertz to Gissing, April 1897, Yale archives, reprinted in *Letters of George Gissing to Eduard Bertz*, 228, 229n.

47. To catalog one's sufferings as a defense of personal beliefs is an important literary strategy in Gissing's final testament. The most famous precedent for such a strategy is Paul's lengthy catalog in 2 Cor. 11: "Thrice was I beaten with rods, once was I stoned, thrice I suffered shipwreck, a night and a day have I been in the deep," etc. Gissing makes all too clear in *Ryecroft* that the aestheticism of the present makes no sense without the context of the earlier privations.

48. Irving Howe, *Politics and the Novel* (1957; New York: Avon, 1970), 158.

49. But is the reception of an independent living the cause of moral refinement or the confirmation of already superior character? Gissing vacillates on this. At one point in *Ryecroft*, the narrator suggests that even when he was living in deprivation, full of resentment toward the rich, he was "all that time one of 'the privileged'" (13). On the other hand, Rolfe's reflections in *The Whirlpool* suggest that the getting of money was the beginning of the process of moral refinement:

"The possession of money had done him good. It clarified his passions, or tended that way. A self-respect, which differed appreciably from what he had formerly understood by that term, began to guard him against grossness; together with it there developed in him a new social pride which made him desire the acquaintance of well-bred people" (332–33). In either case, we are in the presence of Pip wiggling between Miss Havisham's talons.

50. Tindall, *The Born Exile*, 35.

CHAPTER FIVE

1. H. G. Wells, *Tono-Bungay* (1909; Lincoln: University of Nebraska Press, 1978), 317.

2. Richard Le Gallienne, *Rudyard Kipling: A Criticism* (London: John Lane, 1900), 128.

3. Henry James to Grace Norton, December 1897, in *Henry James, Letters*, ed. Leon Edel (Cambridge: Harvard University Press, 1984), 4:70, reprinted in *Henry James, the Critical Muse: Selected Literary Criticism*, ed. Roger Gard (Harmondsworth: Penguin, 1987), 326.

4. Martin Green, *The English Novel in the Twentieth Century: [The Doom of Empire]* (London: Routledge & Kegan Paul, 1984), ix–xii. Green states: "When I speak of what Kipling meant to later writers, therefore, I sometimes mean his presence (a culture-criticism concept) rather than his influence (a literary criticism term). Kipling was powerfully present to people who never read him—who reacted to the idea of him" (xii).

5. Robert Buchanan and Sir Walter Besant, *The Voice of "The Hooligan": A Discussion of Kiplingism* (New York: Tucker, 1900), 25. Gissing, in his article "Tyrtaeus" (*Review of the Week*, 4 November 1899, reprinted in the *Gissing Newsletter* 10 [July 1974]), asked "should not even the laureate of the Empire think twice before he blows that ringing clarion of his, and ask himself whether his laurels are more likely to be lasting for having been dipped in blood?" (2).

6. Joseph Conrad, *The Rescue: A Romance of the Shallows* (1919; Garden City: Doubleday, Page & Co., 1923), 3.

7. Martin Seymour-Smith, *Rudyard Kipling* (London: Queen Anne Press, 1989), 70.

8. Buchanan and Besant, *Voice of "The Hooligan,"* 6–7.

9. Most recently, two chapters in Edward Said's *Culture and Imperialism* (New York: Knopf, 1993) provide ample opportunity for making some comparisons: "Two Visions in *Heart of Darkness*" (19–31) and "The Pleasures of Imperialism" (132–62), which addresses specifically *Kim*.

10. David H. Stewart gives a good summary of critical works juxtaposing the two writers' work in "Kipling, Conrad and the Dark Heart," *Conradiana* 19 (1987):

195–205. Included on his list are Sandison's *The Wheel of Empire* (1967), Jonah Raskin's *The Mythology of Imperialism* (1971), Jeffrey Meyer's *Fiction and the Colonial Experience* (1973), John A. McClure's *Kipling and Conrad: The Colonial Fiction* (1981), and Benita Parry's *Conrad and Imperialism: Ideological Boundaries and Visionary Frontiers* (1983). Stewart does not mention Robert F. Lee's shrill right-wing treatment, *Conrad's Colonialism* (The Hague: Mouton & Co., 1969), which blurs practically every ideological distinction between Kipling and Conrad and makes Conrad out to be an uncritical advocate of the imperial "idea." Lee's book, for instance, argues that Kurtz's disaster does not represent the failure of the "idea" but rather one man's failure to live up to the idea's standards. What is ironic is that Lee, usually ignored, substantiates to a large extent Achebe's argument.

11. Chinua Achebe, "An Image of Africa," *Research in African Literatures* 9 (1978): 1–15. See also Frances B. Singh, "The Colonialistic Bias of *Heart of Darkness*," *Conradiana* 10 (1978): 41–54, and Susan L. Blake, "Racism and the Classics: Teaching *Heart of Darkness*," *College Language Association Journal* 25 (1982): 396–404. Among the many responses to Achebe, perhaps the strongest are Hunt Hawkins, "Conrad's Critique of Imperialism in *Heart of Darkness*," *PMLA* 94 (1979): 286–99, and Cedric Watts, " 'A Bloody Racist': About Achebe's View of Conrad," *Yearbook of English Studies* 13 (1983): 196–209. Two voices that mediate the gap between Conrad's racism and anti-imperialism are Ian Watt, *Conrad in the Nineteenth Century* (Berkeley: University of California Press, 1979), esp. 157–61, and Patrick Brantlinger, "*Heart of Darkness*: Anti-Imperialism, Racism, or Impressionism?," *Criticism* 27 (1985): 363–85. Brantlinger's essay seeks to mediate the debate that has embroiled *Heart of Darkness* since Achebe's attack, and summarizes the quandary thus: "*Heart of Darkness* . . . offers a powerful critique of at least certain manifestations of imperialism and racism, at the same time that it presents that critique in ways which can only be characterized as both imperialist and racist" (364–65). Brantlinger expands on this view of Conrad's fundamental hesitancy to make any explicit commitment in his *Rule of Darkness: British Literature and Imperialism, 1830–1914* (Ithaca: Cornell University Press, 1988), 264.

12. Elliot L. Gilbert, *The Good Kipling: Studies in the Short Story* (Oberlin: Oberlin University Press, 1970), 7–8. See also James Harrison, *Rudyard Kipling* (Boston: Twayne, 1982); Seymour-Smith's introduction in his biography, *Rudyard Kipling*; Michael Brock, " 'Outside His Art': Rudyard Kipling in Politics," *Kipling Journal* 62 (March 1988): 9–32; and Sandra Kemp, *Kipling's Hidden Narratives* (New York: Basil Blackwell, 1988).

13. Charles E. Carrington, *The Life of Rudyard Kipling* (Garden City: Doubleday, 1955), 261n.

14. Frederick Karl, *Joseph Conrad: The Three Lives* (New York: Farrar, 1979), 472–73.

15. Conrad to Pinker, 11 October 1906, and Conrad to Galsworthy, 14? October 1906, in *Collected Letters of Joseph Conrad*, ed. Frederick Karl and Laurence

Davies (Cambridge: Cambridge University Press, 1988), 3:365, 366, respectively. The note from Kipling to which Conrad refers is in fact the only letter from Kipling to Conrad which survives. It is in the Berg Collection.

16. Conrad to Unwin, 22 April 1896, in ibid., 1:276.

17. Conrad to Cunninghame Graham, 5 August 1897, in ibid., 369.

18. Conrad to Cunninghame Graham, 9 August 1897, in ibid., 371.

19. Conrad to Edward Garnett, 2 February 1898, and Conrad to E. L. Sanderson, 3 February 1898, in ibid., 2:32-33, 34, respectively.

20. Zdzislaw Najder, *Joseph Conrad: A Chronicle* (New Brunswick: Rutgers University Press, 1983), 226.

21. *Collected Letters of Joseph Conrad*, 2:138.

22. Joseph Conrad, *Lord Jim*, ed. Thomas C. Moser (New York: Norton, 1968), 205-6. Subsequent quotations from the novel are cited parenthetically in the text and are from this edition.

23. Albert J. Guerard, *Conrad the Novelist* (Cambridge: Harvard University Press, 1958), 413, 401.

24. John Feaster, "The 'Privileged Man' in *Lord Jim*: A Speculative Note," *Conradiana* 10 (1978): 81-84.

25. Linda Shires, "The 'Privileged' Reader and Narrative Methodology in *Lord Jim*," *Conradiana* 17 (1985): 19-30.

26. Stephen Barza, "Bonds of Empathy: The Widening Audience in *Lord Jim*," *Midwest Quarterly* 25 (1984): 228.

27. James Dale, " 'One of Us': Craft and Caste in *Lord Jim*," *English Record* 15, no. 4 (1965): 7.

28. The miscegenation theme is as central to Conrad's early work as to Kipling's early Indian stories; *Almayer's Folly* (1895; Garden City: Doubleday, 1923) can be read as the tragic story of a half-caste, Nina, who finds no acceptance by either Malay, Arab, or white, and finally embraces her "savage" rather than "white" nature. As Conrad writes, when she consciously chooses the Malay culture over against her white father's, her lover Dain "felt the subtle breath of mutual understanding passing between their two savage natures" (63). There are strong overtones of Kipling's "Lispeth" here. Similarly, in *An Outcast of the Islands* (1896; Garden City: Doubleday, 1923), Conrad describes Willems's encounter with the native Aissa this way: "He seemed to be surrendering to a wild creature the unstained purity of his life, of his race, of his civilization" (80); when he returns to Almayer's house, Almayer reproves him: "This is a civilized man's house. A white man's" (88). The final curse on Willems comes from Lingard himself who shouts, "Nothing can help you. Nobody will. You are neither white nor brown. You have no colour as you have no heart" (276).

Critics find it all too easy to comment on Kipling's racism—for example, Jeffrey Meyers's claim in *Fiction and the Colonial Experience* that "Kipling is neither willing to permit Indians to marry whites nor to allow Indians a viable emotional and cultural life of their own" (17). In fact, one of Kipling's early short stories, "Yoked with an Unbeliever," ends comically with a happy Indian-white marriage in which a wayward Britishman is more educated by his wife than the other way around. The charge that Kipling denies his Indians a cultural life of their own is greatly exaggerated. True, more often than not Kipling's white-native liaisons end in tragedy. So do Conrad's. A close reading of both writers' earlier work shows parallel racial attitudes, although it has been altogether easier to pound away on Kipling's than on Conrad's. J. I. M. Stewart speaks a minority view when he argues in *Joseph Conrad* (New York: Dodd, Mead, 1968) that "Conrad is in fact immensely less tolerant than is the much-maligned Kipling of remote races and primitive cultures, and the degradation of 'going native' is as vivid to him as it is to his hero [in *Almayer's Folly*]" (39, 40).

29. Conrad to Cunninghame Graham, 19 December 1899, *Collected Letters of Joseph Conrad*, 2:228.

30. "Correspondence Related to *Lord Jim*," *Lord Jim*, 302.

31. Harold Orel, *The Victorian Short Story: Development and Triumph of a Literary Genre* (Cambridge: Cambridge University Press, 1986), esp. chap. 7, "Rudyard Kipling: The Anglo-Indian Stories," 138–59.

32. "Textual History," *Lord Jim*, 256.

33. Quotations from Kipling's poems are from *The Portable Kipling*, ed. Irving Howe (New York: Penguin, 1982).

34. *Heart of Darkness*, in *The Portable Conrad*, ed. Morton Dauwen Zabel (New York: Penguin, 1976), 495–96. Subsequent quotations from the novel are cited parenthetically in the text and are from this edition.

35. John Buchan, *A Lodge in the Wilderness* (Edinburgh: W. Blackwood & Sons, 1906), 369.

36. Alan Sandison, *The Wheel of Empire: A Study of the Imperial Idea in Some Late Nineteenth and Early Twentieth-Century Fiction* (New York: St. Martin's, 1967), 149.

37. Avrom Fleishman, *Conrad's Politics: Community and Anarchy in the Fiction of Joseph Conrad* (Baltimore: Johns Hopkins University Press, 1967), 97–98.

38. Raymond Gates Malbone, "'How To Be': Marlow's Quest in *Lord Jim*," *Twentieth Century Literature* 10 (1965): 179.

39. Elizabeth Brody Tenenbaum, "'And the Woman Is Dead Now': A Reconsideration of Conrad's Stein," *Studies in the Novel* 19 (1978): 335–45.

40. Sir F. Younghusband, "Inter Racial Relations," *Sociological Review*, III (Sherratt & Hughes, 1910), reprinted in *Documents from Edwardian England 1901–1915*, ed. Donald Read (London: Harrap, 1973), 174.

41. George Orwell, "Rudyard Kipling," in *George Orwell: A Collection of Essays* (San Diego: Harcourt, 1946), 119.

42. As Francis Singh puts it in "The Colonialistic Bias of *Heart of Darkness*," *Conradiana* 10 (1978), the "'unlawful' ways" which Kurtz adopts in Africa "seem

to be nothing more than Kurtz's adoption of the customs of an African tribe" (49).

43. Michael P. Jones, *Conrad's Heroism: A Paradise Lost* (Ann Arbor: UMI Press, 1985), 83.

44. Ibid.

45. Orwell, "Rudyard Kipling," 121.

46. J. Hillis Miller, "The Interpretation of *Lord Jim*," in *The Interpretation of Narrative: Theory and Practice* [Harvard English Studies 1], ed. Morton W. Bloomfield (Cambridge: Harvard University Press, 1970), esp. 211-13, 215. Patrick Brantlinger's comments about *Heart of Darkness* in "*Heart of Darkness*: Anti-Imperialism, Racism, or Impressionism?," 381, are equally applicable to *Lord Jim* in this regard.

CHAPTER SIX

1. D. S. Savage, *The Withered Branch: Six Studies in the Modern Novel* (London: Eyre & Spottiswoode, 1950), 46.

2. Lionel Trilling, *E. M. Forster* (Norfolk: New Directions, 1943), 123.

3. Wilfred Stone, in *The Cave and the Mountain: A Study of E. M. Forster* (Stanford: Stanford University Press, 1962), remarks that "houses have the symbolic role in this novel that rooms had in the last" (237). This is true, but we must add that Forster is also concerned with houses in all their literalness and with how those houses, those spaces, impinge on the inner life of values. Especially useful to this examination of the connection between living space and inner values are Malcolm Bradbury, "*Howards End*," in *Forster: A Collection of Critical Essays*, ed. Bradbury (Englewood Cliffs, N.J.: Prentice Hall, 1966), 134, and Paul B. Armstrong, "E. M. Forster's *Howards End*: The Existential Crisis of the Liberal Imagination," *Mosaic* 8 (1974): 187. Crucial architectural reading that further explains the reverential Edwardian attitude toward the country house includes Clive Aslet's *The Last Country Houses* (New Haven: Yale University Press, 1982), Mark Girouard's *The Victorian Country House* (New Haven: Yale University Press, 1979), and especially Hermann Muthesius's *The English House*, ed. Dennis Sharp, trans. Janet Seligman (1904-5; Oxford Professional Books, 1987).

4. E. M. Forster, "The Challenge of Our Time," in *Two Cheers for Democracy* (New York: Harcourt, 1951), 56.

5. E. M. Forster, "What I Believe," in *Two Cheers for Democracy*, 74.

6. Richard Rorty, *Contingency, Irony, and Solidarity* (New York: Cambridge University Press, 1989), xiv.

7. Trilling, *E. M. Forster*, 13. C. B. Cox notes in *The Free Spirit: A Study of Liberal Humanism in the Novels of George Eliot, Henry James, E. M. Forster, Virginia Woolf, Angus Wilson* (London: Oxford University Press, 1963) that "to make liberalism more aware of its own deficiencies has been the life work of Trilling . . . and

he has chosen to write about Arnold and Forster because in them he finds a similar purpose" (5). Proclamations of liberalism's imminent death have become part and parcel of academic discourse and by that constant repetition been rendered less than shocking, or even persuasive. But at the same time, there has been an opposite temptation in the wake of the Cold War to proclaim liberalism as the final triumph over every ideology. Francis Fukuyama's *The End of History and the Last Man* (1992) is the most familiar example of such hubris, and Rorty himself may be accused of the same when he makes utterances such as these: "my hunch is that Western social and political thought may have had the last *conceptual* revolution it needs" (*Contingency, Irony, and Solidarity*, 63).

8. Trilling, *E. M. Forster*, 9.

9. M. M. Bakhtin and P. N. Medvedev, *The Formal Method in Literary Scholarship: A Critical Introduction to Sociological Poetics*, trans. Albert J. Wehrle (Cambridge: Harvard University Press, 1985), 19–20.

10. Trilling, *E. M. Forster*, 118. For a complete discussion of the various elastic uses of the term "middle class," see Raymond Williams, *Keywords: A Vocabulary of Culture and Society* (New York: Oxford University Press, 1976), 51–59.

11. Trilling, *E. M. Forster*, 125.

12. E. M. Forster, *Howards End* (1910; New York: Bantam, 1985), 25. Subsequent quotations from the novel are cited parenthetically in the text and are from this edition.

13. C. F. G. Masterman, *The Heart of the Empire: Discussions of Problems of Modern City Life in England. With an Essay on Imperialism* (T. Fisher Unwin, 1901; Brighton: Harvester Press, 1973), 7.

14. Ibid., 8.

15. C. F. G. Masterman, *From the Abyss: Of Its Inhabitants by One of Them* (London: R. B. Johnson, 1902; reprint, New York: Garland, 1980), 31.

16. Jack London, *The People of the Abyss* (1903; New York: MSS Information Corporation, 1970), 47.

17. Stone, *The Cave and the Mountain*, 247.

18. John Colmer, *E. M. Forster: The Personal Voice* (1975; London: Routledge & Kegan Paul, 1983), 95.

19. H. A. Smith, "Forster's Humanism and the Nineteenth Century," in Bradbury, *Forster: A Collection of Critical Essays*, 111n.

20. Peter Widdowson, *E. M. Forster's "Howards End": Fiction as History* (London: Sussex University Press, 1977), 90–92.

21. C. F. G. Masterman, *The Condition of England* (London: Methuen, 1909), 25.

22. Jamie Camplin, in *The Rise of the Plutocrats: Wealth and Power in Edwardian England* (London: Constable, 1978), cites a number of Edwardian commentators to this effect, quoting, for instance, L. G. Chiozza Money's *Riches and Poverty* (1905):

"more than one-third of the entire income of the United Kingdom is enjoyed by less than one-thirtieth of its people" (147).

23. Ibid., 149.

24. Colmer, *E. M. Forster*, 100.

25. F. R. Leavis, "E. M. Forster," *Scrutiny* 7 (1938): 193.

26. Masterman, *From the Abyss*, 43.

27. Ibid., 41–48; London, *People of the Abyss*, 27–29. In chapter 6 of the novel, Forster provides a rough summary of the same process.

28. John Edward Hardy, *Man in the Modern Novel* (Seattle: University of Washington Press, 1964), 43.

29. Virginia Woolf, "The Novels of E. M. Forster," in *The Death of the Moth and Other Essays* (1942; San Diego: Harcourt, 1970), 169.

30. The most comprehensive study of this pastoralism is Raymond Williams's *The Country and the City* (New York: Oxford University Press, 1973). Among the many other critics who have remarked on the phenomenon specifically in *Howards End*, see John Batchelor, *The Edwardian Novelists* (London: Duckworth, 1982), 9–10, 227; Samuel Hynes, *The Edwardian Turn of Mind* (Princeton: Princeton University Press, 1968), 68; Stone, *The Cave and the Mountain*, 266; and Widdowson, *E. M. Forster's "Howards End,"* 89–90.

31. As C. B. Cox notes in *The Free Spirit*, the misguidedness of this brand of liberalism also becomes evident in the Leavisite version of idealized country living (90).

32. Hynes, "Undecided Prophets," in *Edwardian Turn of Mind*, 68.

33. Thomas A. Spragens, Jr., *The Irony of Liberal Reason* (Chicago: University of Chicago Press, 1981), 190.

34. Rorty, *Contingency, Irony, and Solidarity*, 68.

35. Richard Rorty, "Method, Social Science, Social Hope," in *Consequences of Pragmatism: Essays, 1972–1980* (Minneapolis: University of Minnesota Press, 1982), 210. This observation, by way of a footnote, follows the more explicit defensiveness of Rorty against a socialist perspective: "there seems no particular reason why, after dumping Marx, we have to keep on repeating all the nasty things about bourgeois liberalism which he taught us to say. There is no inferential connection between the transcendental subject—of 'man' as something having a nature which society can repress or understand—and the disappearance of human solidarity. Bourgeois liberalism seems to me the best example of this solidarity we have yet achieved, and Deweyan pragmatism the best articulation of it" (207). Rorty does not explain why the imperative for "human solidarity" should be any more convincing than an argument for common "human nature." Nor does he provide any clue as to how bourgeois liberalism can be translated into solidarity. He simply asserts that to be the case. Frank Lentricchia's criticism of Rorty in *Criticism and Social Change* (Chicago: University of Chicago Press, 1983) is most

apt: "Is there culture that is not covert politics?" (14). Rorty's cultural liberalism runs the risk of skirting questions of political commitment, which might give its "solidarity" content. Interestingly, Rorty himself seems aware of this weakness, which explains why so much of his writing since *Contingency, Irony, and Solidarity* has taken on an explicitly political tone.

36. Jeffrey Stout, *Ethics after Babel: The Languages of Morals and Their Discontents* (Boston: Beacon, 1988), 229–30.

CHAPTER SEVEN

1. H. G. Wells, *Tono-Bungay* (1909: Lincoln: University of Nebraska Press, 1978), 221. Subsequent quotations from the novel are cited parenthetically in the text and are from this edition.

2. Irving Howe's essay, "Mass Society and Postmodern Fiction," in *Decline of the New* (New York: Harcourt, Brace & World, 1963), makes the first critical connection between mass culture and postmodern art. His introduction to *The Idea of the Modern in Literature and the Arts* (New York: Horizon Press, 1967) is also crucial in raising the problems implicit in periodicizing literary history—of particular importance to use of the term "postmodernism." Do we mean by that term a definable period or body of work? Or do we mean more vaguely a process, an impulse of ongoing avant-gardism? This same essay also points to the exhaustion of modernism and outlines some of the features of the literary movement following it, features which had become more explicit by the time the next generation of critics began to tackle the subject. My reading of postmodernism in this chapter relies particularly on the following: Hal Foster, ed., *The Anti-Aesthetic: Essays in Postmodern Culture* (Port Townsend, Wash.: Bay Press, 1983); Todd Gitlin, "Postmodernism: Roots and Politics," in *Cultural Politics in Contemporary America*, ed. Ian Angus and Sut Jhally (New York: Routledge, 1989); Gerald Graff, *Literature against Itself: Literary Ideas in Modern Society* (Chicago: University of Chicago Press, 1979); Jurgen Habermas, "Modernity—An Incomplete Project," in *The Anti-Aesthetic*; Fredric Jameson, "Postmodernism and Consumer Society," in *Postmodernism and Its Discontents: Theories, Practices*, ed. E. Ann Kaplan (London: Verso, 1988); and Jean-François Lyotard, *The Postmodern Condition: A Report on Knowledge*, trans. Geoff Bennington and Brian Massumi (Minneapolis: University of Minnesota Press, 1984).

3. Gitlin, "Postmodernism," 347.

4. The idea that literature should function in some oppositional way to the culture at large is one that retains its vitality for literary critics of virtually every political stripe.

5. See, for instance, Nancy Miller, *Getting Personal: Feminist Occasions and Other Autobiographical Acts* (New York: Routledge, 1991), and G. Douglas Atkins,

"The Return of/to the Personal," in *Estranging the Familiar: Toward a Revitalized Critical Writing* (Athens: University of Georgia Press, 1992). The recent spate of autobiographies and memoirs by critical theorists in the academy is too numerous to list.

6. Lyotard, *The Postmodern Condition*, 81.

7. Gitlin, "Postmodernism," 349.

8. H. G. Wells, *Experiment in Autobiography* (New York: Macmillan, 1934), 420.

9. H. G. Wells, *An Englishman Looks at the World* (London: Cassell and Co., 1914), 169, 151.

10. As both Jameson and Graff observe, following an earlier observation by Howe in *The Idea of the Modern*, capitalist culture is endlessly assimilative; there is practically nothing that cannot be turned into commodity.

11. The title of Hal Foster's collection of essays, *The Anti-Aesthetic*, summarizes perfectly Wells's aesthetic stance.

12. David C. Smith, *H. G. Wells: Desperately Mortal* (New Haven: Yale University Press, 1986), 462.

13. The best summary of the difficulties inherent in defining "literature" is still found in Terry Eagleton's *Literary Theory* (Minneapolis: University of Minnesota Press, 1983). And this matter has particular application to Wells's own status within the English literary canon, as Patrick Parrinder makes plain in *Wells's Literary Criticism* (Sussex: Harvester Press, 1980): "if the word 'prophet' is, together with 'novelist,' that which best sums up his multifarious activities, this is not only on account of his preoccupation with the future, but because it draws attention to his affinities with such nineteenth-century forebears as Carlyle, Emerson, Ruskin, and William Morris—writers whose work is equally diverse, and whose literary eminence is equally difficult to justify from a strictly formalist point of view" (17).

14. Henry James, in *Henry James, Letters*, ed. Leon Edel (Cambridge: Harvard University Press, 1984), 4:379, reprinted in *Henry James, the Critical Muse: Selected Literary Criticism*, ed. Roger Gard (Harmondsworth: Penguin, 1987), 427.

15. James, "The New Novel," in *Henry James, the Critical Muse*, 606.

16. H. G. Wells, *Boon: The Mind of the Race, the Wild Asses of the Devil, and the Last Trump* (New York: George H. Doran Co., 1915), 110.

17. Walter Allen, *The English Novel: A Short Critical History* (New York: Dutton, 1954), 379, 380.

18. Ibid., 374.

19. Mark Schorer, "Technique as Discovery," *Hudson Review* (Spring 1948), reprinted in John W. Aldridge, *Critiques and Essays on Modern Fiction 1920-1951* (New York: Ronald Press, 1952), 67–82. Aldridge notes in his preface the "strong formalist bias" of all the articles collected in this volume (iii).

20. Barthelme's short story, "Me and Miss Mandible," in *Come Back, Dr. Caligari* (1964) is an early source for this phrase. The narrator of that story speaks of

"the debris of our civilization . . . the world as a vast junkyard." The junkyard corresponds nicely with Wells's "hotch-potch."

21. Schorer, "Technique as Discovery," 72, 73.

22. David Lodge, " 'Tono-Bungay' and the Condition of England," in *Language of Fiction: Essays in Criticism and Verbal Analysis of the English Novel* (London: Routledge & Kegan Paul, 1966), 215.

23. Kenneth B. Newell, *Structure in Four Novels by H. G. Wells* (The Hague: Mouton, 1968), 73-83; see also Bernard Bergonzi's essay on Wells in *The Turn of a Century: Essays on Victorian and Modern English Literature* (New York: Barnes, 1973).

24. J. R. Hammond notes this tendency in *H. G. Wells and the Modern Novel* (New York: St. Martin's, 1988), 16, 17.

25. A considerable body of secondary literature refutes the notion that Wells was at heart a meliorist technocrat. See, for instance, Lodge, " 'Tono-Bungay' and the Condition of England," 242; Mark R. Hillegas, *The Future as Nightmare: H. G. Wells and the Anti-Utopians* (New York: Oxford University Press, 1967), 16; William J. Scheik, *The Splintering Frame: The Later Fiction of H. G. Wells* (Victoria: University of Victoria Press, 1984), 9; John Batchelor, *H. G. Wells* (Cambridge: Cambridge University Press, 1985), 79; John R. Reed, *The Natural History of H. G. Wells* (Athens: Ohio University Press, 1982), 95-109; Samuel Hynes, *Edwardian Occasions* (New York: Oxford University Press, 1972), 8; Peter Kemp, *H. G. Wells and the Culminating Ape* (New York: St. Martin's, 1982), 131-37.

26. Bergonzi, *The Turn of a Century*, 94. C. F. G. Masterman was first to appraise the novel's importance this way in *The Condition of England* (London: Methuen, 1909), 234-41.

27. J. R. Hammond, *Wells and the Modern Novel*, 87-89. Scheik's *The Splintering Frame* likewise finds the book to be most compelling on account of its being an "open" rather than "closed" text.

28. Hammond, *Wells and the Modern Novel*, 87.

29. John Batchelor, *H. G. Wells*, 79. Jonathan Rose, in *The Edwardian Temperament, 1895-1919* (Athens: Ohio University Press, 1986), describes the mood of the book as "an almost manic-depressive vacillation between bouncy Wellsian fun and total despair" (188).

30. Alfred Borello, *H. G. Wells: Author in Agony* (Carbondale: Southern Illinois University Press, 1972), 23.

31. Batchelor, *H. G. Wells*, 68.

32. Philip Rieff, *Freud: The Mind of the Moralist* (1959; Chicago: University of Chicago Press, 1979), 320.

33. Ibid., 321-22. It should be noted here that another critic has previously used Rieff as the interpretive grid for reading Wells: William Bellamy in *The Novels of Wells, Bennett and Galsworthy: 1890-1910* (New York: Barnes, 1971). Bellamy sees this novel as Ponderevo's act of self-therapy in a world of cultural disintegration

(134-35); yet, erroneously, I think, Bellamy misunderstands Rieff to be affirmative of this postcultural world. This misreading of Rieff is difficult to fathom in light of much of Rieff's writing in *Freud: The Mind of the Moralist*, as well as Rieff's sharply articulated attack on the Freudian legacy, *The Triumph of the Therapeutic: Uses of Faith after Freud* (New York: Harper, 1966; Chicago: University of Chicago Press, 1987).

34. Geoffrey Galt Harpham, "Minority Report: *Tono-Bungay* and the Shape of Wells's Career," *Modern Language Quarterly* 39 (1978): 54. For full discussion of this episode as a parody of Conrad, see Batchelor, *H. G. Wells*; Bergonzi, *The Turn of a Century*; and Hammond, *Wells and the Modern Novel*.

35. *The War in the Air* (1908), which Wells worked on concurrently with *Tono-Bungay* (see Smith, *H. G. Wells*, 203), predicted massive destruction through saturation bombing, and *The World Set Free* (1914) predicted the atomic bomb. Numerous nuclear physicists read Wells and were particularly interested in his reflections on science and political power. On this subject see Richard Rhodes, *The Making of the Atomic Bomb* (New York: Simon and Schuster, 1986). Maybe of even greater interest are the uncanny parallels between Ponderevo and Oppenheimer. At one point, Rhodes notes, Oppenheimer, who "professed at various times in his life to be dedicated to *Ahimsa* ('the Sanskrit word that means doing no harm or hurt,' he explains)," corresponded with Fermi on the possibilities of poisoning half a million German citizens with the radioactive isotope strontium 90 (511). As compared to the egregious crimes of the Reich's scientists, Oppenheimer's moral ambiguities about what he was creating make him a more interesting study.

36. Don DeLillo says it best in *End Zone* (1972; New York: Penguin, 1986): "Weapons technology is so specialized that nobody has to feel any guilt. Responsibility is distributed too thinly for that" (86).

37. Gitlin, "Postmodernism," 348.

38. Howe's discussion of "mass society" and "consumers" in "Mass Society and Postmodern Fiction" gets shaped into a more rigid Marxist (and I think eschatological) tag in Jameson's vocabulary: "late capitalism." Though we can quarrel with that term, Jameson is absolutely correct when he suggests that critics on both the left and the right desire for literature a stance of oppositionality (28).

39. This is a sweeping historical generalization that I want to qualify. It should be read in the same way we read Northrop Frye's schematization of literary modes and literary history; not as taxonomically airtight but rather impressionistically useful. There are critics who would insist that some of the bloodiest Renaissance tragedies were intended as farce; and in the Roman arenas actual combat was maybe invested with comic properties by practiced spectators. Certain Biblical stories of assassination and death, particularly in Genesis and Judges, seem morbidly funny. The problem here is the perennial one of pinning down irony; only ungifted writers, like ungifted comics, need to tell us when the irony light is on. Nevertheless, postmodern handling of violence shows a rather consistent urge to

take traditional feelings of seriousness about, and revulsion toward, violent death and to turn it into something else. This, in tandem with film's grindingly repetitious depiction of death in slow motion, suggests there is something new going on, and that we have not, in fact, been here before.

40. The global capitalist cartel as the ultimate conspiracy nightmare figures most prominently in Pynchon's *Gravity's Rainbow* (1973).

41. The erosion of the status and function of the nation state in the web of late capitalism, the perception that power will increasingly reside in transnational corporate boardrooms and not necessarily government offices, is a mainstay not only of postmodern novels such as *Catch-22* or *Gravity's Rainbow*, but also of critical works such as Lyotard's *Postmodern Condition*.

42. I am indebted to filmmaker David Murdock in New York City for his observations on this subject.

43. Bellamy, *Novels of Wells, Bennett and Galsworthy*, 133.

44. Harpham, "Minority Report," 56, 57, 60; Kemp, *H. G. Wells*, 177. Lucy Herbert's "*Tono-Bungay*: Tradition and Experiment," *Modern Language Quarterly* 33 (1972): 140–55, makes the most shrill argument to this effect, but the oversimplifications are obvious: all Wells's narrators equal Wells himself, and all his plots can be reduced to the single formula of cataclysm leading to world peace.

45. The most thorough discussion of this arms race is Robert K. Massie's *Dreadnought: Britain, Germany, and the Coming of the Great War* (New York: Random House, 1991). See especially chaps. 26 and 33.

46. Linda Anderson, "Self and Society in H. G. Wells's *Tono-Bungay*," *Modern Fiction Studies* 26 (1980): 211.

47. Gitlin, in "Postmodernism," maintains the most passionate antipathy against the postmodern spirit in the arts: "theoretical nihilism" (358), getting "involved with nothing" (359), and "disengagement" (359).

48. Judith Shklar, "The Liberalism of Fear," in *Liberalism and the Moral Life*, ed. Nancy L. Rosenblum (Cambridge: Harvard University Press, 1989), 29.

49. Henry S. Kariel, *The Desperate Politics of Postmodernism* (Amherst: University of Massachusetts Press, 1989), 116, 117. Unlike Gitlin, Kariel remains hopeful that a postmodernist art can actually excite genuinely subversive political consciousness, rather than reify cynicism, by way of endlessly parodic laughter.

50. Linda Hutcheon's *The Politics of Postmodernism* (London: Routledge, 1989) makes this point repeatedly.

CONCLUSION

1. Giles Gunn, *The Culture of Criticism and the Criticism of Culture* (New York: Oxford University Press, 1987), 68.

2. Dennis Donoghue, *The Old Moderns: Essays on Literature and Theory* (New York: Knopf, 1994), 52-53.

3. Ibid., 34.

4. Stanley Weintraub's *Disraeli: A Biography* (New York: Dutton, 1993) contains this valuable synopsis of the Young Tories' politics: "Young England would proselytize for a nostalgic Old England that never was as 'Merrie' as its proponents described it, and revolved about attachment to the land through the institutions of Monarchy, Aristocracy, and Church, and their noblesse oblige toward a peasantry that now included the industrial labor force. It was a myth that gained power from the revival of a romanticized medievalism in art and architecture as well as in literature—and, through the Oxford Movement, an Anglicanism ritualized almost into Romanism. The Church of England . . . had to lead the spiritual revival against materialism, which had degraded society" (207).

5. Virginia Woolf, "Modern Fiction," in *The Common Reader* (1925; San Diego: Harcourt, 1984), 148.

6. E. P. Thompson, "The Peculiarities of the English," in *The Poverty of Theory and Other Essays* (New York: Monthly Review Press, 1975).

7. Eugenio F. Biagini, *Liberty, Retrenchment and Reform: Popular Liberalism in the Age of Gladstone, 1860-1880* (Cambridge: Cambridge University Press, 1992), 50, 15-20.

8. Ibid., 50.

9. Judith Shklar, "The Liberalism of Fear," in *Liberalism and the Moral Life*, ed. Nancy L. Rosenblum (Cambridge: Harvard University Press, 1989), 21-38.

10. Both the substance of this attack and the liberal response to it are given ample explication in Steven Holmes's *The Anatomy of Antiliberalism* (Cambridge: Harvard University Press, 1993). See especially chaps. 7, 8, and 9: "The Community Trap," "Antiliberals as Historians of Liberal Thought," and "The 'Atomization' of Society?"

11. Woolf, "Modern Fiction," 148.

12. Martin Buber, *The Knowledge of Man* (London: Allen & Unwin, 1965), 123.

13. Mikhail Bakhtin, "Toward a Reworking of the Dostoevsky Book," trans. Caryl Emerson, quoted in Caryl Emerson, "The Outer Word and Inner Speech: Bakhtin, Vygotsky, and the Internalization of Language," in *Bakhtin: Essays and Dialogues on His Work*, ed. Gary Saul Morson (Chicago: University of Chicago Press, 1986), 33.

14. Frank Lentricchia, *Criticism and Social Change* (Chicago: University of Chicago Press, 1983), 1-2.

15. Buber, *Knowledge of Man*, 146.

INDEX